IS THAT YOU, PETULA?

# Is That You, Petula?

## AN AUTOBIOGRAPHY

# PETULA CLARK

## WITH IAN GITTINS

EBURY
SPOTLIGHT

EBURY SPOTLIGHT

UK | USA | Canada | Ireland | Australia
India | New Zealand | South Africa

Ebury Spotlight is part of the Penguin Random House group of companies
whose addresses can be found at global.penguinrandomhouse.com

Penguin Random House UK
One Embassy Gardens, 8 Viaduct Gardens, London SW11 7BW

penguin.co.uk
global.penguinrandomhouse.com

Penguin
Random House
UK

First published by Ebury Spotlight in 2025

2

Typeset by seagulls.net

Printed and bound in Great Britain by Clays Ltd, Elcograf S.p.A.

The authorised representative in the EEA is Penguin Random House Ireland,
Morrison Chambers, 32 Nassau Street, Dublin D02 YH68.

A CIP catalogue record for this book is available from the British Library

ISBN 9781529955095

MIX
Paper | Supporting
responsible forestry
FSC   FSC® C018179
www.fsc.org

Penguin Random House is committed to a sustainable future
for our business, our readers and our planet. This book is
made from Forest Stewardship Council® certified paper.

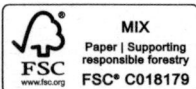

*I would like to dedicate this to all those
who love music and nature. To my family,
and the many I have not named but have admired
and loved so dearly. You are with me always.*

# CONTENTS

# INTRODUCTION

## IS THAT YOU, PETULA?

It was a low hum, a collection of whispers, but it was impossible to miss. Every time I spoke, the voices coming back at me from the darkness of the packed auditorium I was playing to were telling me that they really didn't like what I was saying.

Or, rather, they didn't like the language that I was saying it in.

It was 1 June 1969 and I was performing at the Place des Arts concert hall in Montreal. I'd played the city several times before with great success. Four years earlier, when my life and career were based in France, I'd toured Canada with a one-woman show entirely in French. It had been rapturously received.

My life had changed somewhat since then. In the interim, I'd enjoyed a lot of success in America, and by now had a wide repertoire of hit songs in English *and* in French. So, on my latest return to the province of Quebec, it seemed to make sense to do a bilingual show, in which I sang and talked to the audience in both languages.

*Erreur!*

These were sensitive political times in Montreal, and in Quebec as a whole. Two years before, French president Charles de Gaulle had visited the city and said, '*Vive le Québec libre!*' –

1

'Long live free Quebec!' His speech was seen as giving support to the movement for Quebec independence, and for it to be a French-speaking land.

So, that night, I had wandered onto a battlefield. The Montreal audience knew me as a French star and that was who they wanted. Each time I spoke, or sang, in English, indignant voices hissed back at me from the darkness: '*Pas en anglais!*' People seemed to be taking everything I said in my native tongue as a personal insult: '*En français!*'

Nor was the vitriol one-sided. When I switched to the French-speaking section of my show, the exact opposite occurred. I could hear voices complaining, 'No, no – sing in English!' If I'd hoped that singing in two languages would please everybody, I was clearly pleasing nobody at all.*

People were making their feelings very known and I was stuck in the middle. I didn't know what to do, or say, so I just carried on as well as I could. It was difficult, and disturbing, and when the show ended and I could finally escape backstage, I was in tears.

The team of people I was with were trying to console me and telling me not to worry and that it didn't matter. But I didn't agree. I was upset and thought that it *did* matter. I felt inconsolable. And, suddenly, I realised *exactly* who I wanted to talk to about it.

I had seen on the news – it was hard to miss: it was a worldwide media event – that John Lennon and Yoko Ono

---

* I should say that I've played bilingual shows in Montreal so many times since and never had the slightest problem. This night was, in so many ways, a one-off.

were doing their second bed-in for world peace just down the street in Montreal, at the Queen Elizabeth Hotel. I'd never met them, but John was a star who'd entertained millions of fans in his career. Maybe *he'd* know what to do.

So, I left the theatre on my own and walked the short distance through the night streets of Montreal to their hotel. I still had my stage make-up on and I was crying. Not only that but it was pouring with rain and I didn't have an umbrella. I got to the hotel, ten minutes later, with mascara streaming down my cheeks. Not the best look.

Somehow, the concierge recognised me. 'Madame Clark!' he exclaimed.

'I want to see John Lennon,' I said.

'Ah, yes, he is in room 1742,' he replied, pointing me towards the lift. Clearly, the security in that hotel was not all that it might have been.

I took the lift to nearly the top of the hotel. The door to room 1742 was slightly ajar, so I pushed it open. I stood in the doorway, still crying, make-up smeared all over my face like a clown, dripping water all over the posh carpet. John and Yoko were in bed in their nightwear. John squinted over at me, and looked gobsmacked.

'Is that *you*, Petula?' he asked me.

'Yes,' I sobbed.

'Come here!' he said. I shuffled over, sat on the bed with him and Yoko, and he gave me a big hug. 'What's going on?' he asked. Between sniffles, I told him the story of the gig, and the crowd, and the way they'd made their displeasure known all through my show. John listened carefully, and nodded, and then he delivered his verdict.

'You know what?' he said. 'Fuck 'em!'

This was certainly forthright advice! *Well, it's John Lennon talking!* I thought. *He may be right!* 'You need a drink,' John added. 'Go in there and get one!' I walked into the suite's living room, where a few people were hanging out. I knew one or two of them, such as Tommy from The Smothers Brothers. Someone gave me a glass of wine.

I sat down and started to relax and cheer up. Some gentle music was playing in the background. A guy handed out lyric sheets and we all began singing. It was fun: I had no idea we were being recorded. And that was how I ended up singing along on John and Yoko's anti-war single, 'Give Peace a Chance'.

I'd never met John before but I was to bump into him a few times in subsequent years, until he was taken from us, and I found him a wonderful guy. He never forgot about our first meeting. And I reckon those first words he said to me have a wider significance in terms of me, and my life: 'Is that you, Petula?'

I wasn't born Petula. I was christened Sally Olwen Clark. Not that I can remember anyone ever calling me Sally. My father quickly invented the name Petula for me: don't ask me why. He said that he came up with it by combining the names of two of his old flames: Pet and Ula. I still wonder what my mother thought about that.

I've always felt ambivalent about the name 'Petula'. Of course, I've got used to being called it now, and I like it more than the diminutive 'Pet': I've never cared much for that. But the honest truth is that I love the name Sally. I think it suits me. All through my life, I've always felt more like a Sally than a Petula.

*Ah, well. It's too late to change it now!*

I'm quite surprised, not to mention apprehensive, to find myself penning *Is That You, Petula?* It's the book I swore I would never write. I've been asked to put my memories to paper so many times by publishers, and my response has always been a firm 'No, thank you'. So, why have I changed my mind, this late in the day?

There are a few reasons. Maybe it's to do with time running out. And my late husband, Claude Wolff, who died in 2024, wanted me to write my autobiography. Claude said that if I don't do it myself, someone else will do it when I'm gone, and probably get most of it wrong.

So, I'll do my best to get most of it right. For Claude, and for me.

In truth, nostalgia has never appealed to me. I'm not the kind of person who sits around talking about 'the good old days'. They weren't *all* that good, and they're gone! I rarely listen to my old records or rifle through old photos. I much prefer to live for today. I always have. I've even released an album called *Living for Today*.

But maybe, hopefully, that's what *Is That You, Petula?* is – a book about a life spent living for today. I know that looking back can be painful, but I am going to try my hardest. So, as a friend of eighty-four years, Julie Andrews, used to sing, *let's start at the very beginning ...*

# CHAPTER 1

# HOW GREAT WAS MY VALLEY?

*… it's a very good place to start.*

I was born on 15 November 1932, in West Ewell in Surrey. Not that I tell anyone that if I'm abroad. No one's ever heard of it. If you say 'Ewell' to a French person, they'll reply, '*Quoi?*' Or '*Où ça?*' So, I say I'm from Epsom, which is nearby. It has more of a ring to it, and people abroad have vaguely heard of it because of the Derby.

My mother gave me my Welsh middle name, Olwen, in memory of one of her two younger sisters. I never got to meet Aunty Olwen: she'd died young, before I was even born. I only recall ever seeing one family photo of her. She had dark hair and was very beautiful.

There was a big mystery surrounding Aunty Olwen's death. I remember, when I was little, asking why she had died so young, and at first I was told that she hadn't been well and had died of pneumonia. Then, later, someone said that she died of a broken heart. *What?* I wondered. *Who was this person who broke her heart?*

It's not a phrase you hear today, thankfully, but I was told Olwen had 'fallen in love with a Jew boy'. 'What's a Jew boy?'

I asked. It didn't mean a thing to me at the time. Of course, the irony is that I was myself later to fall in love with a Jewish man, Claude, have three kids with him, and stay married to him for sixty-three years.

But that's all to come. I'm getting ahead of myself.

My mother, Doris Phillips, was a very pretty, petite Welshwoman. She had auburn hair, blue eyes, high cheekbones and a strong Welsh accent, which I loved. She also had a lovely singing voice. She hadn't had any training: the Welsh tend not to need it. But she'd never sing in public. She was too shy.

Mum was kind and loving, and cooked for us and looked after the family, but my main memory is of her being ill. She was quiet and not very talkative and never seemed well. She was often poorly in bed, and I suspect now that she was suffering for years from the tuberculosis that was eventually to kill her.

Well, that was my mother. My father was a different kettle of fish. Leslie Norman Clark was a dashing, handsome man. He was an extrovert and, with his dapper moustache, looked like a suave movie star, a cross between Errol Flynn and Ronald Colman. I loved having a dad who was so good-looking. Any little girl would.

Dad came from Chichester and had always wanted to be an actor. I never got the full story, but I know that in his teens, he ran away with a travelling theatre company who came to town. His parents tracked him down, dragged him home in disgrace, and he was never allowed to mention acting again.

It made Dad a frustrated performer. Could he have made it as an actor? Who knows? He had a slight accent, what they call a Sussex burr, but he was charming and had a lot of charisma.

When I was little, I worshipped him and I thought he could do no wrong.

My mum and dad had met when they both worked as nurses at Long Grove Hospital, a mental hospital in Epsom. Dad carried on working there after I was born. He didn't talk about it much, but he did once tell me about a patient who, when the leaves fell in autumn, went around trying to tie them back on the trees.

When I was four, my beloved little sister, Barbara – Babs – came along. We always got on well and we still do today, even though our lives took us in very different directions. We were both shy children but, growing up, Babs was even more introverted than me. I have old photos where I'm smiling at the camera and Babs really doesn't want to be there.

Ewell is a suburb of London, and our early life there was very suburban. We were a typical middle-class, middle-of-the-road family and lived in an ordinary semi-detached house. Babs and I shared a bedroom. A year or two after she was born, we moved to a similar house, in a nearby area called Hook.

Our new home in Hook had a willow tree in the back garden. I used to spend a lot of time in it. I'd climb up and sit there with the birds for hours. Everything looked wonderful from up there. I loved that tree, and I still have a passion for trees and for nature. That's always stayed with me.

As a young child, I lived in my own little world. I'd tell myself stories, made up from my very vivid imagination, which I still have today. And I had music going on in my head all the time. I was always singing.

I'd sing anything and everything. We'd listen to the BBC Home Service, which played the popular hits of the day *and* classical music. I loved all of it. I'd float around the house singing songs by Bing Crosby or Anne Shelton (a great British singer). If I went to see a movie, I'd come out singing the incidental music.

My father would work nights in the hospital and then come home, go to bed and sleep in the daytime. Once, he was woken up by my singing, and shouted to my mum: 'Will you turn that radio off? I'm trying to get some sleep!'

'It's not the radio,' Mum answered. 'It's Pet.'

Pet, you see? Not Sally.

I sometimes wonder if my father would have liked to have a son, because he schooled me in some very masculine pursuits. He used to take me to boxing matches and explain the finer arts of that sport. He also gave me some boxing lessons in the back garden. Apparently, I had a very good left uppercut. Not that I've ever used it. Yet.

My dad also tried to teach me to ride a bike, which I found quite traumatic. Try as I might, I just couldn't get the hang of it. And my father's way of checking that I could swim, after he'd explained the basics of how to do it, was to chuck me off the pier at Bognor Regis. It was a question of sink or swim – literally!

I have such fond memories of family holidays in Cornwall. I can remember the immense beaches, long walks on cliff tops, beach picnics with sandy salmon sandwiches with lemonade and, now and then, the big treat: a cream tea. And always, over and above everything else: the sea.*

I gave my first ever live musical performance in 1939. We used to go to Kingston-on-Thames on the number 65 bus. In

---

* I formed a passion in my childhood for seas, rivers and streams which has never left me. I still love Cornwall today and I adore the Lake District: there is an atmosphere of poetry and peace there that I have simply never found anywhere else.

those days, Kingston had a huge department store called Bentalls, which I loved going to. It had an escalator hall by the entrance with a kind of raised platform at the top of the escalators.

One day, my dad took me to Bentalls and there was an orchestra up on the platform, playing to the customers. I'd never seen an orchestra before. I'd heard them on records, but I had no idea what they looked like. Now, here one was, right in front of me. It both looked and sounded wonderful.

'Would you like to sing with them?' my dad asked me.

'Yes!' I said. And, being the man he was, my dad went up to the conductor and told him: 'My daughter would like to sing a song with you.' For whatever reason, the man smiled and agreed. And, aged six, I climbed up on the platform and sang with an orchestra for the first time.

I wish I could remember what I sang but that is lost in the mists of time. But what I *can* recall is how much I loved doing it. The managers at Bentalls must have been suitably impressed with me, because they gave me a tin of toffees as a reward. I guess that made it my first paid gig.

Around the same time as this impromptu live musical debut, my father took me to see a play. It was *Mary Tudor*, starring a brilliant actress (or actor, as we say nowadays), Flora Robson. Simply being in a theatre was wonderful for me. Just being with so many other people, all staring at the stage, felt new and thrilling.

I was so young that I could only half-follow the story, and what was going on, but I was transfixed by Flora Robson. She wasn't a beautiful woman but she was a great actress. She had such presence and such power over the audience. She gave them her amazing talent. I never met her but I will never forget her.

I was mesmerised by the whole experience. I remember that, afterwards, I was on the top of a bus with my father, going home, and he asked what I was thinking about. 'That's what I want to do when I grow up,' I told him. 'I want to do what *she* does.'

What I am about to say now may sound strange, but because I got well known so young, *I hardly remember any of my life before I got famous.* I do remember that I was hopeless at school. I liked English, and history, where I could use my imagination. But maths, or anything to do with numbers? I didn't have a clue. Still don't.

At Moor Lane School in Hook, I was in the choir. The songs were all too high for me, as I have what's called a mezzo-soprano voice.* I couldn't sing that high, so I started singing harmony. I thought it sounded pretty good, but it didn't go down well with the teacher: she rapped me on the knuckles and kicked me out of the choir. So that was that.

My early school years were shaped by my shyness. I had a couple of friends who, like me, were very quiet. In a way, I'd have loved to have been one of the girls running around playing netball and doing all that stuff. But it just never happened. Yet on the whole I was a happy child, and I've no doubt when I was happiest. And that was every time we went to visit my mum's parents in Wales.

\* \* \*

Mum had grown up in a tiny Glamorgan mining village called Abercanaid. It stood right on the River Taff. On the other side of the river was a neighbouring village, Pentrebach. They were

---

* Not that I knew anything about that then!

two halves of the same place, really. Pentrebach had a train station that served both of the villages.

I adored Wales. I loved how everything there was different. I loved the accents and the Welsh language, even though I couldn't understand it at first. I loved the mountains and the coal tips. I even loved how Abercanaid *smelled*, due to the coal dust. It all felt unusual and exciting.

We didn't have a car in those days, so we would go to Wales by train. Even getting on those old steam trains was wonderful. We'd leave from Paddington, change at Cardiff, then get the local train through the valley to Pentrebach. And arriving there was always a thrill.

We'd cross the Taff and walk to my grandparents' house. It was in a row of about twenty in something called a *cwm*, which was a tiny, narrow street, if you can call it that. You'd never get a car down there. Not that anyone in Abercanaid had one, anyway.

Along the *cwm* stood five or six taps. This was because there was no running water in the houses. Nor electricity. We'd walk to our grandparents' old stone cottage and up its whitewashed front steps. And once we got in, to my eager eyes, everything about that house, and life inside it, was extraordinary.

My grandfather, William Phillips, was a coal miner. He was a good-looking man who would come back from the pit with his face black with coal dust, which made his blue eyes look even more sparkling. He was very funny, always telling jokes, and he used to sing, beautifully. I adored him.

My grandmother, Jane, cooked meals on a coal-burning stove. She was a small, plump, rather bossy lady who was always bustling around cleaning the steps, or polishing the brass and black lead around the fireplace. She spoke Welsh and hardly said a word in English. Although I think she understood it, she preferred not to speak it.

When my grandfather got in from work, my grandmother would go to the *cwm* to fetch water from a tap. She'd heat it on the stove, pour it into a tin bath in front of the fire and he'd climb in and have a bath. Later that evening, Babs and I would share a bath before we went to bed.

The toilet was in a shed at the end of a long garden. You had to be brave to go there at night (if we couldn't face it, we had a potty under the bed). But, to me, that garden was magic. The earth was black, and strawberries, raspberries, blackcurrants, gooseberries and beautiful flowers all grew amazingly well. It was nothing like our London garden.

We used to visit Wales in our school holidays and I would count the days until it was time to go. And then, suddenly, we were going there a lot more. Because Britain was at war.

* * *

I vaguely remember World War II starting. Well, that's not quite right. I was only six and I didn't know what a *war* was. We kids all wondered: *we're at war? What does that mean?* We knew there was a baddy called Hitler, but that was about it. We only saw what 'war' meant when the bombs began falling.

In Hook, we were on the flight path for the German planes coming in to bomb London.* Soon, we'd hear the Luftwaffe engines overhead every night. They had a very different sound

---

* Hook is close to Chessington Zoo. Recently, I drove past it, for the first time in years. I remembered how, during air raids, we used to hear the terrified animals roaring and howling in the night.

from our British planes. The Messerschmitts, Heinkels and Junkers had a very distinctive low throb.

They weren't actually dropping bombs on our suburban bit of London but the RAF Hurricanes and Spitfires were trying to shoot them down. We saw dogfights going on up in the sky. And it might sound awful to say, but Babs and I thought it was an amazing spectacle.

We had an RAF station near us and they'd send up barrage balloons to defend ground targets. We lived close to a railway line and we'd see a huge gun rattling down the track at night, firing at the enemy planes. For us, and a lot of other children, it was all a thrilling contrast to our humdrum everyday lives: *Well, this is different!*

I won't say we *enjoyed* the war. That feels wrong. But we were too young to understand the human tragedy of it all. It just felt exciting to us: a wild time. We weren't scared. I don't really know why, except that children just go along with things.

We had an air-raid shelter in our garden, like most families, but we didn't like it. It was made of corrugated iron, smelled horrible and was full of sandbags, worms and spiders. So, my father dug a proper Army-style trench just outside our kitchen door, and we'd leap into that instead.

Later in the war, the Luftwaffe began dropping V-1 flying bombs: doodlebugs. We'd hear a throbbing noise. When it stopped, we had to run for cover. Babs and I played 'chicken', waiting for the buzzing to stop before we ran and dived into the trench. Then, the next morning, we'd be out looking for shrapnel. All the kids did that.

In school, we kids spent as much time in the air-raid shelter as the classrooms. There were a lot of us, and a lot of air raids, so it made sense to have lessons in there rather than running back and forth. But the oil lamps didn't give out much light, and we could hardly hear the teachers. So, to keep things going, they would skip the lessons and get us to sing, or tell stories. All the kids would have a go, but usually I'd volunteer to go first.

Because I'm basically very shy, singing helps me to express myself. Why is this? In fact, the need to sing is very deep inside of me. It always has been, and it's when I'm singing that I've always felt the most free.

My father joined the Army during the war. He signed up for the armoured corps and rose through the ranks to Lance Corporal. It meant he'd go away to Farnborough for days at a time. But he was often given compassionate leave to come home, as our mother was still so ill.

* * *

By 1941, the Blitz had begun. The German air raids grew even more frequent and intense, and my mother and father packed Babs and me off to Abercanaid, where it was safer, to stay with our grandparents. And, OK, there was a war going on, but I had the time of my little life.

I started going to school in Abercanaid. It was difficult at first because the lessons were in Welsh and I didn't speak a word. But I picked it up quite easily. Kids are so good at learning and assimilating quickly. After a few weeks there, I was speaking fluent Welsh.

At first, the other kids were a bit: *who's this, then?* I was a curio to them because I was new, and I was English. But on the whole, they were pretty welcoming. And I enjoyed it because it seemed a lot more relaxed and laid-back than my school in Hook and, of course, there was lots of music and singing.

I'd often go off to the mountains on my own. Even though I was still very young, kids were allowed to do such things in those days. I'd spend my day clearing the stones from a little mountain stream so the water could run more swiftly. It made me feel as if I was doing a good deed. I'd sing and tell myself stories as I did it.

After a day in the mountains, I'd go back to my grandparents' house with my hair all over the place, and my face almost as black as my grandfather's when he came home from the pit. I think I've always had a tomboy side* and Wales allowed it to manifest itself. I was very, very happy indeed.

It rained a lot in Wales and there was nothing to do when we stayed home. Babs and I used to sit in front of the window and go through a box of buttons that my grandmother kept on the windowsill. Some of them were such beautiful shapes and colours.

My grandmother was very religious (my grandfather wasn't) so we weren't allowed to do anything much on Sundays. Instead, we went to chapel in Abercanaid two or three times. At least we could sing there. Sometimes, I even sang solo.

I enjoyed chapel. The service was in Welsh, and could be hard to follow, but I loved the *sound* of it, and all those glorious voices raised in song. It was all about the music. And, in any case, it wasn't like there was anything else for us to do. Going to chapel was our Sunday entertainment.

---

* You know what? I still do!

Sometimes, my grandfather would take me down the local pub, the Colliers Arms. The locals would stand me on the table and I'd sing for them. There was also a sweet old man at the bottom of the *cwm* who'd give me a ha'penny if I sang him a couple of songs. Which I was more than happy to do.

A big thrill was getting on the bus to go to the nearest town, Merthyr Tydfil. It was such a rickety old bus that I'm surprised it ever got anywhere. Merthyr was great on market days. My grandmother would bustle around buying coloured wools and all sorts of stuff. I can still picture her buying peanuts. At home, she kept them in her apron pockets so that us kids could get to them.

Even more exciting for Babs and me was going to a small town called Pontlottyn, where our cousins Shirley and Clive lived with our aunty Emma and uncle Bert. More than eighty years on, I can still picture the journey. We'd get the Merthyr bus to a place called Dowlais, which was really just a windy hilltop, and change for Pontlottyn.

Aunty Emma was my mother's other younger sister (besides the late Olwen). She was dark-haired, curvaceous and very pretty. She was a midwife, which meant she had a car: very rare in those days. Aunty Emma was always dashing off up into the mountains delivering babies. I thought she was terrific.

Her husband, Uncle Bert, was a quiet man who ran a grocer's shop in Pontlottyn. It was a proper old grocer's, lit by gaslight, where you cut the cheese with a wire, and the sugar and flour were kept in sacks and served in paper bags. I adored being in that shop, especially when Uncle Bert let me help him serve the customers.

My cousin Clive was the same age as me. He had been a twin, but his twin sister had died very young. I think that I kind of replaced her for him. I loved Clive, and we had all sorts of ridiculous, often dangerous, adventures together.

When he came to Abercanaid, we'd slide down the coal tips around my grandparents' house on tin trays. We'd slide, as fast as we could, straight into the River Taff, and try to skim all the way across to the other side. I think Clive even made it once. Or maybe that's my memory playing tricks on me.

In Pontlottyn, our big thing was trying to get into the local cinema. It was really grotty, a proper fleapit: the sound was terrible and the projector was always breaking down. If you've ever seen *Cinema Paradiso*, the State Cinema in Pontlottyn was exactly that. We were too young to get in, but we were determined to do it.

We'd try all sorts of schemes. We'd dress up in our parents' clothes: Clive, aged nine, in Uncle Bert's trilby, and me with my mum's lipstick. Other times, we'd climb in through the toilet window. We hardly ever made it and, if we did, we got kicked straight out again. We didn't care. It was the whole adventure of getting in that mattered.*

Aunty Emma and Uncle Bert lived in a flat over the grocer's shop. It was bigger than my grandparents' house, so I quite often went to stay with them for a few days at a time. I used to sleep in Clive's bed with him. In fact, Clive's was the first willy that I ever saw.

When you're eight or nine, that kind of thing is quite interesting, so I mentioned it to his mum and dad. My parents were also

---

* Sadly, Clive died recently, but before he did, we met up for dinner and a laugh about our old adventures. I said, 'We got up to so many things because you were a naughty boy.' 'What?' Clive laughed. 'You were the one that got me to do all that stuff!' That surprised me. Maybe I was more of a daredevil than I remember?

there and were horrified. Needless to say, I was never allowed to sleep in with Clive again. I wondered: *what's the problem?* It didn't traumatise me and, well, it was always going to happen one day …

There were a few other shops on the same street as the grocer's. There was a chemist up on the corner, owned by a family with the good local name of Evans. Aunty Emma and Uncle Bert were friends with the family who ran it and we'd sometimes pop round to see them.

I'll never forget walking into the flat over the chemist one night. The mother was making ointment in front of a crackling coal fire like a scene from *Macbeth*, smoking a cigarette as she stirred the mixture. The ash from her fag was dropping into the ointment. *Hmm, maybe that's a magic ingredient!* I thought. I'm sure it was on sale in the shop the next day.

Wales always seemed full of funny, offbeat people like that. Going there was an adventure, but it also touched something deep in me from the very first time. It still does. There's a certain Welshness that has stayed with me, and in me, all of my life. And I'm grateful for it.

\* \* \*

My first experience of singing to a real audience came about in a very haphazard way. I suppose you could call it my big break into show business but it wasn't planned in any way, shape or form. It just sort of happened.

During the war, the BBC's Overseas Forces Service used to record a programme called *It's All Yours* at the Criterion Theatre in Piccadilly Circus. This was a show where children could send messages to family members who were away serving with the Armed Forces in far-flung corners of the globe.

The Criterion Theatre had been requisitioned by the BBC because of one crucial factor. It was situated underground. This meant that even though it was right in the centre of London, and the Blitz was still hammering the city, it was a safe place for them to record and broadcast programmes.

Now, let me confess: I'm terrible with dates. It may be something to do with how I was so bad at maths at school: I can't deal with anything to do with numbers. But I know the date that I went along to that fateful recording of *It's All Yours*. It was 17 October 1942, and I was nine years old.

It was my father's idea for us to go. I was to send a message to a relative whom I used to call Uncle Dudley. He was in the Army. We hardly ever saw him, and I didn't really know him that well, but he was apparently stationed in Iraq, having fought in the Anglo–Iraqi War the previous year.

We arrived at the Criterion and went down the stairs to a lovely theatre that was full of sandbags.\* Really, it was a glorified air-raid shelter. My dad looked handsome in his Army uniform. When we got in, they gave us kids name tags to pin on our chests, so that the announcers could read our names. We settled down and they began a rehearsal.

The producers were deciding among themselves which order we kids would read out our messages in, and there was a full orchestra onstage, warming up. And then, suddenly, from nowhere, Messerschmitts zoomed into the skies over London and there was a full-blown air raid.

---

\* It's strange how the memory works: I went back to the Criterion more than seventy years later to see a play, and as soon as I walked in, I swear that I could still smell those sandbags.

The Luftwaffe were really going for it this time. The noise was terrible and it felt as if the building above us was shaking. I didn't think too much of it. I was quite blasé, because I was a London kid who'd watched dogfights over Hook. But a lot of the other children were up from the country. They'd never been in an air raid before and they were terrified.

With the noise of the bombs, and lots of children crying in the audience, there was no way to continue the rehearsal. So the *It's All Yours* producer, a lovely man called Stephen Williams, asked if anyone would like to go onstage to sing a song to calm everyone down.

Nobody else was volunteering, so I put my hand up. 'I'll sing a song,' I said. I walked down and got up on the stage. The big BBC microphone was way too high for me, so they put a box in front of it so that I could clamber up to reach it.

I began to sing 'Mighty Lak' a Rose', a sweet little song that was popular at the time. I think I'd heard Paul Robeson singing it on the Home Service. And as I was singing, a truly great thing happened. The orchestra started playing behind me, just like in the movies. I can't tell you how wonderful it sounded, and felt.

I guess I must have sung the song quite well, because the show's producers up in the control room liked it. They asked my father and me if I'd sing it again for broadcast on the actual show, as well as sending my message to Uncle Dudley. My father was very keen, and I thought, *why not?*

This may sound odd, but I wasn't nervous. I never was, as a kid. It felt the same to me as singing at home, or in the chapel or the pub in Wales. *I just loved singing*. It never occurred to me that millions of people would be listening to that radio broadcast. Any nerves came much later in my career.

When that edition of *It's All Yours* was broadcast, there was a huge reaction both from the Forces and the BBC. One soldier sent in a letter that said: 'Petula's voice reminded us of chapel bells on a Sunday morning in England.' My father kept that letter. And the BBC asked if I would go back and sing on the show again.

And that was how it all began.

# CHAPTER 2

# A SOLDIER'S CHILD

After I made my unexpected singing debut on Forces Radio, I very quickly became what I suppose you'd call, for want of a better phrase, a 'child star'. It all took off at lightning speed. Looking back, the whole thing was extraordinary. At the time, as a kid, I just went along with it all.

The first thing that happened was the BBC immediately asked me to go on *It's All Yours* again. I went back to the Criterion a month later and sang 'Ave Maria'. And, after that, my father taking me down to Piccadilly to appear on the show became a very regular occurrence.

As well as singing, sometimes, the producers would give me poems to read. I've since been told that they contained coded messages for our secret agents and spies who were listening in. I don't know if that is true but it's certainly possible. After all, that sort of thing happened.

Then, just before Christmas 1942, a few weeks after I turned ten, I went on a show that was broadcast not just on Forces Radio but also on the Home Service. This meant that I was heard in Britain, as well as by overseas listeners, and it changed my life. Because, overnight, I became famous.

The show was a birthday party to celebrate the tenth anniversary of the BBC British Empire Service, which was the precursor of what is now the World Service. It was quite an extravaganza, and it was broadcast from a theatre venue called the Queensberry All-Services Club in the heart of Soho.

The invitation to this show, and many others that followed, was extended by a man called Cecil Madden. He was a senior executive at the BBC who had been at the first Criterion show and who took a keen and supportive interest in me. He was a huge factor in my early career: I owe a lot to dear old Cecil.

The British Empire Service party was big news so it had big guests. Arthur Askey, or 'Big-Hearted Arthur' as he used to be known, was always on the radio back then and was the most famous comic in Britain at the time. I felt slightly over-awed to meet him but there was no need, because he was funny and kind to me.

Also on were Elsie and Doris Waters, who used to appear on the Home Service as a comedy duo called Gert and Daisy. They were lovely, too. Elsie and Doris were the sisters of the music hall star Jack Warner, who went on to become a famous actor. I was to work with Jack a lot a few years later.

At home, I used to do impressions of singers I would hear on the radio, so I got onstage and did a couple of impersonations. I balanced fruit on my head to impersonate Carmen Miranda, the 'Brazilian bombshell', as I sang her famous song 'When I Love, I Love'. Then I did Sophie Tucker, the big-voiced American star, belting out 'Some of These Days'. It must have come over as cute because the audience loved it.

The show's headliner was Vera Lynn. I impersonated Vera, too, but I'd certainly never have dared to do it in front of her!

I've no idea if she ever heard my impersonation. I hope not. But I always loved the way Vera sang, with that little break in her voice which made her so original.

Vera was always gracious to me when we met over the years. She was the Forces' Sweetheart, and the BBC billed me that 1942 night as 'A Soldier's Child'. The idea was that Vera represented the wives and girlfriends left behind by the men who'd gone off to fight, and I represented the children.*

I suppose it made sense but, looking back, I hated some of the other labels that they tried to stick on me. I remember, once or twice, getting described as the 'English Shirley Temple', which was ridiculous. I didn't even have any dimples! I was a skinny little thing.

Also in 1942, I started going off on what they called 'troop trains' to entertain the Forces. My father and I would get on trains and travel through the night to Army camps up and down the country. We'd be in darkness throughout the journey because of the blackout. It felt like an adventure.

We'd arrive without a clue where we were and get whisked off for me to sing for the soldiers. Sometimes they were British, other times American or Canadian. Or a mixture. The shows were always fantastic fun. During 1942 and 1943, I performed in at least a hundred such troop shows all over the country.

I wasn't the only person doing it, of course. I often travelled with a fellow child star called Julie Andrews. Julie was

---

* I kept in touch with Vera over the years. I'd occasionally call her. The final time was in 2017, to congratulate her on turning 100. And, talking to her on the phone, she sounded exactly the same as ever. The same as she had the day that we met.

three years younger than me: she was only seven. If the trains were packed, as they often were, she and I would get put in the luggage racks to sleep.

Each troop show had a varied bill. I'd sing swing-type songs such as 'When That Man Is Dead and Gone', which was about Hitler and so always went down well. I did comedy sketches like 'Movie Mad', about a housemaid who wants to be in films. My dad wrote one called 'Lizzie the Land Girl from London', in which I brandished a pitchfork.

Julie used to perform with her parents, Ted and Barbara Andrews. Barbara played the piano and Ted and Julie sang. Even as a child, Julie had this exquisite, pure singing voice. I loved listening to her. But I think I had more sense of rhythm than she did when I sang. I suppose we were a bit yin and yang.

Julie and I never looked on each other as rivals, but I have a feeling that our parents did, in a 'my little girl is better than *your* little girl' kind of way. A funny thing is that, a few years ago, Julie and I had a long chat in New York about those troop shows, and she remembers them well. They were special times for both of us.

I also used to sing sometimes at Rainbow Corner on Shaftesbury Avenue, a club for American GIs who were stationed in London. We children loved the GIs. They were so generous. They'd turn up at shows with their hands full of oranges and Hershey bars for us.

Because I was entertaining the troops, my father used to get leave from his own Army posting to take me around the country. This suited both of us. I loved travelling around with him because I idolised him. And as for my dad … well, he loved what we were doing, too.

Ever since his parents had stopped him running away to join the theatre, my father had longed to be in show business. My sudden rise to fame had given him the chance and it opened up a whole new life for him. He was managing me … well, sort of. He didn't really know much about the entertainment industry.

My father loved the glamour of showbiz, so was delighted in 1943 when I got to sing at the Royal Albert Hall. It was a charity concert for the London Fire Service with a host of big names, including Tommy Handley from the radio show *It's That Man Again* and Anne Shelton, but I was totally unfazed by the experience.

I remember that I was sitting backstage reading a comic, probably *Radio Fun* or *Film Fun*, and somebody tapped me on the shoulder and said, 'You're on!' I dog-eared my place in the comic, ran up the ramp to get onto the stage, and absolutely pulled the place down.

I sang 'Ave Maria', acted out the 'Movie Mad' sketch, took my bow, ran back down the ramp and went back to my comic as if nothing had happened. I had no sense of fear at all. In later years, however, I occasionally got stage fright at the Albert Hall and had to be almost pushed up that ramp. But that first time just felt easy and natural.

Around that time, my father would also drive me around Britain to play theatre concerts. One time, we were heading home from something or other. Someone at the event had given me a piece of paper. I looked at it and thought, *What's this?* I threw it out of the car window. It turned out it was my payment: a £5 note. My father was furious. That was a lot of money in those days.

More usually, we travelled around by train. We always seemed to be getting to the station late, or just in the nick of time. I got used to running along station platforms and leaping onto moving trains as they pulled out. Thinking back, it was a health-and-safety nightmare.

\* \* \*

I was still doing plenty of BBC Radio shows. I went on *Variety Bandbox*, which featured entertainment chosen by the overseas Forces. And, because I was doing so many of their shows, the BBC sort of took me under their wing and decided I should go to a good school.

When I was eleven, I left Moor Lane and got moved to a very *nice* all-girls school called St Bernard's, down the road in Surbiton. The Beeb paid for Babs to go there, as well. And we both learned to be very *nice* young ladies.

Actually, I quite liked St Bernard's. It was a bit posh but it had a lovely atmosphere and attractive grounds. I still wasn't any great shakes in the classroom, but at lunchtimes I'd hide away in the shrubbery around the playground and chatter to my friends, or sing and tell myself stories. The bushes were where the dreamers went.

St Bernard's was fine, but my education was skimpy at best. I kept being taken out of lessons for days at a time to do troop shows. When I got back to school, I'd be out of step with the other kids – not that I was ever *in* step with them, really. And that got worse when I started making movies.

It turned out that a famous British film director, Maurice Elvey, had been at the Royal Albert Hall show and was impressed by me doing the 'Movie Mad' sketch. He contacted my father to offer me a part in a film that he was just about to make called *Medal for the General*.

*Making a movie!* I thought the idea sounded terrific. My dad often took me to the pictures and I loved everything about it: seeing the organ rise up at the start from who-knows-where, and, of course, watching the films. Occasionally, we'd go to a posh cinema where we could also have tea. *That* was special.

To me, movies meant excitement, escapism, magic and Hollywood glamour. And then I went to Elstree Studios to make one, and you know what? It was nothing like that whatsoever.

From the outside, the studio building looked like a factory. And when you got inside, being on the set was intimidating. By now, I knew all about getting onstage with a band and a microphone, singing songs to a live audience and getting a reaction from them. But making movies was completely different.

The studio was very dark except for the part of the set where a scene was being shot. Everything would be focused on that spot, with loads of people crowded around the actors and actresses with lights and cameras. The rest of the studio was dark and silent. It felt strange, even a little scary.

Despite that, I soon found that I loved acting, and that acting and singing to me were almost the same thing. I was *using the same part of me* to do them. Because singing isn't just about staying in tune and keeping the rhythm: it's about using your voice to express something you have inside of you. And I think acting is like that, too.

The big star of *Medal for the General* was Godfrey Tearle. If I'm honest, I'd never heard of him, but he was charming. A handsome man in his sixties, he was American-born but often portrayed the quintessential English gentleman. In this film, he played a retired general who tries to enlist in the war but gets turned down because he's too old.

I had a small part in the film as Irma, a precocious little urchin who is evacuated out of London during the Blitz to live with the general, along with five other working-class kids. I liked it because Irma was relatable, a normal little girl, and it gave me a chance to try out my Cockney accent. I love accents.

Mind you, I can't pretend that I understood the storyline of *Medal for the General* when we were making it. I didn't have a clue. I'd just wait around with my father until I had to shoot a scene, and then do, and say, exactly what Maurice Elvey told me to. But I can remember that, when it came out, seeing myself on a cinema screen felt great.

After *Medal for the General*, I was put under contract to the Rank Organisation as a child actress. For the next few years, pretty much any role for a little girl in a Rank film would land in my lap, although there were other, older girls around such as Sally Ann Howes and Jean Simmons. I suppose we were all rivals.

My next movie, in 1945, was *Strawberry Roan*, starring William Hartnell, who was to go on to be Dr Who on TV. I played a little girl living in the West Country. My part was so small that if you blinked, you'd miss it, but at least it gave me a chance to try out another accent. And I found that I was start-ing to enjoy being around film studios.

As I say, my father enjoyed it even more. As a frustrated actor, he loved a side of show business that I wasn't aware of. Even as a girl, I never had any desire to 'be famous' but my dad loved the glory, or maybe *reflected* glory, of it all. Being around glamorous people in movie studios, he felt as if he was an inte-gral part of this glittering scene.

One unfortunate side-effect of me being so busy as a child star was that my family got split in two. I was travelling here, there and everywhere around the country with my father, making movies, doing radio shows and singing at Army camps, and my mother stayed at home with Babs.

When I was home, my mum never really asked me any questions about my singing or acting. Unlike my dad, she didn't seem at all excited by that side of things, although it may have been because she was still very ill. She'd often go away with Babs and stay in the country for her health.

At home, it could be pretty tense. The atmosphere was strange, and strained. My mother and father weren't getting on and would have verbal fights. I knew my mum was unhappy but if I had to take sides, I was on my dad's, because I still worshipped him. In truth, I was just a kid who didn't know what was going on.

Looking back, it was not a normal household or a normal family situation. And it got even stranger when my father started seeing a woman called Annie.

I want to say, right from the start, that Annie was a lovely lady. I don't know how my father met her, but suddenly there she was, travelling around to my shows with my dad and me. Sometimes she'd be there as 'my tutor', because I was supposed to be getting at least some token education while I was working in film studios.

Annie was great to me. She was friendly, and funny, and in a way almost became more of a mother than my real mother, because she was with us all of the time. I quickly grew fond of her and close to her, especially as I could see how happy my father was around her. They were very much in love.

Even so, I can see now that it was not a good situation. My father liked Annie to be thought of as my mother, and he told me to call her 'Mummy'. As a naïve little girl, I figured if my dad said to do it, it must be OK. But it meant I sometimes had to lie to my real mother. It was not a good position to put a child in.

Annie was also married, to a man called George, and had a son, a great little boy called Malcolm. We'd meet them sometimes. George was a draughtsman, and I remember that when he ate, he'd cut his food up just like a draughtsman: very methodically and precisely. It used to fascinate me.

I went along with what was happening. Children can sometimes get drawn into strange situations without realising they are strange. My father, Annie and I were having a good time and it didn't feel as if anything bad was going on. In any case, I didn't know many other children, or how other people lived.

*It was what it was.* I didn't analyse it. Even so, I have to admit that as I grew older, and I understood more about the situation, I had very bad feelings about it all. And it somewhat turned me against my father.

This was all going on while I was still working like mad. By now, we had a telephone in our home: quite a luxury for the time. Rank would call and say, 'We want Petula next week, for this or that movie, at Elstree/Pinewood/Shepperton studio.' I'd never have a clue what the movie was about, or what my part was, until we turned up on the day.

The next film I made, also in 1945, was *I Know Where I'm Going!* which has since become a cult movie. It was directed by Michael Powell, half of the film-making duo of Powell and Pressburger, and it was a proper movie made in a proper studio, Denham – a big step-up from Elstree.

I played a rather snooty, aristocratic child in horn-rimmed glasses, which was a new one for me. The movie was set in a castle which was supposed to be in Scotland. Obviously, most of the cast, including me, never went anywhere *near* Scotland.

*I Know Where I'm Going!* was a very good movie, and had big-name stars in Wendy Hiller, Roger Livesey and Catherine Lacey, but I didn't much enjoy making it. It was shot on a very dark set, and I was afraid of Michael Powell. He was never directly unkind to me, but he was a hard director. In truth, I thought he was rather a bully.

In one scene, Catherine Lacey had to ask Roger Livesey if he played cards. He replied, 'I'm sorry, no,' and she had to say, 'Oh!' with disappointment in her voice. I lost count of how many times Michael Powell made her do that one line. Every time she tried, he just snapped, 'NO – *not* like that!' By the end, Catherine was in tears.

It seemed to me downright sadistic, and I became petrified of Michael Powell. In my first scene in the movie, I was sitting in a baronial hall, wearing a pair of jodhpurs. As we were film-ing, I needed to go to the toilet, but I didn't have a stand-in, and I was too scared to ask to go to the loo.

So, I sat in my baronial chair in that baronial hall for an entire morning, desperate to go for a wee. I actually wee-weed in my jodhpurs. I had to wait until lunchtime for everyone to leave the set so I could scuttle off and hang them on my dressing-room radiator to dry.*

---

* Nearly eighty years later, in 2024, Martin Scorsese made a tribute documentary, *Made in England*, to the genius of Powell and Pressburger. He included a clip of *I Know Where I'm Going!* – and there was I, a lifetime ago, acting away. Hopefully in dry jodhpurs.

Something else that happened in 1945, which was definitely somewhat more important than me making movies and weeing in my jodhpurs, was the end of the war. It felt as if it would go on forever, so it was almost impossible to believe on 8 May when the BBC announced that World War II was finally over.

I can still picture the huge crowds in Piccadilly on VE Day. I was twelve by then, but still petite, so my dad put me on his shoulders so I could see everything. Everywhere I looked, people were dancing. Babs and I joined in. I faintly recall that I sang a song at a big celebration in Trafalgar Square.

We all loved the street parties, but life after the war wasn't easy from day one. Everybody was on rations and there was a greyness to life which went on for a long time. Even as a girl, I think I had a feeling of disappointment. There was a sense of *Well, OK, good, the war is over – but now what?*

At the start of the war, I had been an anonymous six-year-old girl who loved playing in the streams in the mountains in Wales. By the end of it, I was almost in my teens and I had become famous. And that fame just carried on. It never really stopped.

# CHAPTER 3

# BINDING IN MY BOSOM

As soon as the war was over, Rank put me into a film that was unlike anything I'd done before. In fact, it seemed to represent an end to the grim austerity of wartime, and the start of something bigger, brighter and, maybe, more hopeful.

The movie was called *London Town* and it was a musical with a huge orchestra, dance routines and lavish costumes. The producers made a big deal of the fact that it would be the first British musical to be shot in glorious Technicolor™, as they called it in those days. It was clearly going to be a very *big* movie.

Of course, I was excited by this. My father had taken me to the cinema to see all these great musicals with Fred Astaire, and Betty Grable, and Rita Hayworth, and suddenly I was to make one! But it didn't work out exactly how the studio had planned.

It had an American director, Wesley Ruggles, which made it feel even more glamorous. Wesley was very nice to me, but apparently his career was in decline and he wasn't the creative force that he had been. Not that I knew the first thing about that, obviously, at twelve years old.

The strange thing was that although *London Town* was a musical, and I had become well known as a singer, I didn't sing in it. Instead, I played the daughter of the main star, Sid Field, who was an extremely famous music-hall star and comedian of the time.

I liked Sid enormously. He was very funny and kind to me, and made me laugh a lot. Apparently, he had a drinking problem, although, again, I didn't know that at the time. I guess it was probably true, because poor Sid was to die from a heart attack four years later, aged only forty-five.

The female lead was Kay Kendall, making her first movie. Kay was tall and graceful and extremely talented. She was later to make a wonderful comedy movie called *Genevieve* which made her a big star. Sadly, Kay was also to die young, of leukaemia, when she was only thirty-two.

Also in *London Town* was the famous Welsh entertainer Tessie O'Shea, who used to be known as 'Two-Ton Tessie'. One day on the set, Tessie took it upon herself to sit me on her rather plump knee and tell me the facts of life. I have to admit that I found this a bit alarming.

The studio had spent a fortune on *London Town* but I don't think it was a terribly good movie. It didn't do very well critically or commercially and, in fact, I believe it is now viewed as one of the biggest flops in British cinema history. In my defence, I don't believe that was my fault.

However, one funny thing that I learned recently was that apparently, after *London Town* had bombed, the producers took Sid Field's sketches out of it and made them into a half-hour comedy special that became all the rage in Hollywood. Frank Sinatra used to show it at his parties. So, I guess at least Rank made *some* money back.

Rather less glamorously, around the same time I made an educational film for children called *Trouble at Townsend*. It was about a city boy and girl going to the countryside and having adventures. The little boy in the film with me put on weight and got too plump for his costume. We filmed some of it on a farm, and I got chased and butted by a goat.

\* \* \*

Just after the war ended, I went abroad for the first time. I flew to Dublin with my father. These were the days when you dressed up and wore hats just to get on an aeroplane. It was incredible to land in Dublin and see the lights on all over the city. I was so used to wartime blackouts.

It was equally amazing to find food freely available everywhere there, which it still wasn't in London. Of course, that didn't mean there wasn't poverty in Ireland. As far as I remember, I was there to perform at a fundraising event to help to buy shoes for children who didn't have any.

It was around now that I also saw the French Riviera for the first time, when my dad took me and Babs on holiday. We left London on a cold, early-spring morning and arrived in what felt to us like paradise. The perfume of roses and mimosa and the extraordinary blue of the Med were overwhelming.*

Back in England, the BBC started putting me in a few TV shows. I must admit that I can't remember them all. I'm told that in 1946 I did a show called *Cabaret Cartoons*, where a

---

* And I still get the same feeling every time I go back to the Côte d'Azur. It never fails, or fades.

cartoonist called Harry Rutherford drew his guests as they sang, then showed them his sketches at the end.

Apparently, Harry had a strong Manchester accent, so the BBC bosses wouldn't let him speak on air in case his voice should offend their viewers, who were accustomed to only ever hearing received pronunciation on the Beeb. Can you believe it? How times have changed.

I *do* vaguely remember singing a few songs on a short (fifteen-minute) TV programme called *Petula Clark* that was shown on Sunday afternoons. But a bit more interesting, I think, was a radio show that I started doing in 1947 called *Cabin in the Cotton*. This starred Edric Connor as Uncle Remus, a slave who sang 'Songs of the South' and told stories. Edric was a Trinidadian, and the first Black person I'd ever seen: there weren't many around in England in those days. He was a wonderful man and we got on very well.

Edric was a very emotional performer. When we sang together, he squeezed me tight. After the show, my father and I would eat whale steaks, of all things, in a little restaurant in Soho. They weren't bad! There were a lot of women hanging around outside. I was too naïve to know they were ladies of the night (and, by the look of it, of the daytime, too).

As I was getting into my mid-teens, I changed schools. The BBC moved me from St Bernard's to Romanoff School for Girls, in Surbiton. And I didn't like a single thing about it. The uniform was purple, which I found a bit sinister. The other girls were snobby and spiteful and they weren't nice to me. I had no friends. Most mornings, I'd cry my way to school.

The girls at Romanoff didn't like me because I was famous, and I guess they were jealous. And I was worse than ever at lessons. Because I was away for weeks at a time making movies, when I got back to school, I was miles behind with the syllabus. I'd have no idea what the teachers were talking about.

The other girls found this hilarious. They'd laugh at me and say, 'You might be a star, but you can't do algebra, can you?' They took the mickey out of me non-stop. One or two of them took it upon themselves to be particularly cruel. I can see why, but it was tough for me.

Despite my fame, I was never a spoiled showbiz child. My father was very strict, and I had to take my work seriously. I didn't have a lot of friends. Looking back, now, I didn't get on well with many people, and I very often felt as if I was *outside of everything*.

You know what? In a way, I still do.

* * *

My father would sometimes take me Up West. We'd go into Soho and occasionally have lunch in smart restaurants such as L'Escargot and Quo Vadis. There was also a wonderful place called Isow's – it's long gone now – that did fantastic Jewish food. Going there was always a highlight.

On our trips into town, my dad and I would head down to Denmark Street, London's Tin Pan Alley. I liked it because it always felt lively and happening. And, when we were there, we'd call into the music-publishing companies. That was always fun.

The street was wall-to-wall music and instrument shops. As soon as the publishers heard I was in Denmark Street, they'd run down and meet us on the pavement. They'd invite Dad and me up to their offices, sit us down and try to persuade us that I should perform their latest songs.

Somebody would play us a song on a guitar or piano. We'd listen, and Dad or I might say, 'Oh, I like that one!' They would give me the lyrics to sing along, to see if my voice suited the song. Publishers used to like artists to sing medleys, because then they got paid for more than one song.*

One day in 1947, we went to one of the big publishers – the Peter Maurice Publishing Company – and I met a pianist called Joe Henderson. He was such a great player that he was to become known as Joe 'Mr Piano' Henderson. Joe was a sweet, quiet, charming man and a joy to sing with.

Rank were still sending me off to make their movies, and in 1948, I filmed one that was a hoot. It was a comedy called *Vice Versa* and it was so much fun. We laughed through the whole thing, from start to finish. This was down to the director, who was a crazy young whizz-kid called Peter Ustinov.

Peter was still only twenty-seven and was quite off-the-wall as a director. He was a genius: intelligent, very warm and not at all snobby. He was extremely talented musically. He had a piano on the set and sometimes he'd play during breaks from filming, or I'd play it by ear, and we'd all sing together.

While we were at Denham making *Vice Versa*, Laurence Olivier was in the next studio doing *Hamlet*. He was very strict about visitors, and pinned a notice on his studio door:

NO VISITORS.
KEEP OUT.
THIS MEANS YOU.

---

* And I suppose it was also the days of payola.

When Peter saw it, he pinned a sign on *our* studio door:

## VISITORS WELCOME. COME ON IN!

And that was exactly how it worked out. All the people who couldn't get in to see Olivier came in to see Ustinov.

My character in *Vice Versa* had the splendid name of Dulcie Grimstone and was the daughter of a headmaster played by James Robertson Justice. James was physically a big man, had a huge personality and always played overbearing authority figures. Thankfully, he was nothing like that in real life. He was friendly and a good laugh.

But I was more excited to meet Anthony Newley.

Anthony was a year older than me. He was handsome and brilliant and, importantly, funny: that's always been the clincher for me. I had a crush on him as soon as I met him. But I knew that, as the old song used to go, I didn't stand a ghost of a chance with him. He was a lad, flirting with all the ladies, and I still seemed like a little girl.

I was fifteen by now but, in my films, I still had to be a child. It was how the studio and the movie audiences liked me. They didn't want me to grow up. I was much more useful, and lucrative, to Rank as a child than a teenager – in fact, teenagers hadn't even been invented yet. *They* only came along later.

In the 1940s, adolescence, with its spots and gawkiness, had to be hidden away. No one wanted to see it. In America, Shirley Temple was a child star, but vanished when she became an adolescent. They brought her back later as a woman, but people didn't *want* Shirley Temple as a woman. They wanted that cute little girl.

It was the same for me. Rank wanted me to carry on being a child star. So, they kept putting me in kiddie parts and dressing me up in ankle socks and little-girl dresses. I had no say in it: I was contracted to them and had to do what I was told. But it was tough for me, emotionally and psychologically.

When I began growing boobs, the studio powers-that-be bound my bosom in and made me as flat-chested as a seven-year-old. I hated that. I was growing up, my figure was developing and I wanted to show off my curves. But that simply wasn't in Rank's script. In any of them, in fact.

Annie was still in my dad's life, and therefore also mine, and coming to the studios with us. She was a huge help to me. She told me all about stuff like periods, which I knew nothing about. Let's face it, puberty is a confusing time, and Annie helped to guide me through it.

There were a lot of affairs going on in the studios, and sex talk that I didn't understand. One make-up guy only talked to me in double meanings and innuendos. He was hitting on me, really, and toying with the fact that I didn't know how to deal with it. I never told anyone, but it made me uncomfortable.

I was still in ankle socks in the next film that I made. It was called *Easy Money* and I played a daughter in a working-class family who win the pools. *Except that I'd forgotten to post the coupon.* The movie had a famous close-up of my face when I confessed my mistake, and everybody in the cinema went, 'Oh, no!'

*Easy Money* went down well and it led to a cinematic series: the Huggetts movies, about the adventures of an ordinary London family. Jack Warner was the father, Kathleen Harrison was the mother, and they had three girls. I played the youngest daughter (well, obviously!), called – guess what? – Pet.

Jack Warner was a lovely man. He'd spent a lot of time in France, including working as a test driver, and spoke excellent French (later, of course, he became a national treasure as *Dixon of Dock Green*). Jack was like a second father to me. In fact, making those films, I thought of him as a father figure.

The Huggetts did feel like a proper family. We all got on so well. We made the movies in a strange, grotty little studio in Islington. I remember, when we first went there, seeing a Scottish guy in a flat cap standing outside. He was a union leader, and informed us, 'Ah can close this studio any time ah want!' And, now and then, he did.

The Huggetts wasn't high art but it was fun. The director was a nice guy called Ken Annakin. Years later, in his memoir, he said he'd never really wanted to do the Huggetts: he wanted to make more ambitious films. He went on to direct *Those Magnificent Men in Their Flying Machines* and a big war film, *Battle of the Bulge*.

I shared a dressing room in the Huggetts films with Susan Shaw, who played one of my older sisters. Susan was lovely and I adored her. She was very beautiful, with blonde hair and green eyes. She had been through Rank's 'charm school' (I've no idea what they taught there: I was too young to go) and she was everything I wanted to be.

Susan liked a drink. She used to drink gin and orange in the dressing room. I saw her and thought, *Well, that's pretty cool! Maybe I need to do that if I want to be like Susan!* So I started knocking back gin and oranges as well. I didn't particularly enjoy the taste, but I liked feeling sophisticated.

My father had got me an agent. He was called E.W. Kent, and he was a funny little man with thick Coke bottle glasses.

One day, he came to see me at the studio, took me for lunch and casually said, 'You're drinking too much.' I was horrified. It was like a slap in the face. I stopped right away (it was easy, as I didn't enjoy it anyway).

Susan and I lost touch in later years. She had a lot of boyfriends, I believe, and married an actor called Bonar Colleano, who died in a car crash. Susan was broken-hearted and I think her life and career began to go downhill. But I didn't know how badly until, years later, I bumped into her.

One day in the late 1970s, I was crossing the street near Leicester Square when I saw Susan. Or was it her? I wasn't even sure. She looked scruffy, and dirty. 'Hello, Susan?' I said. She looked at me … then looked away. It *was* her, but she didn't want me to see her in the state she was in.

Apparently, she had become a virtual down-and-out, living on her own in Soho. She died soon afterwards, from cirrhosis of the liver. The Rank Organisation paid for her funeral. It was such a tragedy, and I still find it extraordinary that someone who had everything, and whom I had idolised so much, could have ended up so sadly.

The first Huggetts film was *Here Come the Huggetts*. I sang a song in it called 'Walking Backwards', written by my father. That was a regular sideline for Dad. As well as managing me and my career, he liked to write and sell songs and scripts whenever he could.

*Here Come the Huggetts* was a big success in Britain. Cinemagoers loved it and fell in love with this funny, quirky family. So, naturally, Rank wanted to make more. The second movie in the series was *Vote for Huggett* and it featured a very voluptuous, spectacular new star called Diana Dors.

Diana was only a year older than me, but how different two girls could be! Even as Rank were binding in my bosom and trying to keep me a child star, they were pushing Diana as a sex symbol: a British Marilyn Monroe or Jayne Mansfield. It was a bit of a stereotype image, but Diana carried it off brilliantly.

The running joke in *Vote for Huggett* was that the men all went to pieces and got tongue-tied around her. I think Diana was used to that, both onscreen and off. But if she was, it hadn't gone to her head. She was down-to-earth and nice to be around, and she and I got on very well.

I used to work with a lot of the same stars in my movies because they were contracted to Rank, like me, and Anthony Newley was also in *Vote for Huggett*. I was just as smitten with him as before and, once again, he never even noticed me. Like all the men, he was more interested in Diana Dors.

But I soon became friends with Anthony. Whenever a film we were in came out, Rank would send us off around the country together to do promotional events. We'd go along to premieres in Birmingham, or wherever, meet the mayor and local dignitaries, and sign autographs.

We'd get sent to factories, have to look interested in whatever was going on, and get our photos taken by the local paper. I remember us going to a factory in Exeter that made pies and sausages. We were ankle-deep in cow's and pig's blood. It was *horrific*. And, for lunch – guess what they gave us? Yep, pies and sausages!

Sometimes, rather than just saying hello to local film fans, Tony and I would put on a double act for them. We'd sing 'Anything You Can Do (I Can Do Better)' and silly songs like that. It was fun, and I think that was what got Tony interested in the idea of having a singing career alongside his acting.

* * *

During all this, my family dynamic hadn't changed. We were still firmly split in two. My father and I were away, with Annie, making movies and doing concerts and radio shows, while Babs stayed at home with my ailing mum. Babs was doing very well at her studies in school – far better than I ever had.

In 1948, we moved to a bigger house in East Molesey, near Hampton Court. When I say *bigger*, it wasn't a mansion, or anything: just a semi-detached, mock-Tudor place that we thought was quite nice. The best thing was that we had the River Ember flowing at the end of our garden.

We didn't live extravagantly but the one luxury my father indulged in was cars. He adored them. Our first was an SS Jaguar sports car, then he had a Bentley, then an American automobile called a Cord, then a shooting brake. They weren't brand new, but they were smart. I think it was all part of my dad's image. He loved being seen in a grand car.

Not that I was involved with anything to do with money. I just sang my songs, and made my films, and my dad handled the finances. I don't imagine that I was making a huge amount of money, certainly compared to young stars nowadays, but it must have been reasonable.

I was still under contract to Rank, who paid me whether I was working or not. I was doing live shows (and no longer throwing my fees out of car windows!). But I was totally in the dark about my income. In my teens, I'd occasionally ask,

'How much money do we have?' 'Oh, don't you worry!' my dad would say. 'You are a very rich young lady!'

I was to find out this was far from the truth.

The final Huggetts film, in 1949, was *The Huggetts Abroad*. In this one, the family had decided to emigrate to South Africa and, for some reason, to drive all the way there across African deserts. Naturally, the cast never left Islington. The producers simply scattered sand over the studio floor.

*The Huggetts Abroad* didn't get as good reviews as its predecessors, but I was totally oblivious to that. I never used to read critics' reviews of films or shows that I'd done, and I still don't. What's the point? As far as I'm concerned, once I've done something, it's done. It's gone. Time to move on.

I was still heading off to the publishers in Denmark Street to try out new songs with Joe Henderson. It was always a joy to sing with him. There are lots of wonderful pianists but so few great accompanists, and Joe really was one. He made me feel comfortable and confident, as a good accompanist should.*

Joe Henderson also introduced my father to a young music publishing executive called Alan A. Freeman. Alan wanted to form his own record company and my dad was just as keen on the idea. So, the two of them got together and began setting up a label called Polygon Records.

I was so busy at this time in my life and I liked that. My next movie for Rank was a comedy called *Don't Ever Leave Me*. I enjoyed shooting this one because it was the first time I'd had

---

* Around this time, Joe conducted the orchestra on my first single for Columbia Records, 'Put Your Shoes On, Lucy'.

a lead role and I actually played a grown-up character for once. So, at least my bosom went unbound in this one.

* * *

Really, my adolescence was a difficult time. I was still young for my age, yet at the same time I was quite sophisticated. I was mixing more with adults than with other children, particularly in the film studios, yet I was simultaneously still naïve about a lot of things. And I was a very shy young lady.

I had a strict life. It was fun, in a way, but also extremely controlled, mostly by my father. I certainly never had any boyfriends, or anything like that. And one of the first times that a boy showed an interest in me ended in … well, I'm not quite sure if you'd call it disaster, tragedy or comedy?

Now we'd moved to East Molesey, I spent a lot of my spare time wandering around Hampton Court, just down the road. The place fascinated me. I loved the history of it, and the sense of strangeness. (I also ventured alone into the maze once, before bottling it and making a quick exit the same way I'd gone in.)

One day, I was at Hampton Court sitting on a bench by the Thames when a boy came up to me. He was a tall, handsome, blond chap. By this time, I was quite well known, but this guy clearly had no idea who I was. 'Ah, hello!' he said.

'Hello!' I replied.

The boy introduced himself as Truls and explained that he was from Norway. He sat down on the bench with me and we began chatting. He was nice. 'Do you come here every day?' he asked me.

'Well, quite a lot,' I replied.

'Will you be here tomorrow? Can we have a cup of coffee?'

I liked Truls, so I agreed. The next day, I met him again and we drank coffee, walked and talked. We were having a nice time. Then we sat on a bench again to chat a little more … and he suddenly grabbed me and kissed me. And, when I say he kissed me, I mean he *really* kissed me! Full-on: lips, tongues, the works!

*What?* I was shocked! It was the first time I'd ever been kissed like that – or at all, really – and I recoiled and slapped his face. *Really hard.* I properly whacked him. Truls, bless him, looked gobsmacked. He rubbed his cheek and asked me, 'Huh? What was *that?*'

'*That's it*, is what it was!' I told him. 'Goodbye!'

I jumped up and walked quickly all the way home. I didn't look around, but Truls must have followed me. Because that evening, when I was up in my bedroom, I heard a noise from outside. I looked out of the window … to see Truls climbing up the drainpipe.

Now, *this* I hadn't expected! Truls was a big, strapping lad, so the pipe was creaking and looking like it might come away from the wall. Downstairs, my father also heard it, and ran out of the house just as Truls fell off. Truls tried to explain, or apologise, but my dad was *livid*. He chased him out of the garden.

It was a shame, really. Truls was only being a boy. He must have been a bit smitten with me because he wrote me a few letters from Norway. It turned out he was from quite a good family who owned a shipbuilding company, or something like that. I wrote back to him once or twice, but then it fizzled out. As these things usually do.

My love life was going nowhere fast but that didn't stop me making a film called *The Romantic Age*. It was quite risqué for its time. I played the daughter of a schoolteacher who gets seduced by a sultry pupil into having an affair and running off to Paris. I don't imagine that a comedy with *that* particular storyline would get made nowadays.

The teenage seductress was played by a gorgeous Swedish actress named Mai Zetterling. Mai and I got along very well. Five years earlier, she'd starred in a film written especially for her by a fellow Swede, Ingmar Bergman. I was still too young to have heard of Bergman then, but I rapidly came to really admire his work.

Bergman was a great director. Very real. Very gritty. He directed women really well. I was absolutely blown away by one film, *The Virgin Spring*. So, why did his movies affect me so much (and still do)? I think it's because they speak to a part of me I've rarely had a chance to express in my work.

Being a Scorpio, I've always had a fascination with *the dark side of things* and I used to read a lot of Edgar Allan Poe. I've always been very aware of, shall we say, the bogeyman in the corner. I may have been playing very light movie roles in my late teens, but what was going on in my mind was very different.

I often think I've spent a lot of my life pretending that everything was OK, even when it wasn't. I never let that side of me show – what would be the point? But even as a child, playing up in the mountains in Wales, I was very aware of … let's call it *the strangeness of life*. So, no wonder that I took to Bergman.

But my mind was on far lighter matters when I made my next movie, in 1950. It was called *Dance Hall* and it was the only time in my Rank contract that they let me go off and make an Ealing Studios film. I was excited about this one … and the main reason was that I would get to kiss Anthony Newley.

I played Georgie, a factory girl who wanted to become a ballroom dancer, and Anthony was my boyfriend, Peter. We had to become good dancers for the movie, so the studio sent us off to a dance school in Kensington. It was great because it meant that Anthony was holding me in his arms every day.

When the filming began, I couldn't wait for our big kiss scene to come around … but then, suddenly, Anthony wasn't there anymore. He got conscripted into the Army and was replaced in the movie by Douglas Barr, who was a nice boy but a lot younger and kind of pale, spotty and, frankly, uninteresting. So, my hopes were dashed.

Despite this setback, my life was OK at this point. I'd left school, so I no longer had to suffer the teasing and torments of Romanoff. I was busy making both records and movies and I liked the constant activity. I'd always enjoyed singing to an audience, and now I'd got the hang of making movies and I loved that, too.

Yet life has this way of sometimes stopping you in your tracks just when everything seems to be going smoothly. And that happened to me and Babs in 1950 when our mother died.

It was a strange chain of events. Mum had been ill for years, but Babs and I had never even thought that she might die. We were so used to her being unwell. But the TB that she had by now been diagnosed with was getting worse.

In June, my dad sent us girls off to stay with family friends in Brighton for a few days. And when Babs and I came back, our mother had gone. She had died, and been buried already. Not only that, but the house had been redecorated, and Annie, who by now had divorced her husband, had moved in. My father told the two of us that *she* was going to be our mother now.

It was all so strange, but even stranger was that Babs and I never questioned it. I don't know why, but we said nothing. We thought that, well, maybe that was the way things worked: *that was how it was.* It was probably harder for Babs than me: she'd spent so much more time with Mum than I had. Her death must have been a huge trauma for her.

I have to say, again: Annie was a wonderful woman. She was very much in love with my father and they were to marry and have a son, Chris, whom I adored, and still do to this day. And yet, though I became closer to Annie than I ever was to my own mother, I never could bring myself to call her 'Mummy'.

It was such a weird thing to go through: my mum dying, and Babs and me not being part of it, or allowed to mourn her. After she had gone, we were discouraged from mentioning her, and there were no photographs of her around the house. I didn't even know where she was buried for years.

As a confused teenager, it made no sense to me. As usual, I just went along with what my father said. Yet as I grew older, became an adult and understood more about life, love and emotions, I realised what an awful way it was to treat two young, vulnerable girls who had lost their mother.

It wasn't until I became a mother myself that I came to realise how painful life in our family must have been for my mum. And the hardest thing for me to accept: that the responsibility lay with my father, whom I'd always adored, for creating a situation that I rather feel damaged us all.

CHAPTER 4

# A PINK CAR TO GO
# WITH MY HAIR

The strangest thing about my mother dying when I was seventeen was probably that I never took, or was given, any time to grieve. I think there was a numbness. Emotionally, I was obviously affected and hurt by the loss. How could I not be? But my day-to-day life and work routine just went on as if nothing had happened.

The BBC kept giving me more to do. I acted and sang in a radio programme called *Study in A Flat*, recorded weekly at the Aeolian Hall in New Bond Street. This was quite an arty, highbrow show and it had some great music, thanks to the esteemed composer and conductor Frank Cordell and his chamber orchestra.

I was also appearing regularly on a show named *Calling All Forces*, where I sang requests sent in from servicemen overseas. I can remember that the musical director, Bob Sharples, would often make the arrangements so complex that they were difficult for me to sing along with. Just another challenge.

I didn't mind *that*, though. My only gripe with *Calling All Forces* was that the BBC initially tried to bill me as 'the Forces'

Sweetheart'. I was firmly against *that*. As far as I was concerned, the Forces' Sweetheart was Vera Lynn, and Vera alone. So, they called me 'the Singing Sweetheart' instead. Which I suppose was slightly better.

The other big news around now was that the Beeb gave me my own weekly TV show. It was called *Pet's Parlour*, and while I wasn't wild about the title, it turned out to be very popular. The producer was a legendary BBC figure, Michael Mills, and his assistant was Yvonne Littlewood. There were virtually no female TV producers in those days, so Yvonne was a groundbreaking figure. She and I were to work together for decades to come.

*Pet's Parlour* was an intimate little show, and the format was simple. Joe Henderson would play the piano and I'd sing. Sometimes, my sister, Babs, would come on the programme, we'd have a little chat, and then she'd join in with a few of the songs. It was probably slightly coy but people enjoyed it.

We'd have special guests on *Pet's Parlour*. The very first, in 1950, was Max Bygraves. Max was a very funny man, who in his later years went to live in Australia. I met up with him out there when I was on tour many, many years later.

With all due respect to Max, though, I was far more excited when Spike Milligan visited *Pet's Parlour*. I used to adore *The Goon Show*. I thought everything about it was weird and wonderful, and Spike was the weirdest of the lot. So, it was great when he came on the show and also signed a couple of his books for me.

One reason that I loved *The Goon Show* was that they always had great music. This was due to a terrific musical director, Wally Stott, whom I was to get to know really well. Wally began to do some musical arrangements for me in later years, and I'd go to his house and meet his wife and children. I was very fond of him.

I liked doing *Pet's Parlour* but the show had its frustrations. I used to adore Peggy Lee, the great American singer and songwriter, and one week I sang one of her songs, '(Ah, the Apple Trees) When the World Was Young'. It was a song from the perspective of a grown woman looking back at her youth and 'lying in the hay / The games we used to play'. Well, when I sang it, there was quite a scandal! Viewers wrote in complaining that I shouldn't be doing 'sexy' songs like that. They all still wanted me to be 'Our Pet', or 'Little Pet', trilling cutesy numbers in those white ankle socks. 'What does *Pet* know about love?' they asked. Which, of course, was true.

After that hoo-ha, I had to be more careful which songs I sang, but *Pet's Parlour* was so well liked that, in 1950, I was voted 'Outstanding Female TV Personality of the Year' by a newspaper's readers. I won a trophy in the shape of a microphone. I've never really been bothered about awards, but that was the first one I ever got. I still have it.

While this was all going on, my recording career was still developing. My father and Alan A. Freeman had got Polygon Records up and running. They set up an office in Grosvenor Place in Belgravia – which can't have come cheap – and got to work. And while Polygon was quite an amateurish operation, they were very enthusiastic.

Alan, who was a dear man, produced all the records himself. He'd get them pressed at Decca, then stick them in his battered old Ford Standard and drive around all the record shops delivering them. Those old 10" 78rpm shellac discs were so heavy that the back of his car scraped the road. I imagine we had a few breakages.

Polygon also released songs by Jimmy Young, a young crooner who'd just come out of the RAF. Jimmy was to go on to have big hits (not on Polygon) like 'Unchained Melody' and 'The Man from Laramie'. He became most famous, later on, as a radio DJ, hosting his 'JY Prog' on Radio 2 for nearly thirty years.

Jimmy and I did a duet called 'Mariandl'. It was a weird experience. Jimmy's wife was his manager. He and I shared a microphone in the studio and, as we sang, she stood behind Jimmy pushing him closer to the mic, while my father stood behind me and shoved me closer, too. The poor bloke in the control room had to hold it all together.

I was spending a lot of time making movies. My next film was a serious drama, set in a hospital, called *White Corridors*. The leads were Googie Withers, whom I adored, and Godfrey Tearle from my very first movie, *Medal for the General*. Except that he was now *Sir* Godfrey, as he'd just been knighted in the King's Birthday Honours list.

I played a nurse in the film and I found shooting it a little harrowing. This was especially true of a scene with Bernard Lee. He played a patient whose badly burned face was bandaged up, and I had to help unwrap his dressings.*

*White Corridors* was fairly dark but it was a good film and did very well. It was one of the top ten box-office movies of that year. Or so I've been told. If I'm honest, it didn't mean anything to me. I wasn't interested in that business side of things at all.

---

* Bernard, of course, later became famous as M in the early James Bond movies.

At least my role in *White Corridors* was an interesting part. Sadly, my next movie was a very different matter. It was called *Madame Louise* and it was a vehicle for the comedian and actor Richard Hearne, and his comic alter ego, Mr Pastry. He had his own TV show, *Mr Pastry's Progress*.

By now, I'd grown from a little girl into a young woman and I longed to play more serious roles. The problem was there weren't many around for women. They all went to men like John Mills and Jack Hawkins. They'd be going off to war, or doing heroic things, and we women would be stuck in the background, weeping and waving them on.

In *Madame Louise*, I played an assistant in a dress shop, but it was a role of no depth or significance. It was all a bit slapstick and I had very little to do. I was basically a stooge to a comedian. Richard Hearne was nice enough, but I thought the film was naff and I didn't find it remotely funny.

*Madame Louise* turned me right off films where I was just a cutesy little lady feeding men their lines and I decided not to do any more. When Rank told me next to make a movie called *Trouble in Store* with Norman Wisdom, I refused. I knew Norman, and I liked him, but I'd had enough. So, I said no.

Rank were very annoyed by this. They were used to me being a sweet, pliant little child star, and they didn't like me standing up for myself: '*Who does she think she is?*' Plus, I was supposed to do what I was told, so I was in breach of my contract. They promptly suspended me from that contract.

If I'm honest, I thought, *Who cares?* I had plenty of other things to do. I didn't depend on films for my career, so I just got on with my singing, my radio shows and working out what I wanted to do with my life. Obviously, my father saw things differently.

Being used to having total control over me, my dad didn't like the fact that I was pulling at the leash as I was growing up. I wanted to make my own decisions and make my own mistakes. I'd begun questioning what I was doing, which I'd never done as a child, and it strained our relationship.

And my father was certainly not impressed with what I did next. Because I fell in love.

It happened at Hampton Court again. I was still pretty naïve and, please believe me, I wasn't in the habit of going down there to pick up men. I simply loved wandering around the grounds and going horse riding in Bushy Park, which is next to the palace.

Unknown to me, there was an American military camp nearby, and one day a GI was walking in the park. He introduced himself as Bill and we began talking. He invited me for a cup of coffee, so I hitched the horse to a post and we headed off to Hampton Court café. Bill was great and we got on well. We quickly fell in love.

Bill and I began seeing each other whenever we could. When I wasn't busy doing TV or radio programmes, or playing shows, I'd zoom down to Hampton Court to meet up with him. We'd walk, and talk, and kiss, and we developed very strong feelings for one another. He was my proper first love.

My father knew about Bill, and met him, but he didn't approve of our relationship. He didn't *dislike* Bill, but I think he was worried about what might happen. Would I vanish to America and abandon my career, which he'd been carefully organising and controlling? Bill just didn't fit into his plans for me at all.

After two or three months, Bill's posting in the UK ended and he had to go back to the States. But if my dad hoped that would be the end of it, he had another think coming. I was heartbroken, and spent all my time reading Bill's many letters over and over, and writing back to him. So, my father agreed to take me out to America to see him.

At the end of 1951, right after Christmas, we flew into Idlewild Airport (as JFK was still known then). It was my first time in New York and it felt like being in a movie. The accents and the yellow taxis and the cop cars ... it all knocked me sideways. A little part of me thought, *Can this be real? Or are they putting on a show, just for me?*

Bill's family lived in the Catskills, out in the country. We drove up and it was wonderful to see him again. I met all his family. His parents were very nice and typically American. They believed every ad they saw on TV and so all drank prune juice at breakfast to keep themselves regular. 'What do *you* take to help you go to the toilet?' they asked me.

My dad, Bill and I drove from New York to Florida for a short holiday. My father was trying to chaperone us, but where there's a will, there's a way. Bill and I managed to slip away a few times, things got quite hot between us, and we went all the way. I wasn't all that impressed with it, frankly. But I knew that I loved Bill.

He felt the same because he gave me an engagement ring and told me that he was going to build a house for us to live in. It sounded a wonderful plan. But my dad was horrified when he saw the ring. Back in England, he wouldn't allow me to wear it on my finger, so I hung it on a chain around my neck.

He did everything he could to break us up, really. There was certainly no hope of a return trip to America to see Bill again. Bill and I wrote and wrote: I waited eagerly for those air-mail envelopes. But long-distance relationships are so hard to do and, after a few months, it inevitably faded away.

* * *

*What could I do?* Life goes on, and it was time for my next movie. *The Card* was a comedy, directed by Ronald Neame. Working with a fellow director, David Lean, he'd previously produced cinema classics like *Brief Encounter* before moving into directing. Lean and Neame are venerated today by American directors like Scorsese and Spielberg.

The male lead in *The Card* was Alec Guinness, a charming man with a very useful ability: he was a huge star, and a great actor who was brilliant at getting into character, but once offstage, he became almost invisible. There was nothing starry about Alec. He could walk down the street and nobody would recognise him.

*The Card* was partly filmed on location in Llandudno, which was great for me because I loved any chance to get back to Wales. It co-starred Valerie Hobson, a brilliant actress.

Alec and I had to kiss right at the end of the movie when he chose me over the character played by the fabulous Glynis Johns. We were a little self-conscious but Ronald put us at our ease.

*How was it?* It was OK, but I wouldn't say the earth moved for either of us. And, of course, he wasn't Anthony Newley.

At least this kiss represented me finally being given romantic roles rather than kiddie parts. Next up, I played a newly married young wife in *Made in Heaven* with David Tomlinson. It was a fun movie to shoot: the best thing about it was that it required me to dye my hair red. I liked it so much that I kept it that way for a long time.

*Made in Heaven* was a comedy (and actually filmed in colour!). While I still harboured closet desires to be in Ingmar Bergman movies, I liked doing comedies if I had a decent part. I'm a solitary person, but I loved acting, and reacting, with my co-actors. It brought out a side of me that I didn't know I had, and rather liked.

Then something happened that I hadn't expected. After I had finally to accept that Bill and I were over, I drifted into a romantic relationship with Joe Henderson.

I hadn't seen it coming but it felt a very natural thing. Joe and I had been great friends and worked together for so long. It slowly dawned on me that I liked a lot more about him than just the way he played piano. It wasn't a passionate love affair, as it had been with Bill, but Joe and I had a close, special bond.

Joe was married, with a son, but he and his wife were separated. He and I weren't a very public couple. But he was a kind, gentle man and we soon settled into a relaxed, easy-going relationship. Mainly, we listened to music. I still recall that it was Joe who first played me Holst's *The Planets*.

Joe and I used to drive a lot out to the country together. He instilled in me a love for the countryside that persists even today. I'm still passionate about going to places like the Lake District, or being by the sea. Joe showed me a lot of the nicer things in life. I can honestly say that I learned a lot from him.

Obviously, my father knew about Joe and me. He knew Joe so well that he couldn't really disapprove of us in the way he had of me and Bill, but I don't think he exactly *approved* of us, either. Or of me being with any man. It probably felt to him like yet another sign of me growing up … and away from him.

It's a topic that I find difficult to talk about even now, seventy years on, but I suspect my dad was a bit like the Rank Organisation – he wanted me to stay a little girl forever. I was still being pushed towards making some quite childish recordings. Let me give you a couple of examples.

In 1952, I made a Christmas single for Polygon called: 'Where Did My Snowman Go?' which I recorded with children from Dr Barnardo's Homes. The following year, at the age of twenty, around the time of Queen Elizabeth II's coronation, I gave the world, 'Christopher Robin Goes to Buckingham Palace'. *Oh dear.*

Early in 1953, I began feeling unwell. I figured it was just tiredness, from my hectic work schedule and the upheavals in my private life, but by the spring, it was clear that it was worse than that. One day, I was in agony and was rushed into St Anthony's Hospital in Cheam, where I was diagnosed with appendicitis.

St Anthony's was a small Catholic hospital staffed entirely by female medics and nuns, so I came to after my appendectomy to find myself surrounded by serene-looking ladies in white habits, wafting around the room. In my delirium, I initially thought that I had died. *Oh, I must have gone. Well, this doesn't look too bad!*

Thankfully, I hadn't passed on, and the nursing nuns were very kind and caring, but they kept me in bed for two weeks or more while I recovered from my operation. They meant well

– but it was to lead to severe problems for me shortly down the line.

When I came out of hospital, I went straight into making another movie. Rank had never forgiven me for turning down the Norman Wisdom film and when my contract came to an end, they didn't renew it. My first post-Rank movie, which I began to film in 1953, was called *The Runaway Bus*.

Written and directed by Val Guest, this was a comedy set on a replacement bus for air passengers whose flight was cancelled due to thick fog. I played an air hostess. I wouldn't call it a classic of cinema, but it was fun to make – well, except that every day, the producers filled the studio with a toxic, oil-based fog. The cast had to drink gallons of milk to protect our stomachs.

The male lead was Frankie Howerd. Frankie had a bizarre, sticking-up hairpiece that I could never quite work out, and was so off-the-wall that I was constantly thinking, *Huh? Why did he say THAT?* He certainly wasn't a straightforward kind of person. But I really liked working with him, and he was brilliant at what he did.

I was excited to meet the film's other big star, Margaret Rutherford. I'd admired her ever since I'd seen her magnificent performance as a psychic in *Blithe Spirit*, so it was great to get the chance to work with her. They say you should never meet your heroes, but that wasn't true with Margaret. She was adorable.

*Less* adorable was what happened to me a few months afterwards. I was recording yet another chirpy, kiddie-friendly single, 'Poppa Piccolino', when I suddenly felt ill and collapsed in the studio. Alan, who as usual was producing the song, drove me home, and I felt a bit better when I got to bed.

Not for long. I woke up in the middle of the night in such agony that my first thought was, *This is it. I'm dying.* The pain in my stomach was so excruciating that I could barely cry out for help. Annie woke up and came in to me. 'Oh, it's just period pain,' she said. 'I'll tell you what's good for that – hot gin!'

She made me one and I drank it. I think I passed out, either from the gin or the pain, but I woke up again, at 3am, feeling even worse. Annie and my dad called an emergency doctor, who arrived in his pyjamas and dressing gown. He took one look at me and said, 'She has to go to hospital. *Now!*'

An ambulance arrived and rushed me to the South London Hospital for Women in Clapham.* It was a dark, imposing, old-fashioned hospital with, once again, an all-female staff. I was drifting in and out of consciousness, but the pain seemed to be easing as they put me into a bed and I fell back to sleep.

When I woke up later, I saw a washbasin in the corner of my room and got up to clean my teeth. I never made it. I fell on the floor and passed out again. And I have no memory whatsoever of what happened for the next few days.

I later learned that they'd rushed me into theatre for exploratory surgery. They didn't know what was wrong, but a brilliant female surgeon opened me up and diagnosed that I had strangulation of the intestine. It had almost certainly been caused by the nuns leaving me in bed for so long as I recovered from my appendix operation.

They told me later that it was a very serious condition. Gangrene had set in and I could easily have died. The surgeon

---

* It's now a Waitrose, by the way.

took part of my intestine out. I spent the next three days unconscious, in intensive care with a nurse by my beside. Or so I was later told. I didn't know a thing about it.

When I finally came to, I felt relaxed. The sun was streaming through the window. I thought, *This is nice. I'm warm; I'm comfortable; the pain has gone. I think I'll go back to sleep.* And then an alarm went off in my head: *ding-ding-ding!* Somehow, I sensed that if I fell asleep, I would never wake up again. It was literally a life-or-death moment.

That was the point when I began getting better. I lay in bed, slowly recuperating, for days. My family and Joe visited. The first day I was allowed to get up, I walked very slowly down a long, dark corridor. At the end, I saw a lady sitting on a chair. As I got nearer, I saw it was Margaret Rutherford, holding a bunch of violets. What a great lady.

I was in hospital for six weeks. Before I came out, a gynaecologist, part of the surgical team who'd operated on me, came to see me. She advised me that *if* I ever got pregnant – which she made to sound very unlikely – I should go back to that hospital to have my baby. 'Because at least *we* will know what was done to you,' she explained.

When the press got wind of my illness, they made a song and dance about it. For some daft reason, they reported that I had had a colostomy. So untrue. It was a very serious operation, and I was lucky to survive it. But all I have left from it today is a bad memory and a small, faded scar.

\* \* \*

Just after all that hospital palaver, I turned twenty-one. It's what they call coming-of-age, and I certainly did. I was now a fully grown, independent adult, and I decided that there were going to be a few changes around here.

I asked my father for, and was given, my first cheque book for the bank account that he had always controlled. I'd also recently learned to drive, after being taught by a police driver, and passed my test first time. So, I bought my first car.

I *adored* that car. It was a pink Turner sports car with the numberplate PET1. Why pink? Well, I still had red hair after the *Made in Heaven* movie, and my hairdresser had advised me that the colour pink looked great on redheads. 'OK, then!' I replied. 'I'll get a pink car!' Which is what I did.

The Turner was made of fibreglass, so it probably wasn't what you'd call a classic sports car, but I couldn't have cared less. I loved driving it very fast, and even tuned the engine myself. When I had the hood down, it looked like I was driving a bath. With the colour and the numberplate, it certainly got attention.

Around now, my music career went up a gear. The UK pop charts had launched in 1952, but none of my Polygon releases had troubled it so far. That all changed at the start of 1954 when I put out a single called 'The Little Shoemaker'.

It was originally a French song called '*Le petit cordonnier*' and it was quite a child-like song, really, but I liked it as soon as I heard it. Its catchy melody was punctuated by a tap-tap-tap representing the cobbler's hammer. I recorded it and people seemed to love it. It was a top-ten hit, and even went to number one in Australia.

I suppose it was quite a breakthrough, but I had so much else going on. That same year, I did my first stage play when I starred in *The Constant Nymph,* based on a classic Bohemian novel by Margaret Kennedy, at the Q Theatre next to Kew Gardens. My co-star was John Gregson, who had a string of West End plays and hit movies behind him.

The Q was a funny little theatre. It had a toilet right by the side of the stage, so if anyone went to the loo during a performance and pulled the chain, you heard it on the stage. That was peculiar. But I enjoyed doing the play. I was surprised to learn you can get live feedback from an audience when you're acting just as much as you can when you're singing.

*The Constant Nymph* wasn't without its mishaps. I had a dramatic death scene at the end, where I had to fall onto a bed with John. Well, one night we dropped onto it, and the bed collapsed beneath us. I found myself lying on the floor. John was a true trouper: he picked me up, lay me on the bed and carried on the scene seamlessly.

I was biting my lip and trying hard not to laugh (well, I *was* supposed to be dead), but the weird thing was that the audience didn't seem to notice anything had gone wrong. I think they just figured it was part of the script. We also took *The Constant Nymph* to Brighton. It was a great experience and whetted my appetite for doing more theatre.

The BBC gave me a part in a new radio sitcom, *A Life of Bliss*. I played the girlfriend of the main character, a hapless bachelor played by George Cole (who, years later, went on to become famous as Arthur Daley in *Minder*).

*A Life of Bliss* was quite an off-the-wall series, and the way that it was produced was even more eccentric. It was recorded weekly in front of a live studio audience at the Playhouse Theatre near to Embankment. It was a comedy series, but our problem was that the man writing the scripts appeared to be having a nervous breakdown. He'd never have the full script finished by the time recording began.

We'd normally have the first few pages. We'd act them out to the studio audience as the poor guy was downstairs, in the basement of the theatre, hurriedly bashing out the next bit on his typewriter. It might take him an hour. He'd run up with those pages, we'd perform them, and the process would continue until the episode was finished.

It left us with a lot of time to kill. As we waited for the scripts, I'd sing a song or two, a cappella, for the audience. Percy Edwards, the famous animal impersonator, was in the cast, playing a dog called Psyche. Percy would get up and run through his extensive repertoire of animal noises and bird calls to keep people entertained.

It would take ages to finish an episode, but the audiences loved it. As well as seeing the sitcom recorded, they were basically getting a free variety show chucked in. We started noticing the same people turning up every week, clutching drinks and snacks to keep them going. Some even brought sleeping bags. I loved doing that show.

I can't say the same about the next film I did. I'd sworn not to make any more movies where I played second fiddle to a comedian, and yet, somehow, I found myself doing another one. It was a comedy about greyhound racing called *The Gay Dog* (would you believe?) and it was a vehicle for a jocular Yorkshire radio host, Wilfred Pickles.

Wilfred presented a very successful radio show called *Have A Go*, where he'd travel around the town halls of Britain with his wife, Mabel, asking locals quiz questions and giving them the chance to win cash prizes. Wilfred had tons of catchphrases that he'd spiel out during his show. The most famous was 'Give 'em the money, Mabel!'

Wilfred was all right to work with. Mabel wasn't. She came to every day of filming of *The Gay Dog* and, any time I had a close-up, would sit beside the cameraman timing the scene to the second, to ensure I didn't get too much screen time. I found the whole film to be a waste of time and making it was a drag.

I felt like I needed a holiday after that silly saga, and I got one. Alan Freeman had been ill and was in need of some rest and recuperation. He invited Joe and me to go with him to Majorca on holiday. Back then, it was a beautiful, unspoiled island, hardly touched by tourism, and the three of us had a wonderful break.

Then the strangest coincidence occurred. As soon as we got home, I was offered a song called 'Majorca' to sing. It was a gentle little tune, written by Louis 'Loulou' Gasté, husband of Line Renaud, the legendary French singer and actress. I recorded it in a church with big acoustics, and it became my second British chart hit.

Although I was always on BBC Radio, off duty I listened more to Radio Luxembourg. The good old Beeb were a bit stuffy and not quite there yet when it came to pop music, so I'd tune in to 208MW, with its crackly reception. So, it was nice when the station asked me to do a show with them.

It was called *Pet's Song Party*. Every week I'd visit Dr Barnardo's Village Home in Barkingside, Essex, for a sing-song with the orphan girls who lived there. I did a lot of things for

Barnardo's over the years. I also got taken out to Luxembourg to meet the great group of people at the station, including the DJ Pete Murray.

\* \* \*

Around this time, I had to tell my father that I no longer wanted him to manage me. We had outgrown that situation, and I felt that it was ruining our relationship as father and daughter. Living together, with him also being my manager, had grown too awkward and claustrophobic.

We were arguing and it was a difficult situation all round. We'd have a meal together at home, he'd say something about work, and I'd wonder, *OK, who am I talking to here – my dad, or my manager?* Things were not good between us. Plus, I was in my mid-twenties. It was time to leave home and go out into the world.

My father was upset by my decision but I knew it had to be done. Babs also felt ready for a change of scenery, so the two of us moved out together and found an unfurnished rented flat in Westminster, not far from Victoria Station. And then I was hit by a bombshell.

I went to see an accountant to check on my finances. I'd never had anything to do with them: as I said earlier, my dad had always handled everything. Whenever I asked about money, he'd just say I was a 'wealthy young lady'. Well, this accountant sat me down, went through all the figures, and exploded that particular fiction.

'Miss Clark, you have £500,' he told me.

I couldn't believe my ears. '*£500?*'

'Yes. I'm afraid that's all you've got right now.'

*What? How could this be?* I'd been working hard for fifteen years by now. We'd never spent money extravagantly – the semi-detached house in East Molesey, and my dad's cars, yep, but that was it. *Where had the money gone?* On Polygon? Did my dad gamble? I didn't know and, in all honesty, seventy years on, I still don't.

I asked my father about it, of course. It was tricky. Dad professed to be as baffled by it as me. Then, after we went our separate ways, he gave up show business completely and moved, with Annie and their son, Chris, to a pretty village called Lodsworth in Sussex to run a local shop. He and I hardly spoke for months as the wounds healed.

So, I was broke, or close to it, and living in a flat with no furniture and, come to that, no heating. We'd moved in towards the end of the year, and I still recall that the first night I was there on my own, and Babs was out, was New Year's Eve. I still didn't have a bed. I lay on the carpet and heard Big Ben strike midnight just down the road.

Well, this was a curious situation, to say the least, for a 'star' with a long broadcasting, movie and music career to find herself in. I must admit, I was devastated, but *what can you do?* There was no point in despairing. I had to take a deep breath, soldier on and find a way forward.

This was when Babs came into her own. My sister had her own career by now, working at a record company, and she was a rock for me. She was so supportive and courageous as we recovered, and I would certainly have found it a lot harder to battle through that tough time without her.

I can remember one particular turning point. We didn't have a fridge, or any money to buy one. An iffy cabaret club somewhere up north offered me a gig for £75. I found my way there with a dodgy accompanist (Joe was busy), played the show to a tipsy crowd, got back home, and spent the £75 on a new fridge.

*A-ha!* I thought to myself. *So THAT'S how supporting myself works!*

It was a challenge, but over the months I got used to having more say over my career as I rebuilt my life and my finances. I was in a low-budget crime movie, *Track the Man Down*, and scored another top-ten hit, 'Suddenly There's a Valley'. It may have helped that my father and Alan had by now sold Polygon to Pye Records, who *didn't* distribute their discs by driving them to record shops in a battered old Ford Standard. They also put out my first 10" album: *Petula Clark Sings*.

One major change in my life around now was that Joe and I stopped seeing each other. We'd been low-key lovers for two or three years and I think it had probably just run its course. It's never easy when a relationship ends but it felt like it was time to move on.

Joe was developing his own successful career as a composer and performer and our lives were moving in separate directions. But we knew that we'd always be close, and stay friends, and that's how it worked out. Joe was a wonderful person, and I have only good things to say about him.

Despite Joe and me finishing, and the fact that my money struggles were not fully over, I was quite content at this point in my life. I was enjoying my independence, and loving living with Babs in our by-now-at-least-partly-furnished flat. I felt as if I was emerging from a difficult time into a kind of happy place.

It got happier when I found a new boyfriend. His name was George, and it's weird, but I can't for the life of me remember how I met him! But he was a brainy, gorgeous Irish guy who was studying Art at Manchester University. He was a passionate man and he got me very interested in art and literature.

George used to call me Psyche. I've no idea why: I can only hope it was complimentary. At least it wasn't Psycho! By now, I'd upgraded my pink sports car to an MG and I'd drive up to Manchester to see him (it used to take quite a while – the M6 didn't exist yet). We'd sleep on the floor in his bohemian lodgings.

George would also get the train down to London to see me in Westminster. I'd look forward to his visits. He and I would have proper, deep conversations about literature, and life, of the sort I'd never had before. We saw one another for probably about a year. It was a very good year.

I was enjoying my new freedom in London. I was friends with a few other young actors and entertainment people and we'd often have parties. We normally used to gather in one friend's nearby apartment, hang out, play music and drink gin and Merrydown cider (yes, really). There was a grand piano in her living room.

One guy who used to come along was a young hopeful called Sean Connery. Sean was a show boy at the time. He and I seemed to always end up lying under the piano, chatting. (In future years, whenever I bumped into Sean, we reminisced about those parties. He remembered them clearly.)

I headlined a tour of seaside towns. Unlike many enter-tainers that I know, I've always enjoyed being out on the road, seeing the glorious British countryside, and performing to audiences. They may be similar but no two shows are ever exactly the same. There is something unique and special about all of them.

Music-wise, this was an interesting era in Britain. The first wave of rock and roll was breaking from America. Initially, I was indifferent towards it. I was a Count Basie and Peggy Lee girl, and when I heard Bill Haley's 'Rock Around the Clock', I just didn't get it. I thought it was lumpy and uninteresting. I wondered, *Where's the musicality?*

I've always loved dancing but Bill Haley didn't do it for me. But then I heard people like Elvis Presley, who had a great voice and more of a Black music influence. Little Richard was quite the show and Jerry Lee Lewis was amazing. And I thought, *I think this is going to fly* (clever girl!).

My own music was ploughing a different furrow. I had more choice now over the songs I recorded and I had a hit in 1957 with a love song called 'With All My Heart'. I followed that up with 'Alone'. They were songs that I loved singing, which hadn't always been the case in the past.

\* \* \*

Dalida, a famous singer in France, often covered my songs. She was to have a French number one with a rewrite of 'With All My Heart' called '*Gondolier*' and sang 'Alone' as '*Je pars*'. My new record company, Pye, had links to a French label called Disques Vogue, co-owned and managed by a man called Léon Cabat, who called me up.

M. Cabat told me that Dalida was 'copying my records' and asked me to go to Paris to perform and 'defend my songs'. I thought, *Well, if she wants to sing them, good luck to her!* I told the label boss: 'After all, we're all copying American songs in England.' I couldn't have cared less and I had no particular desire to go to France.

I'd had mixed experiences of Paris. I'd first been, years earlier, with my father and Alan, on a short holiday. It had tipped it down every second we were there, but I'd found the city fascinating. The people were dashing, the lights glistened off the rainy streets, and the scent of Gauloises hung in the air. It felt magical.*

Yet I'd since returned to Paris. On a couple of subsequent trips, including one to appear on a 1954 Line Renaud television special, I'd found it grubby, smelly and unappealing. I was seriously unimpressed with the stand-up public toilets. You had to virtually get undressed to use them. I used to call them 'acrobat loos' and I really didn't like them.

I was happy in London, enjoying my new life of freedom with my flat in Westminster and my MG and Babs. *No, I'm fine where I am, thank you,* I told M. Cabat. Then a radio station got involved.

Europe n° 1 was a big deal. It was the most important and hippest pop station on the continent, and their head of music, Lucien Morisse (who, oddly enough, later married Dalida), called and said they were to stage a gala called *Musicorama* at the Olympia in Paris. They wanted me to go over and appear at the show.

I said no, again, but Europe n° 1 would not take *non* for an answer. They were super-persistent. They rang and rang and badgered me. 'But I don't even *speak* French!' I protested. 'How can I *sing* in French?' 'You don't have to,' they replied.

---

* That first trip to Paris stayed with me. Seventy years later, when I saw the Paris 2024 Olympics opening ceremony on TV, held in equally torrential rain, it made me catch my breath. *Yes!* I thought. In a Proustian rush, it took me back to that first visit.

'You can sing in English. Just come!' Sighing, I gave in and agreed to go.

The *Musicorama* show was on 24 October 1957. I flew in the day before to discover that the Olympia was hugely presti- gious and basically Paris's equivalent of the London Palladium. *Gulp!* I was nervous about performing there – and it didn't help that I'd arrived in France feeling terrible.

I had a bad throat infection. I could barely speak, let alone sing. I'd wondered if it was even worth going: *How can I do a show like this?* When the people from the record company came to greet me, and saw the state I was in, one of them took me straight to see a doctor.

I sat in a dark waiting room full of Napoleonic antiques and a glass cabinet packed with old medical instruments that looked like weapons of torture. Then *le docteur* called me in and, well, I don't want to be rude, but he could have *been* Napoleon. He was small, with the exact same hairstyle. All he needed was a three-cornered hat.*

'What is ze problem?' he asked. I croaked at him. 'Ah, I see!' he said. He touched me on my shoulders, and the back of my head, but never even examined me. *Odd!* Instead, he wrote out a prescription and handed it to my escort from the record company. Off we trotted to find a pharmacy.

The woman in the chemist gave me some large oval capsules. I was perplexed: 'Er, what do I do with these?'

'Ah, you put them up ze bottom!' she said, miming sticking them up her rear end.

---

* His name was Dr Fouquet. He may have looked like Napoleon, but he was a wonderful doctor and years later became our family doctor.

'Now, wait a minute! I have a bad throat. It's nothing to do with my bottom!'

'No, you will see. They are very good!'

And the weird thing was, they *were*. I woke up the next morning feeling still poorly but at least like I'd be able to sing. Which didn't dispel my growing nerves. I got to the Olympia fervently wishing I'd stuck to my guns and stayed in London. Someone told me how to say '*Bonsoir*' to the audience, and I practised doing this backstage.

I walked out, nervously, wearing a flowing blue dress. I heard some people in the crowd snickering. Chic Parisians, with their understated style, always felt that English women dressed somewhat oddly. And I think they felt I was proving the point for them.

I didn't attempt to say '*Bonsoir*'. I didn't know, with my bad throat, if anything would come out at all when I opened my mouth. But I sang two or three songs, in English. I did 'A Million Stars Above' and 'It's the Natural Thing to Do'. Frankly, I had no idea how it was going to go. But the audience loved me. I pulled the place down. It was extraordinary.

Nevertheless, I still felt ropey the next morning when I had a meeting with Léon Cabat at Disques Vogue. I had a bright red nose, the sniffles and wanted to be back home and tucked up in my bed with a cup of tea and a hot-water bottle. None of this deterred M. Cabat, who showered me with compliments about my Olympia performance.

'You saw what happened last night,' the record-label boss was saying. 'You were a big success! You must begin recording in French!' I was shaking my head, sneezing and telling him that I didn't care one way or another about launching a French career. And then the two of us were plunged into darkness.

The light bulb hanging over the desk we were sitting at had blown. M. Cabat shouted something in French, and a tall man – well, all I could see was a tall silhouette – opened the door, walked in, climbed on the desk and changed the bulb. The light pinged back on, and I glanced up at the guy who'd sorted it out.

*Ça alors!*

# CHAPTER 5

# *JE SUIS CHAUDE*

The man who had changed the light bulb was very attractive. He was tall, handsome, with beautiful curly hair – I mean, let's not mess about here, he was gorgeous. He jumped down from the desk, smiled and nodded to both of us, then went out of the room without a word.

'Who is *that*?' I asked M. Cabat.

'Ah, that is Claude Wolff,' replied the wily label chief, probably sensing my interest. 'He is our public-relations man. If you decide to record in French, he will be looking after you and going with you to all of your interviews. You will be seeing a lot of him.'

*Now, that might be fun.*

'Oh, OK,' I said. 'I can give this singing in French thing a go, I suppose …'

People have asked me, throughout my life, whether meeting Claude was love at first sight. I'm never sure what to say. It sounds too grand. It may have been *lust* at first sight! I think the best way to put it is just that I fancied him and figured that it might be fun to be taken around Paris by him.

The whole trip had had a kind of dreamlike quality: being in Paris, feeling so ill, and then pulling the house down at the

Olympia. None of it felt like normal life, and now meeting Claude was just one more part of the strange adventure. So, OK, sing a few songs in French if it meant I got to hang out with this gorgeous man? Why not?

So, I returned to London and made my first French recording – four songs, including '*Tout ce que veut Lola*', a cover of Sarah Vaughan's 'Whatever Lola Wants'.* It was pretty bad, because I couldn't speak French! I had to learn how to pronounce all those words. Babs spoke French fluently and gave me some help, but she could only do so much. I felt sure that I was mangling the language. But we got through the session, somehow.

I was looking forward to returning to France and maybe getting to know Claude a little and it happened very quickly when my EP was released early in 1958. I flew back to Paris with my bad record in my hot little hand and he escorted me to a few newspaper and magazine interviews. And I immediately realised how brilliant he was at what he did.

Claude was one of the top PR guys in Paris. He was sophisticated and a true man about town. He was suave and debonair; he knew everybody in French show business and everybody knew him. By contrast, I knew absolutely nobody. I'd just about heard of Maurice Chevalier and Édith Piaf, and that was it.

I wasn't great at doing interviews in English, and obviously I had no chance in French. Claude nursed me through them –

---

* Within two or three years, all the big French artists were recording in London – the studios, and the musicians, were so much better. Later, the Parisian studios became quite wonderful.

at times, he seemed to be doing them *for* me, as I sat next to him. And as the two of us travelled around between my engagements, it wasn't easy for us to talk to each other.

My French was non-existent and Claude spoke very little English. He loved jazz and had worked as a tour manager for the American jazz saxophonist Sidney Bechet, so he'd picked up what English he had from American jazz musicians. It wasn't exactly polite. In fact, it seemed to consist mainly of slang and swearing.

Claude's English was limited and erratic, but it didn't stop him delivering a verdict on a pink dress that I wore for another *Musicorama* Paris show in April 1958. 'You looked,' he said, 'like a sore thumb wrapped in a bandage.' Well, *charmante!* (if, perhaps, true). But he and I got on well and his support was invaluable as I got used to the city.

I found Paris intimidating. The women all looked impossibly chic and sexy. I felt dowdy and frumpy by comparison. I realised just how *English* I was, in my manner and demeanour. My interviewers seemed to find that charming but I felt gauche and awkward. Obviously, not knowing the language didn't help.

*Well*, I told myself, *it doesn't matter. It's just a little adventure and I'll be back home very soon.* I liked Claude, and enjoyed his company, but there was nothing going on between us. Unusually for a Frenchman, he wasn't flirtatious. Our relationship was friendly but very correct and professional.

In any case, I already had a fling going on. I used to play big shows in Denmark, including the beautiful Tivoli Gardens in Copenhagen, and I'd met someone over there. I liked him, he liked me, and our friendship had turned into a bit of a romance. It was fun, if probably ultimately not too serious for either of us.

It was an interesting time in my life. Although I'd enjoyed chapel in Wales, I'd never been a churchgoer, but I met a very charismatic priest who used to visit the London theatres talking to performers. He triggered a latent interest that I'd always had in religion and it made me feel that I should take it more seriously.

In fact, I took it *very* seriously. I studied Anglo-Catholicism in my spare time, becoming so interested that I even got confirmed.* For a while, I felt the need to keep crossing myself as I went about my day. It was that important to me. I also read up on other faiths, including Buddhism. That strong interest in religion has always stayed with me.

While this was all going on, Disques Vogue were still sending me songs to listen to, and later record in my pidgin French in London. Despite my misgivings, they seemed delighted with the results. They would phone me and tell me that my reputation in France was growing fast.

Bizarre as it seemed to me, there was real excitement about me in Paris. I had more big shows coming up. I was to support a very famous French singer and comedian, Henri Salvador, at three weeks of shows in November at a major theatre called the Alhambra-Maurice Chevalier.

To mark the occasion, Disques Vogue commissioned a special song for me. I composed the music, which was then

---

* I was recently in New York, more than sixty years on, and met an English rocker who told me he was confirmed at the very same service as me. Small world, eh?

given to a renowned French literary figure, Boris Vian, to write the words.* Vian called it 'Java pour Petula' (a java is a kind of popular Parisian dance) and sent his lyrics to me. The problem was that I simply could not learn them.

Boris Vian had written the lyrics, about an English girl in Paris, in a French street slang called *argot*. He figured that me singing them, in my English accent, would be cute. He was probably correct, but I couldn't make head nor tail of them. Babs tried to help me, with her excellent French, but she'd never been taught slang. I was getting nowhere.

*What to do?*

The Alhambra show was nearing, and I was beginning to panic. God knows how I came up with this brainwave, but I decided to see a hypnotist. A peculiar little man came to visit me and we went into the sitting room. We sat and chatted for a while, then he put his hand on my shoulder.

'OK, now you learn the song,' he said.

'Wait! Aren't you supposed to hypnotise me?' I asked.

'You *are* hypnotised.'

*Ah*. The guy left me in the room with the lyrics. When he came back, twenty minutes later, I had memorised '*Java pour Petula*'. 'Now you know them,' he said. 'If you feel you are forgetting them, just think of me and they will come back to you.' And, remarkable as it sounds, it worked. I now remembered all the lyrics (and you know what? I still do, to this day).

---

* Boris Vian was a well-known hip French writer (and jazz trumpeter) who was extremely off-the-wall. He wrote a very famous novel in 1946 called *J'irai cracher sur vos tombes* (*I Shall Spit on Your Graves*).

Yet knowing the words was only half of the battle. I also had to know how to pronounce them. I still didn't have a clue how to sing these weird French *argot* lyrics when I arrived at the Alhambra. Which was when Henri Salvador's formidable wife and manager, Jacqueline, entered the equation.

Jacqueline Salvador was a force of nature. A tiny Egyptian woman, she wore clothes slashed to the waist, at the front *and* back, and flamboyant hats, presumably to make herself look a bit taller. When I explained my issues with '*Java pour Petula*', she kindly volunteered to coach me through the pronunciation of the words, line by line.

However, Jacqueline spoke French with a heavy Egyptian accent, extravagantly rolling her *rrrrrs*. The result was that when I came to record, and perform, '*Java pour Petula*', I sang it with both an English *and* an Egyptian accent. For some reason, the French found this irresistible.

The Alhambra shows were a lot of fun. Henri Salvador had a lovely singing voice and, as far as I could tell, his comedy and sketches were very funny. I was wearing a fairly décolleté dress, and every time I bumped into him backstage, he tried to put his hand down the front of it. Those were the days.

I enjoyed my performances far more than I had the first Olympia show. By now, I was more confident. I had a smattering of French and a few French-language songs to sing. I noticed that the more mistakes I made with my French, the more the crowds seemed to love it.

Getting paid for the shows was tough. The Alhambra was run by Jane Breteau, a large, fearsome lady in smoked glasses who had an assistant with equally weird specs: two scary characters. Babs was in Paris with me, and came with me to a very dark, smoke-filled office at the end of each week to support me as we nervously asked for my money (and, eventually, got it).

One evening, when we had a night off from the Alhambra shows, we went to see Billie Holiday play in Paris. It was just her and a brilliant accompanist on piano: every time she went off at a musical tangent, he'd follow her and bring her back. Billie was clearly having difficulties, but it was a privilege to see her perform live. Sadly, she died not long after.

The best thing about those three weeks in Paris was that I got to spend a lot of time with Claude. He was taking me to loads of press and radio interviews, and even some TV: I made my first 'proper' French television appearance on a programme called *La clé des champs* (Dalida was also on, singing a French cover of '*Volare*').

I could feel that things were shifting between me and Claude. We had a new closeness and intensity. It was obvious that we were attracted to one another. I saw him every day of the three weeks that I was at the Alhambra, and that was when I fell in love with him.

One night, I thought that love was doomed. I was sitting in my dressing room when a very elegant, attractive blonde woman strutted in. She ignored me, never said a word, stood in front of my mirror, pouted, primped herself and walked out again. Which, to my English sensibilities, seemed a bit rude.

'Who is *that*?' I asked somebody.

'Oh, that is the girlfriend of Claude,' they replied.

*Wow. Well, that's that*, I thought. *I certainly can't compete with her.*

I could not have been more wrong.

After the last night at the Alhambra, there was a small party backstage. I wasn't really in the mood, so I left early to go back to my hotel. As I stood in the reception area, I heard a squeal of brakes and then the toot of a klaxon. I looked outside to see Claude in his car.

He opened the door. 'Get in,' he said. I did.

Claude drove us to a charming little hotel in Saint-Germain-des-Prés. We spent the night together. It was all very sudden ... but also it had been building up during those intense three weeks in Paris. *And that was it.* The die was cast. The next morning, I flew home to London, feeling very strange and highly emotional. And that everything had changed.

* * *

Back in Westminster, I was confused about that final night in Paris. What had it been? Was it a one-night stand? An adventure? A *dream*? Neither of us had really said very much. Well, we would have to say something soon, because, obviously, Claude and I would have to work together every time I went to France.

Claude phoned me, and it was clear that it hadn't just been a one-off fling. He came over to London for the weekend and stayed with me. We had a great couple of days. He went back to Paris and, because international phone calls were an expensive kerfuffle in those days, we began writing to each other.

Claude's letters were ... *strange*. If his spoken English was eccentric, the written version was something else. There were some very odd phrases. But he did so well to write in a language that he didn't speak, and I loved getting his letters and then attempting to decipher them.

I went to stay with him in France. He had a charming little flat just outside Paris, in a place called Bourg-la-Reine. It was a bachelor pad but cute and smart. We'd go into the city in his car, which he drove like a maniac: very well but very fast. And then I spent 1959 bouncing to-and-fro between London and Paris like a ping-pong ball.

I still had plenty to occupy me in Britain. I appeared at the NME Poll-Winners Party at the Albert Hall in January with Lonnie Donegan, Marty Wilde and Cliff Richard, then went on tour until the spring. And, as a rather unexpected sideline, I taught Anthony Newley to sing.

Anthony and I had stayed friends and he'd just starred in a movie, *Idol on Parade*, about an Elvis Presley-style rock-and-roll singer getting conscripted into the Army. Off the back of it, Anthony had decided to try to launch his own singing career, but he was extremely nervous about doing it.

I went into the studio with him as he did his first proper recordings. Singing is mostly about breathing, so I stood behind him as he sang and literally tapped him on the shoulder to tell him when to breathe. I believe it helped him a lot – and, of course, Tony went on to have an incredible singing and song-writing career.*

Yet my thoughts were with France and Claude. Publishers and writers were still sending songs for me to record in French, which I was now doing with a slightly greater degree

---

* Anthony's music career had so many highlights, from singing number-one singles such as 'Why' and 'Do You Mind?' to co-writing songs with Leslie Bricusse, including 'What Kind of Fool Am I?' (and the rest of the soundtrack to *Stop the World, I Want to Get Off*) and 'Feeling Good', famously sung by Nina Simone and many others.

In Priory Park, Chichester.
I was about 5 years old.

Cousin Shirley, Babs and me sitting
on a wall in Wales.

Standing on a box singing
'Ave Maria' for the BBC at the
Criterion Theatre, 1942.

Rehearsing my impersonation of
Carmen Miranda at our home in
Chessington, 1942.

Going through a script for the BBC with my father, Corporal Leslie Clark, 1942.

Looking snooty in *I Know Where I'm Going*, 1945.

A family shot of *Here Come the Huggetts*, with Jimmy Hanley, Susan Shaw, Kathleen Harrison, Jack Warner, me and Jane Hylton, 1947.

Me with my 'crush' Anthony Newley in *Don't Ever Leave Me*, 1949.

In *Dance Hall* with Natasha Parry Diana Dors and Jane Hylton, 1950.

With Alec Guinness in *The Card*, 1952.

Working with Joe Henderson, 1959.

Church blessing with members of both our families, 1961.

Listening to playback in Pye's studio control room with engineer Ray Prickett, producer Tony Hatch and conductor Johnny Harris, circa 1965.

An early meeting with Mick Jagger and Keith Richards, London, 1965.

US gold record for 'Downtown' with Mike Maitland, head of Warner Brothers Records, Los Angeles, 1965.

With Mia Farrow, Anthony Newley and Claude after my show at the Cocoanut Grove, Los Angeles, 1966.

Chatting with Julie Andrews in New York, 1966.

Splashing around with Bara and Kate in Beverly Hills, 1966.

Happy times with Claude
in London, 1966.

Having fun with Charlie Chaplin at his
home in Vevey, Switzerland (he wrote
'This Is My Song!'), 1967.

With the brilliant French TV
producers Maritie and Gilbert
Carpentier, Beverly Hills, 1966.

With the great English TV director
Yvonne Littlewood on the set of
This Is Petula, 1967.

Maid of honour at Charles Aznavour's wedding to Ulla, with Sammy Davis Jr (best man) at the Flamingo Hotel, Las Vegas, 1967.

Tommy Steele, Jack Warner (of Warner Brothers), Fred Astaire and me having a great time during rehearsals for *Finian's Rainbow*, Hollywood, 1967.

Larking around with Francis Coppola on the set of *Finian's Rainbow*, 1967.

Piggy back with Kate on the *Finian's Rainbow* set, Hollywood, 1967.

With Fred Astaire in *Finian's Rainbow*, 1967-68.

Laughing between takes with the great Peter O'Toole during filming of *Goodbye, Mr. Chips*, London, 1968.

With Queen Elizabeth II at the premiere of *Goodbye, Mr. Chips* at the Empire Cinema, Leicester Square, 1969. Next to me, the film's producer, Arthur P. Jacobs.

of proficiency. They were well received, and I was taking any opportunity I could to go to Paris, promote them and be with Claude.

One thing that surprised me about Paris was that it was extremely fast and efficient. On my previous, flying visits I'd assumed it was a chaotic city, but I now realised this was absolutely untrue. Parisians just had their own way of doing things. Paris worked extremely well.

Despite the language barrier, Claude was able to tell me a bit about himself. He was Jewish and, having been born in 1931, had lived in Paris during Nazi occupation as a boy. We'd had hard times in Britain during the war, especially during the Blitz, but it was nothing compared to what Claude had gone through.

During the occupation, he and his family had had to wear the yellow star.* They had a narrow escape when the French police came to their apartment, but decided not to take them away as Claude's father had served in World War I. These terrifying experiences were to stay with him throughout his life.

Nevertheless, Claude did well at school and had intended to go on to study to become a lawyer. Then he'd discovered jazz. He'd managed a group his friends had formed, helped to run the Vieux Colombier jazz club in Saint Germain, then progressed to looking after Sidney Bechet. He then met Léon Cabat and secured his job at Disques Vogue.

---

* Many years later, Claude and I were invited to a very grand ball in Munich. We were in a lift with two older German men, both sporting military medals. Claude looked fantastic, in a Mao suit with a little red Mao badge on the collar. One of the Germans said, 'Ah, Mao!' and Claude replied, 'Yes, I decided not to wear my yellow star tonight.' Silence. That lift journey seemed to last forever.

While I was hot-footing it to France to see Claude, I made a TV movie there. Co-starring Jean Poiret, *L'anglais tel qu'on le parle* [*English As It Is Spoken*] told the story of a young Englishwoman in Paris who hardly speaks French. So I was perfect casting! It was funny and people liked it, even if I found acting in French quite a stretch.

It was an exciting time, but as it became clear that Claude and I were very serious about each other, the question arose: *where were we going to live?* If we were to be together, then one of us was going to have to uproot and move to the other's country. And the more we thought and talked about it, the more likely it seemed that it would be me.

It made sense. Claude still spoke little English so there was not much he'd have been able to do in London. My French was hesitant but improving, and I appeared to be developing quite a following in France, so I knew I'd be able to work there. Also, beneath it all, I think I was probably ready for a change.

I felt almost imprisoned in England. I say this in the nicest way, but the public had not enjoyed seeing me growing up. It was as if their youth was disappearing right in front of their eyes. I was still having British success with records, but the idea of moving to France felt not just tempting but exciting.

As Claude and I worked towards that decision, I did more British tour dates. I always used to love performing at Blackpool Opera House. The crowds were on their hols and out for a great time, so they were always warm and welcoming. And, on BBC Radio, I did a last joint project with an old flame.

Joe Henderson was still developing his own successful song-writing and performing career, including hits such as 'Trudie', and he and I reunited for a short series called *Pet and Mr Piano*.

Working together again on the show was slightly tricky, but I still loved Joe: just no longer in a romantic sense. Life had pulled me in a different direction.

That direction was Paris, and I went back into IBC Studios in London and recorded another EP in French. The main track was '*Prends mon coeur*', a French-language version of a song called '(Now and Then There's) A Fool Such As I' which had been a US hit for both Hank Snow and Elvis Presley. I have to say, my version wasn't bad at all.

Claude and I had by now resolved that I'd move to Paris. Before I did so, I ticked a silly showbiz box. I had been asked to play the princess in a pantomime, *Humpty Dumpty*, at the Gaumont Theatre in Southampton. *I've never done a panto*, I thought. *I've got to do one now, before I leave!*

It was a hoot. Normally in British panto, the lead 'male' part is taken by a woman but in Southampton, Edmund Hockridge, the Canadian singer, played the prince. Derek Roy, the comedian, was the dame. And the king – the one who sends all of his horses and all of his men, who couldn't put Humpty together again – was Tommy Cooper.

I adored Tommy. All through rehearsals, he played it straight. But once we got onstage, it was mayhem. He just did, and said, whatever the hell he wanted. Once he realised it was easy to make me laugh onstage, every time we shared a scene, he'd come on in a crazy hat, or waving a silly prop.

Claude was coming over to meet my family at Christmas, before I moved to Paris in the new year, and he wanted to come and see me in what he called *Oompty Doompty*. He was curious to see what it was all about (which, actually, was a very good question). So, I gave him instructions to find us.

'Get a train from Waterloo to Southampton,' I told him. 'Then get a taxi to the Gaumont Theatre. There's a little alley-way to the side of it and the stage door is there.'

Well, Claude followed my instructions, and it still went wrong. He made his way to the Gaumont, walked down the alleyway, saw a light over an open door, and walked ... into an Army recruitment centre.

'Hello. Can I help you?' asked the uniformed man behind the desk, with no idea what was playing next door at the Gaumont.

'*Oompty Doompty!*' said Claude.

'Pardon? Are you foreign? This is for the British Army!'

'*Oompty Doompty?*'

Confusion reigned, until Claude got escorted to our stage door. I'm still not sure he understood the first thing about our *Oompty Doompty*. Mind you, it was probably a good job that it was Edmund Hockridge playing the prince rather than a woman. Had the role been taken by a girl, that *would* have thrown Claude completely.

More importantly, that Christmas, Claude made a good impression on my father – after all, he was good-looking, successful, and clearly loved me. It was a relief to me that my dad liked him. After everything, it still mattered.

* * *

I moved to Paris at the start of 1960 and settled into Claude's apartment in Bourg-la-Reine. My emigration made the British papers, and the consensus of their coverage was that I was 'running away' to France in order to get away from my little girl, 'Our Pet' image. Or something like that.

This mystified me because it made no sense. If I'd wanted to 'run away', why would I run to France? Surely I'd have moved to Denmark a year earlier, where I was already a big star, had a Danish boyfriend at the time and people spoke English? No, the only reason I went to France was that I'd fallen in love with a Frenchman. End of story.

I'd pulled up my roots and I got well and truly into French life. There was a lot to learn. I quickly realised that the French have a different way of looking at life. They know all about fashion, and beauty, and perfume, and art, and food, and wine … the sensual things in life, which I knew very little about. And I soaked these things up like a sponge.

I didn't study them: I just picked them up. It was the same with learning the language. I never took lessons: I just listened to the television, and the radio, and, mostly, people talking around me. Really, it was the same as when I'd picked up Welsh as a little girl, twenty years earlier. I learned French by osmosis.

That didn't mean that it was easy, of course. Claude and I would go to dinner with some of his friends. Everyone would be talking French and, in my head, I'd try to work out a phrase to slot into the conversation. By the time I'd done it, they'd have changed the subject! But I kept trying, and kept learning.

I also threw myself into French music and show business, and it helped that, suddenly, I had a big hit. Europe n° 1 and other French radio stations loved the version of '*Prends mon coeur*' that I'd recorded before I left London. They played it a lot, and it became a hit.

I think it did well because by now I was getting surer about singing in French. I'd thrown myself into the song because I was more confident. That's so much of the battle: not being afraid to go for it. Plunge in and give it your all. And, by now, I had begun doing just that.

When I did promotional interviews, it was refreshing that most French journalists knew little about my 'child-star' past and cared even less. They knew that I'd had a successful career, in England, but so what? They just liked me the way I was. It was quite liberating. I still wasn't totally being 'me' because I had this quirky English accent when I sang in French. I couldn't do anything about that. But I was unlike any other female singers they'd heard before.

The French were used to stars like the Spanish-born Gloria Lasso, or the Egyptian-born Dalida, who sang French with a Latin accent. I reminded them slightly of Josephine Baker, the amazing American-born, Paris-based singer who was a huge star.* But I was different again. I sang like an English pop singer, because, well, that was what I was.

The French newspapers and magazines took to calling me '*pétillante*', which translates as sparkling and bubbly (like Champagne!). Or they would write about me under headlines like '*La pétulante Pétula*', which means something very similar. I didn't mind. There are worse things to be called!

I got called a few new names, in fact. A lot of people had only heard my name on the radio and never seen it written down, and therefore assumed that I was called Pétu La Clark. I guess it just looked more French. When I first started receiving fan mail in France, that was how most of the letters were addressed.

It's interesting that I rarely got homesick when I moved to France. The only thing I really missed was the British sense

---

* Although, unlike Josephine, I never did exotic dances in a banana skirt. But I met her many times and she was a great lady.

of humour. Laughing has always been important to me, and French comics left me rather cold.* But I could get my fix every time I popped back across *la Manche* for a few days.

In March 1960, I got asked to do my first French television special: *Rendez-vous avec Petula Clark*. And it was totally different to working on British TV. I was used to the BBC, where great producers such as Yvonne Littlewood made sure everything was perfectly rehearsed, and gave the cameramen a script that they had to follow precisely.

French television was a different story. The cameramen were technicians but they were also artists. If they didn't like what the producers were telling them to do, they'd ignore them, take off their headphones and do their own thing. There was very little studio discipline but the shows were always beautifully shot.

I hadn't had a manager since I'd parted ways professionally with my father, but Claude now assumed the role. We didn't really even talk about it: it just made sense, given that he knew the French entertainment world inside out. And he quickly engaged some really good musicians so I could play live dates.

Newly armed with a band, I set off around the country playing shows. France is very beautiful and very big, and we roamed all over. I soon realised how well known *La pétulante Pétula* had rapidly become. We'd go to towns of all sizes, from Normandy down to the Med, and invariably arrive to find vast crowds eagerly awaiting me.

I found travelling around France fascinating. In the summer, I appeared in spectacular Roman arenas in Nîmes,

---

* Except for Jacques Tati. His movies were silent, so I didn't need to speak the language to find him funny.

Orange and Arles. I'd often be performing after they'd staged a bullfight that afternoon, which would mean blood spatters all over the dressing room. There'd rarely be electricity and I'd have to do my make-up by candlelight. It sounds romantic. It really wasn't.

In other places, we'd play open-air shows in town centres to thousands of people. We would arrive to find that *les gendarmes* had closed off the entire centre of the town. At those gigs, Claude's headache was controlling the tickets and preventing people who hadn't bought them from getting in.

We'd go to places I'd never even heard of. We went to a ravishing little town called Agen in the southwest of the country, constructed largely of Cotswolds-type stone. It is well known throughout France for the delicious prunes that are grown there.

Now, I've never been an enormous fan of prunes, but Agen prunes are *so* tasty and juicy. Claude and I bought a large bag of them, then somehow managed to rip it and spill them in the car we were touring in. For weeks afterwards, we were finding rotting prunes in every corner of it. It put me off them for a while.

In the winter, I'd travel around France performing in packed clubs, theatres and also grand casinos, which would always have very well-dressed audiences. There was a real established circuit in place and, like all of the big, established French stars, I got used to it. I loved trekking around it.

Getting to the shows was an adventure in itself. We travelled across France in a fleet of three Citroën shooting brake cars, carrying our musicians and equipment, and we always seemed to be in a hurry, driving at breakneck speeds to try to make it in time for the next show. Overtaking was terrifying. Death-defying.

These were the days before *les autoroutes*, so we were trying to speed down small roads and even country lanes. In the summer, they'd be packed with dawdling holidaymakers pulling caravans. Belgian tourists were particularly slow-moving. In those days, you didn't need to pass a test to drive in Belgium, and, well, let's just say that you could tell.

I'd be in the first car with Claude, who'd be driving like a maniac as usual. Sometimes, he'd swing off the road and speed through a field to pass slow traffic. One time he did that, I looked behind us to see about fifty cars following us on our improvised short cut. There were clouds of dust everywhere. The poor farmer must have had a heart attack.

My French was improving but I was still dropping howlers. I went onstage in a Roman amphitheatre in Nîmes on a sweltering day and said, '*Je suis chaude.*' The crowd fell about. 'I'm hot' in French is '*J'ai chaud*', but I'd inadvertently said something with a sexual meaning that you really didn't want to announce to thousands of people.

I made that sort of mistake all the time, but you know what? The audiences lapped it up.

This, as you can imagine, was a pretty intense schedule. Claude was having to deal with the business side of it all: finances, organising, contracts. They were totally his department. I sang the songs. We were both thoroughly enjoying this new phase in our lives and learning so much about each other.

We were travelling together and sharing experiences that opened our minds and our hearts. We were a great team. Claude and I discovered that we had a shared love of antiques, and began regularly stopping our little convoy to dive into random antique shops. We'd turn up at gigs with a grandfather clock strapped to our car roof, or an *armoire* squeezed in between the amps.

Yet those French tours could be gruelling, partly because of the huge distances between the shows. Of course, I wasn't the only person on the circuit. Claude knew a restaurant in Provence where all the famous singers used to go to swap funny stories about adventures on tour. There, I got to know some of the biggest names in French music.

Sacha Distel was one of the first stars that I met. I got on really well with him right from the start. Sacha spoke very good English and shared my love of jazz. He and I connected quickly, and he was very good to me for all the years that I knew him.

As I got established in France, Sacha and I did a lot of TV together. A husband-and-wife duo, Maritie and Gilbert Carpentier, produced a string of light-entertainment TV shows that became enormously popular and are now iconic.* Sacha and I would sing and do silly sketches together on those programmes, and on his own show, *Le Sacha Show*.

When I first met Sacha, he'd just stopped dating Brigitte Bardot and he flirted with everyone. He was handsome and charming, and I could see why he had so much success with the ladies. Not that I was ever tempted. I liked him but he just wasn't my type.

Sacha was easy-going and happy-go-lucky. If one thing irked him, it was that the public didn't take him all that seriously as a singer. They liked him but he was seen as a bit of a light-weight. That view only really changed in 1962 when he co-wrote

---

* Even today, these shows sometimes get repeated on French television. There is nothing like them on TV nowadays.

and sang '*La belle vie*' aka 'The Good Life', which was also a big hit in English for Tony Bennett.

Charles Aznavour, whom I met at around the same time as Sacha, never had a problem being taken seriously. Charles was tiny but had such gravitas. He was a true *artiste*. When I first heard his music, before I could speak French well, I couldn't understand a word of any of his songs. But once I did – *wow!* They were incredible.

Charles and I also got on very well and, like Sacha, he and I were to remain friends all through his life. We also sang together on the Carpentiers' TV shows, we'd meet up fairly often and, a few years later, I was his matron of honour when he got married, to Ulla, in Las Vegas. But I'm getting ahead of myself again.

\* \* \*

A great thing about me quickly becoming successful in France was that it opened up other French-speaking nations to me. I began regularly playing dates in both Belgium and Switzerland, and then, interestingly, went further afield to the former French colonies in North Africa such as Algeria, Morocco and Tunisia.

These were wonderful experiences. I remember one afternoon in Algeria we were driving through the desert in a Jeep and stopped at a place where some travelling people, nomads, had set up camp with a few large tents. Some female nomads wandered out to see what was going on. There were no men around: they were all out at work. The women invited me into the tent. It was females-only so the men were not allowed in. Claude and the other guys had to sit and wait in the Jeep.

These beautiful Arab women looked after me for an hour. I watched them doing their cooking, and they fed me. It was fascinating to see how they lived. As I left, they gave me a desert bird as a present: a beautiful little thing. I took it with me and kept it for as long as I could but, eventually, I had to let it fly away.

I played a show in Algeria at a perfect little opera house in Oran. The next morning, when we were due to leave, a huge sandstorm blew in. Sand everywhere. You closed the doors, you closed the windows, but the sand was still in your food. It was a blizzard, and there would clearly be no flights that day.

For something to do, that evening I went back to the opera house with my musical director, Hubert. We were the only non-Arabs in the theatre and watched a local female singer perform. She was clearly an idol. She was wearing a long, flowing dress, and the audience, who were nearly all men, were taking it in turns to go up to the stage and kiss the hem of her dress.

This star had a full orchestra playing her very complicated music and all of her songs were at least ten minutes long. She was like an Arabian Ella Fitzgerald. Her voice was amazing. *I want to learn to sing like her*, I thought. When I got back to Paris, I told Claude my new career plan. 'Are you mad?' he said, laughing.*

And then, back in Paris, at the start of 1961, I witnessed an even more extraordinary performance. In truth, I was not well versed in the music of the legendary Édith Piaf, but when I heard she was playing a rare show at the Olympia, I decided to go along and see her.

---

* A few years later, I played a show in Abidjan, in Ivory Coast. We met a village chief who stroked my cheek and offered Claude twelve cows for me. I was quite flattered: I mean, that's a lot of cows! But Claude declined the offer.

Piaf was clearly not terribly well. She was near the end of her career and suffering from bad arthritis, and she shuffled onto the stage looking extremely frail and thin. The musicians behind her were all in black and the stage was in total darkness except for a single spotlight on her.

Piaf's hair was dyed red and she was wearing a plain black dress – not remotely chic or stylish – with a little crucifix around her neck. There was a big orchestra but no fanfare; no big intro-duction; nothing. I thought, *Uh-oh, I'm not sure I'm going to enjoy this*. And then she began to sing.

Piaf had this amazing voice, rich with vibrato. But she wasn't just singing with her voice: she sang with her heart, body and soul. In her powerful voice – *where is that coming from?* – she sang songs of love, and hate, and madness, and sex, and death. And the way that she sang them was unique.

This was the kind of music that French people listened to. Piaf wasn't really a cult figure: she was a pop singer, as in short for popular. There were other people around who were also singing powerful songs, like Jacques Brel, and Juliette Gréco, and Georges Brassens, but Piaf was her own category. I'd never seen anyone like her.

I'd grown up in the British music-hall showbiz tradition. Piaf had no sequins, nothing flash or phony: as I say, she just sang with her heart and her soul and her guts. She had no tricks. And as I sat in the Olympia and watched her, I thought, *OK, so THAT'S what singing is all about*. It was an education for me.

Remarkably, a year or so after this show, I was voted France's favourite singer in a poll – over Piaf. I bumped into Édith in a Brussels hotel and she kindly congratulated me, but that vote didn't make any sense to me at the time. And it still doesn't today.

Rock and roll was breaking through in France at this time. It was meeting with quite a pushback. The established radio stations wouldn't play it: some of them even smashed rock-and-roll records on air. Stars like Aznavour and Gilbert Bécaud were saying, 'What is this rubbish, coming in from America? It's not real music!'

Claude didn't agree with this and he took the gamble of putting on France's first rock-and-roll festival, *Le Festival du Rock*, in Paris in February 1961. It was a huge success, and it sold out because teenagers and young people were really into the music. The headliner was Johnny Hallyday, and it played a big part in launching his career.*

I didn't 'become French' during this time but France grew in me. I even began thinking in French. I went back to England to do a TV interview and I struggled with my English. There were long pauses as I tried to think of a word and I found myself waving my hands around. People thought I was putting on an act but I really wasn't.

That first year of living in France, and touring here, there and everywhere, was such a special time for Claude and me. They were our halcyon days. We knew that we were building something. Neither of us had much money yet, but we were working hard, and everything was coming together.

I was having the time of my life in France. Did I ever regret moving to Paris? *Non!* Not for one second.

---

\* Johnny was just a teenager himself then, only seventeen, but he was a nice lad. He went on to become France's answer to Elvis. I never thought he was as good a singer as Elvis but by the end of his career, he had got a lot better. And when he died, in 2017, France went into national mourning.

# CHAPTER 6

# JOINING THE HUMAN RACE

Claude and I were very happy. We never actually talked about getting married but things seemed to be heading that way. Yet all through that first year in France, there was a nagging, troubling thought in the back of my head that never went away: *Can I have children?*

The conversation that I'd had with the gynaecologist at the South London Hospital for Women, after my life-saving surgery for strangulation of the intestine, had stayed with me. Because she had appeared to imply that, as a consequence, I'd be unlikely to be able to have kids.

This was a huge deal for me. I didn't for one second think that children are the key to a happy-ever-after marriage. I'd seen plenty of unhappy marriages with kids – including my own parents'. But there was no way I'd ever marry Claude if I knew I'd be unable to give him children. It just wasn't fair on him.

I was thinking, *If I get pregnant, that will be great.* But I wasn't on the Pill and it wasn't happening. So, at the start of 1961, when I was back in London to make an EP, I went to see the gynaecologist again.

'Everything between Claude and me is great, but I'm not getting pregnant,' I told her.

'You're worrying about it too much,' she replied. 'The more you think about it, the less likely it is to happen. Just relax and get on with your life.' She also told me again that, if I *were* to get pregnant, I should have the baby with her, because she knew all about my medical history.

And what do you know? A few weeks later, *voilà*! I was pregnant. I was delighted, and so was Claude, when I told him. And that was when we started talking about getting married.

Being pregnant was great. I felt wonderful. I had this feeling that I was now, somehow … *joining the human race*. Becoming part of civilisation. Before then, I'd thought, *OK, I can sing, but there has to be more to life than this*. Now, I was becoming a woman. I had become what I was made for: *what I was*.

That trip to London was very productive. While I was there, I recorded a new UK single, 'Sailor', with Alan A. Freeman producing. It wasn't the deepest song in the world but I suppose it was an OK little pop tune. Radio stations played it a lot and, after I'd sung it on Cliff Richard's TV show, it became my first ever British number one.

I have to say, this was nice. I've never fixated on the pop charts – they're just a bit of fun, really, and not the best way of judging how good a piece of music is. But there's something special about being number one. Every performer loves it. If they say they don't care, I don't believe them.

Nor was the song's success limited to one side of the Channel. As soon as the single started getting played in Britain, I'd quickly recorded a French version of 'Sailor' called '*Marin*'.

People seemed just as keen on it there, and it went to number two in the French charts.

I was still travelling all around France playing shows and by now I was beginning to earn quite good money. I particularly loved doing concerts in the south of the country. My love for the Med remained as strong as ever, so Claude and I took the plunge and bought ourselves a summer house in Vallauris.

Vallauris is a small town in the hills above the Med, known for its pottery and the fact that Pablo Picasso lived and worked there for a few years. The small farmhouse we bought was in the countryside just outside of the town. It had a magnificent palm tree, a fig tree and three large pigsties, which we eventually turned into guest rooms.

We adored this house. Claude spent hours – no, days – scraping off the old paintwork while I made curtains by hand from a lovely Provençal fabric. We were quite proud of our work. Family and friends came to visit, and we had some of our happiest times in that funky little house in the sun.

\* \* \*

On 8 June 1961, Claude and I got married in our local town hall in Bourg-la-Reine. And it was pandemonium.

There were crowds of fans, reporters and photographers around the town hall. People were literally hanging from the rafters. Even the guy who was marrying us got carried away with it all and was conducting the service in a showy, performative style. It was meant to be a special, personal experience, not a showbiz bash.

I wanted to go somewhere quiet to do it properly so, a couple of weeks later, we had a blessing at the parish church in Lodsworth, the Sussex village where my dad lived. And it was lovely.

It was the perfect English summer's day. My friend Dickie Valentine, the singer, drove us down from London in his cool American car. My family were all there, the tiny parish church at Lodsworth was sweet and picturesque and the low-key blessing was ideal. The day really was everything I wanted.*

After we were married, there was no question of sitting around and waiting for the baby to be born. I was straight back to work. I did a few British shows and then a summer tour of France and Belgium with the singer-songwriter Jean-Claude Darnal, a close friend of Claude's who had been best man at our wedding. And I released a new EP.

'Romeo' was originally a German song and was a very good pop tune which I recorded in London, in both English and French. It was a top-three hit in England in August, but the French-language version did even better. It climbed the chart and was to become my first number one in France.

By now I was heavily pregnant, which raised a few issues when I came to promote 'Roméo' in France. Nowadays, of course, a female singer who is expecting could stroll onto a television show in a T-shirt. Back in 1961, things were very different, and being a pregnant pop star was not a good look.

One French TV show got around this very inventively. The producer stood me inside a suspended metal cylinder which concealed me from my shoulders to my knees. As I sang 'Roméo', this cylinder, with clothes painted on it, revolved

---

* Chris, my half-brother, took me back to Lodsworth church quite recently. It was the most extraordinary experience. The church was empty and silent but, as I stood there, I felt as if Claude and I were there again.

around me, hiding my bump from the viewers. It was bizarre, but I went along with it.

Claude and I had had two wonderful years in the Bourg-la-Reine flat but we realised it wouldn't be big enough for three of us. We rented a larger apartment in Montparnasse and moved from the suburbs into Paris itself. And, as instructed, I dutifully returned to the South London Hospital for Women to have the baby.

I gave birth on 11 December … and what a nightmare it was. The hospital was still as dark, gloomy and forbidding as ever and, as I lay in bed, I could hear women in other rooms crying out in pain. *Gulp.* And when I went into labour myself, things got even worse.

My labour went on for hours. The nurses gave me gas and told me to take a deep breath. Well, I have a singer's lungs and I must have breathed in too much, because it knocked me out. I was unconscious as my daughter was eventually born.

Not only that, but the gas scrambled my mind. While I was under, I had a terrifying experience. I thought I heard a man's loud voice booming at me: 'There's no such thing as love, you idiot. It's all a trick!' It was scary, and I came to feeling as if I was waking from a terrible dream.

My baby daughter's crying was what woke me up. I saw her for the first time. She was exquisite, the most beautiful baby, with lots of lovely dark hair and big blue eyes. Claude and I had already decided to call her Barbara Michèle Wolff, and as I lay and cradled her in that hospital bed, I thought, *I have a child.** And she was wonderful.

---

* When she was a toddler, Barbara could never pronounce her own name. She always said 'Bara', so that was what we called her, and I still do, even today.

Bara was adorable but the bad effects of the gas messed up my head. I stayed in hospital for a couple of days and friends sent me beautiful bouquets of flowers. Yet I couldn't see the beauty. They looked ugly and menacing to me. I've never taken LSD, but it was as if I was having a bad acid trip.

When Claude and I took Bara home to Paris, I had a few more waves of this druggy paranoia for a few weeks. Bara had colic and was awake and crying more than she was asleep, so none of us got much sleep for a while. Well, no matter. She was perfect and I loved becoming a mum.

I went back to work too quickly. I wanted to stay home with Bara as much as I could, but I had signed contracts and had work commitments that had to be honoured. There was no way Claude and I could do them while carrying around a newborn baby so we realised that we'd have to get a nanny.

The first one we hired was a tiny English woman, Nanny Willis. I'm not sure she was even 5 feet tall. She was fully trained and a very serious person, in her grey uniform. She moved into the apartment with us, and it didn't take us long to realise how strict and bossy she was.

A close friend of Claude's, a heart surgeon called Bernard, came to visit us after Bara was born. Nanny Willis answered the door to him. 'Who are you?' she demanded.

'I am Claude and Petula's friend, and I have come to see their baby.'

'Well, you can't come in here.'

I heard the commotion and went over to assure Nanny Willis that Bernard was, indeed, a family friend. She still didn't want to let him in. 'Have you washed your hands?' she barked at him.

Nanny Willis wanted a spyhole put in our front door so she could see who was at the door before she opened it to them. She was so short that, if we had a tall male visitor, all she could see through the peephole was their trousers. Yet she always seemed to know who was outside. 'It's easy – I recognise their flies,' she told me.*

I'd fondly imagined that I would have a baby and then just go back to work as usual. I was wrong. I hadn't anticipated the closeness of the bond between a mother and child. Every time I had to go away and leave Bara, I'd feel guilty. I'd 'hear' her crying, hundreds of miles away. It was very tough.

* * *

At the start of 1962, I gained a wonderful new musical director. Claude and I auditioned a London pianist and MD called Kenny Clayton. And it took us no time at all to realise that he was exactly what I needed. In fact, we hired him on the spot.

Kenny was a real character. He had a wonderful musical brain, a wonderful brain in general – he'd do the *Times* crossword in minutes. He was funny and a brilliant musician. I loved his jazzy style of playing (although I had to ask him to tone it down a bit). Kenny was great fun to work with and to be around. He did a lot of his growing-up in France with me.

---

* We later had a rather large English nanny, Nanny Pat, who'd worked for a lot of *grandes familles* in France and was a bit of a snob. She'd instruct us where to stay and eat while on tour. We were once in Tetou, the famous fish restaurant near Cannes, and Nanny Pat was holding forth when her false teeth fell into the bouillabaisse with a splash. That took her down a few notches. Temporarily.

I then enjoyed another number one in France with an upbeat song called 'Ya Ya Twist'.* When I performed it on Spanish TV – this was under General Franco – they'd only film me from the waist up as my wiggling around was 'too suggestive'. That also happened once on French television. I guess they were my Elvis Presley moments.

Around this time, my musical career took an unexpected new turn when I began singing in other languages. My records were doing well in France, and other countries started to take notice. Disques Vogue asked me to sing not only in French but also in German and Italian.

It was an interesting challenge but it worked out OK, even though I didn't speak either language. In 1962, I recorded a new EP, an original French song called 'Chariot'. It became my biggest hit in French. I also did an Italian version, '*Sul mio carro*' and a German one titled, oddly, 'Cheerio'. There's something to be said for not knowing what you're doing, because it was also a big hit in both countries.

Soon afterwards, I recorded 'Monsieur', a song written for me by two famous German songwriters. I hated it and tried to turn it down but was coaxed into a recording studio. I first recorded 'Monsieur' in German and, a little later, in Italian. And, guess what … it went to number one in both countries.

Singing in the two languages was very different. I liked singing in Italian and I adored going there to perform. I love Italy and Italians and they, in turn, love music and singers. An

---

* 'Ya Ya Twist' was covered around the same time by two other big French artists – Johnny Hallyday and Richard Anthony.

early trip there to appear on a television programme was enjoyable but distinctly off-the-wall.

As we prepared to record the show, we rehearsed all through the afternoon and then the producers said, 'Let's take a break and go and eat.' We had a great meal, and they said, 'You know what? Let's not bother shooting it again – what we already have is good!'

'Hey! Wait a minute,' I said. 'I wasn't wearing any make-up, or the right dress!'

'Oh no, it was fine. We don't need to do it again.' So the rehearsal went out on TV. Well, that's Italy for you.

Germany was a different story. I never really enjoyed singing in German. I wasn't good at the language and I thought some of the songs the record company gave me to sing were dubious. Somebody would coach me through the songs and, after a few takes, would say, '*Wunderbar!*' I'd think, *Eh? Are you sure? Because it sounds awful to me!*

But I recorded in German *a lot*. I remember doing God-knows-how-many tracks in a big, grey studio in Munich. It felt like a factory production line: they even sounded a klaxon when the tapes started rolling. I had a lot of hits in Germany over the years, but I never felt I was singing them properly.

\* \* \*

By autumn 1962, I was expecting again. Claude and I hadn't actually discussed having another child so soon after Bara, but I was delighted and so was he. It was great news. I was lucky enough not to suffer from morning sickness and I loved being pregnant as much as I had the first time around.

Suddenly, our flat was once more not going to be big enough and it was time for me and Claude to move again. This time we went to a big apartment right next to the Bois de Boulogne, overlooking the park. It was a lovely place to be and, a few weeks after we moved there, it gave us a magical moment.

We'd moved in during winter and, the following spring, I awoke one morning to find our bedroom, and the whole of the apartment, suffused in a gorgeous pink glow. It was the reflection of the chestnut trees in the Bois de Boulogne as they came back into flower.* Waking up in that flat at that time of year always felt enchanting.

We settled into our new home quickly and easily – and one of our first guests was a man who was soon to become one of the towering giants of French popular music.

Serge Gainsbourg was not yet a big star when I met him, but I knew his music and I liked his way of singing – he had a very special sound to his voice. Once I got to know him, I liked him even more. He was an ugly-attractive kind of man, if that makes sense; he spoke excellent English and he had a great sense of humour. We got on very well.

Yet Serge was very nervous when he came to our Bois de Boulogne flat to play me a song he'd written for me called '*Vilaine fille, mauvais garçon*' ('Naughty Girl, Bad Boy'). I had a brand-new baby-grand piano, which I was very proud of, and Serge sat down, played me the song and sang it to me. He was classically trained and a terrific musician.

I'd been in France for more than two years by now but some English habits die hard. If ever I had guests at 4pm, I always

---

* As the famous song goes: 'April in Paris, chestnuts in blossom'.

offered them a cup of tea. Maybe because he was nervous, maybe just because he was Serge, he asked me for a beer instead. I fetched him one … and he promptly spilled it into the piano.

Well, Serge was *mortified*. Devastated! He just kept on saying sorry. Frankly, I was pretty horrified, but I tried to hide how upset I was: 'Don't worry, it's OK.' It really *wasn't* OK: I mean, it wasn't a pub piano! It didn't do it any good at all. I got it looked at afterwards and I managed to get it fixed.

The downcast Serge went back to his publisher saying, '*C'est fini avec Petula!*' After that mishap, he feared I'd never work with him. Luckily, I really liked '*Vilaine fille, mauvais garçon*' and gave it its live debut in November 1962 when I headlined the Olympia again.

After that, Serge wrote quite a few songs for me, including '*Les incorruptibles*' and '*La gadoue*'. He'd even sometimes accompany me to London for the recording sessions to help me with some of the pronunciation. A big part of his art was the singular way he both wrote *and* emphasised his lyrics.

Serge changed over the years. When I first met him, he was quite an arty, intellectual singer. Then he altered his image, largely after the success of '*Je t'aime … moi non plus*'. He began chain-smoking onstage and developed a drugged-out, sleazy look as his music and style became more rock and roll.*

Really, he became a provocateur, swearing on television and once, famously, setting fire to a 500-franc note on live TV in a

---

* I once went to a fundraising event in Paris and Serge's widow, Jane Birkin, happened also to be in the audience. Jane and I got up and sang together one of Serge's very earliest songs, '*La Javanaise*'. It was really rather nice: two Englishwomen singing this great French chanson. And we were two women who'd both known Serge well … Jane rather better than me, of course!

protest about French tax rates. He definitely enjoyed this edgy new persona and it helped to make him a lot more successful. He changed a little offstage, as well, but was always polite and gracious with me.

* * *

When it came time to have my second child, there was no way I was going back to the South London Hospital for Women. I was having it in Paris. A lot of mothers were going to the American Hospital, which was quite hip then, but I decided on the English Hospital because I wanted a decent cup of tea after the baby was born.

I talked to our family doctor, Dr Fouquet. 'I don't want any anaesthetic or any messing about,' I told him. 'I don't want anybody to be too gentle with me. I just want a natural child-birth. No medication. I want everything to be straightforward.'

Dr Fouquet said he knew just the person and recommended a Corsican doctor at the English Hospital. He was perfect. On 23 May 1963, I had the most natural birth, with no injections or gas, and I *felt* my gorgeous daughter being born. And I *did* get a decent cup of tea afterwards. Claude and I named her Catherine Nathalie and, from the off, called her Kate.

That summer, the four of us headed down to the house in Vallauris to relax and soak up some sunshine. While we were there, we had a very curious episode. Poor Bara got a bad earache: what the French call *une otite*. She was in a lot of pain and we had to call out a local doctor.

On this same day, a magazine had come to photograph me and my family for their Christmas issue (they were working a long way in advance, as I would be touring later). It was a scorching August

South of France day, but the photographers lit a roaring fire, set up a Christmas tree, and hung decorations all over the place.

The French doctor arrived in the middle of all this. He walked into the living room, gazed all around him, raised an eyebrow and asked me: '*Où est la malade?*' – 'Where is the sick person?' I think he thought there was something wrong with *all* of us.

My pianist and musical director, Kenny Clayton, often came to Vallauris. We were preparing some new songs, and I mentioned to Kenny that I wished I had a piano in the house to work on. He nodded but didn't really say anything, and we carried on as best as we could.

How it happened, I do not know, but a day or two later, a battered old truck turned up with a piano on the back and two guys hanging on to it to stop it falling off. This piano was truly ancient and yet, somehow, it sounded fantastic. I had no idea where Kenny had found it, or if it had fallen off a local lorry. I figured it was best not to ask.

When I got properly back to work later in the summer of 1963, I had the great fortune to do a tour in the north of France with an incredible talent. Jacques Brel was Belgian by birth, of course, but his emotive, passionate songs had made him a massive star in France.

Jacques sang his songs with such extraordinary power: every night, I stood in the wings and watched him perform. The only problem was that he spat a lot because he had quite protruding teeth. The first two rows of the audience used to get sprayed with his saliva. They didn't seem to mind.

Offstage, Jacques was charming and funny. We had a great time together. At the end of the tour, he gave me a gift: a song he'd written for me, called '*Un enfant*', to mark Kate's birth. It's a beautiful song that, over the years, I have sung many times in France and Belgium. I will always treasure it.

Shortly after this, I played a few concerts in Italy. On the way there, I shared a train journey with a teenage Françoise Hardy, who'd signed to Disques Vogue and was having success in Italy as part of the musical yé-yé craze. Françoise was a real beauty but we didn't exactly hit it off on that first meeting.

Françoise wasn't being sociable. She sat and read a book, and didn't talk to me for the entire journey. I guess she and I were so different: she was tall, elegant and cool, and I was *La pétulante Pétula*: small, bubbly and smiley. But I loved her records and the way she sang, and I suppose that aloofness was all part of her image and appeal.

My life was now fully centred on France. For two years, I'd done very little work in the UK. But that didn't stop British TV producers springing a major surprise on me at the start of 1964 when I made a flying visit to London.

Yvonne Littlewood had asked me to appear in one of her TV variety productions at the BBC Television Theatre. At the end, the cast were all lined up taking our bows, when I suddenly spotted the television presenter Eamonn Andrews appear on the edge of the stage with his famous big red book.

There were quite a few stars in the line-up, like the pianist Russ Conway and the French violinist Stéphane Grappelli, so I didn't imagine that Eamonn was there for me. But he walked along the row of performers, stopped in front of me and said those dreaded words: 'Petula Clark – *This Is Your Life*!'

How did I feel? Shocked, initially, with a side order of *oh, no!* I've always been a private person, and I wasn't sure I fancied the minutiae of my life being laid bare on British TV. At the same time, I knew it was an honour, and … what choice did I have? I couldn't leg it out of the theatre! I had to go along with it.

Claude had known all about it and helped to set it up, of course, and he was waiting as the show began. So many faces from my past reappeared: Jack Warner, Anthony Newley (on the phone), Joe Henderson and even Percy Edwards, and at the end Babs came on with Bara and Kate. Which was the best bit.*

Also in 1964, I performed in Romania while it was still under the jackboot of the Soviet Union. It was a strange and difficult experience. I have seen poverty in my life many times, but here was a different, dreadful kind of poverty – a total spiritual and emotional impoverishment.

We knew that we were being watched, and our hotel rooms were bugged, but the worst thing was observing the kind, warm-hearted people living lives of misery. We had flown into Bucharest from Paris, and all of our French newspapers were confiscated as soon as we arrived at customs.

The authorities gave us a lovely translator who was an ex-ballet dancer. She never left our side. As we got to know each other, this woman asked if I had anything from France that she could read. I fished out a copy of *Marie Claire*, which was buried deep in my luggage and had been missed in the airport search. 'Would you like this?' I asked.

The lady gave me a horrified stare: 'No! I can't take that,' she answered. She knew that she'd be in big trouble with the authorities if she were caught with a Western magazine. Yet she

---

* The *This Is Your Life* producers were to nab me twice more – once in 1975 and again in 1996, when I was in *Sunset Boulevard*. That third time, I went backstage and told my dresser: 'Not again! I can't face it.' She gave me a large vodka and tonic and somehow, after that, it wasn't so bad at all.

wanted it so much. In the end, I very carefully wrapped it up in a local newspaper for her so she could sneak it out.

We played what was called the People's Palace: the equipment was state-of-the-art and the audiences wonderful. But the trip was so depressing. We were there for a week or so then flew out to Vienna. It was a culture shock to see joy there, and people actually looking happy, again. It took me a while to get over our trip to Romania.

\* \* \*

I had known Tony Hatch for a few years. He was an up-and-coming young producer who worked for my British label, Pye Records. I had first met him, around five years earlier, when he was a junior recording manager who was assisting Alan A. Freeman while Alan was producing my London recording sessions.

By now, these sessions were mostly in French. Tony wasn't choosing the songs because he didn't speak the language, but he would book the musicians and an engineer, the wonderful Ray Prickett (the very best at the job, in my opinion). Tony was very talented, and he was nice, and I liked him.

Tony and I soon grew close, and Claude and I invited him down to Vallauris. We always had a great time together. When Alan got promoted at Pye, Tony took over his job, producing records by bands like The Searchers. He became my main producer and also began writing his own songs.

Tony and I soon developed a good working system. Every now and then, he'd come to our apartment in Paris and play me a handful of song demos, plus maybe a couple of his own compositions. I'd select the ones I liked, then fly to London to record them with him a couple of weeks later.

On these visits, Tony was mostly playing me French songs selected by the team at Disques Vogue. I was hardly recording in English at that point. It wasn't a conscious choice, as such: it was more that my career in Europe was going so well that the whole English side of things had been slightly put on the back burner.

*That was about to change.*

In the late summer of 1964, Tony returned to our apartment in the Bois de Boulogne with the usual demos of French songs. We listened to them and I picked out the best ones. Then Tony said to me, 'You really should be recording in English again.'

I laughed. 'Listen, Tony!' I said. 'I've got quite enough on my plate recording in French, Italian and German, and looking after two kids! But I *would* like to sing in English again. We just need to find the right song. Do you have any ideas?'

'Well, I've just started writing a song,' he said. 'I don't have very much yet, no lyrics – just a melody, really. Would you like to hear it?'

'Of course!'

It was four o'clock, so I headed into the kitchen to make us some tea. Tony sat at my piano and began to play this tremendous melody. *Hmm, that's not bad at all!* I thought. In fact, the second I heard it, I really liked it.

I walked back into the room and put the tea tray down. 'That sounds great, Tony!' I said. 'If you can write a lyric up to the standard of that music, I'll definitely record it. Do you have a title yet?'

'Yes,' he replied. 'I'm going to call it "Downtown".'

# CHAPTER 7

# WHEN AMERICA CALLS, YOU PICK UP

It was two weeks later that I flew to London to record a few tracks at Pye Studios at Marble Arch. And when I got there, it was clear that Tony Hatch had used that fortnight very productively.

The skeleton of a song that Tony had called 'Downtown' had been fleshed out. It had these great lyrics about fending off feeling alone and lonely by going to the beating heart of a bustling city: 'the lights are much brighter there'. It was about going out, shaking off your problems and *feeling alive*: 'Forget all your troubles, forget all your cares'.

Tony was to tell me later that he'd had the idea for the song a few weeks earlier, on his first ever trip to New York. He'd wandered from his hotel on Central Park down to Times Square and Broadway and thrilled to the buzz of Manhattan. He said the melody had come to him as he waited to cross 48th Street.

Yet even before I heard the lyrics, I walked into Pye Studios and heard Tony conducting a huge orchestra through the arrangement he'd written for the song. Tony was simply a brilliant orchestrator and what he'd come up with for 'Downtown' was amazing. As I took my coat off, I couldn't wait to get up to the microphone and sing it.

I think we did three takes. We used the second one. There was no messing around, no musical tricks or special effects: just me singing this great song that Tony had dreamed up and given a fantastic accompaniment. Although Tony wasn't actually conducting the orchestra as I sang – he was producing it all in the control room.

Did we know we'd recorded a monster song? No, not really. You can never know that. If we all knew the formula to writing huge hits, life would be a lot easier! We never decide which songs become enormous: record buyers do. All that I knew, as I flew back to France, was that we had made a very good record.

Tony said that when he first played 'Downtown' to the high-ups at Pye, they weren't too sure about it. But then Joe Smith entered the picture. Joe was a funny, very short guy – I could see eye-to-eye with him – who worked at Warner Bros in Los Angeles. Pye had a link with Warner, and Joe used to go to London to find British material to release in the US.

Joe was a man who knew what he liked and, as soon as he heard 'Downtown', he loved it and pencilled it in for immediate release in America. Tony was surprised by this and asked Joe if it wasn't a 'very English' song. 'No,' replied Joe. 'It's an observation of America from the outside, and it's beautiful and perfect.'

Joe was on to something. Warner released 'Downtown' in November 1964 and it was in America's *Billboard* charts by Christmas. By the second week of January, it was in the top five. I had never remotely imagined having success in the US. It's not a thing you can plan – it has to just happen. And, suddenly, it seemed to be happening.

The funny thing was that while this was going on, I was in North America – but not in the States. I was on a tour of French-speaking Canada, doing a two-and-a-half-hour, one-woman show entirely in French. And loving it.

It was such a fascinating tour. I started with a week at the Comédie-Canadienne Theatre in Montreal. Montreal is a bilingual city, of course (which was to lead to the onstage mishaps a few years later that would send me running to John and Yoko). But this first time, I was booked to perform solely in French.

Claude and I had taken Bara and Kate with us, as usual – we hated to leave them. It was the first time the girls had stayed up and seen one of my shows. When I went backstage during the intermission, they were excited. Bara came running up to me, beaming, and said, 'Mummy! Mummy! We've just seen Mummy onstage!' Then she stopped dead, and looked rather embarrassed, as if she realised she'd just said something silly. It wasn't. It was adorable.

That Canadian tour was amazing. I played Québec City then smaller towns such as Saint-Jérôme, and Chicoutimi, and Trois-Rivières in the depth of winter. I've never seen snow like it, before or since. And *so cold*! It was −50°C every day. I remember the Saint Lawrence River was frozen over. The boats had to use ice-cutters to get down it.

We did the whole Canadian experience. We drove Ski-Doos on iced-over lakes and fished through holes in the ice. Two local guys came with us, looked after us and showed us the ropes. They drank like fishes but they were great fun.

I had to wrestle with the local accent. As we travelled around, I realised that French–Canadian French is *very* different from the French I'd learned by ear in Paris. It was a mixture of very old French, or *real* French, and American phrases. I'd do radio interviews and find I couldn't understand the questions I was being asked. I didn't want to offend anyone, so I had to quickly get my ears tuned in.

While we were in Canada, 'Downtown' was still going up the *Billboard* chart. Claude would get an update every week. And on 23 January 1965, the single went to number one in America.

How did I feel when I heard? If I'm honest, totally taken aback. As I say, success in America was never on my radar. I was happy with my career in France and Europe, and raising my family. I know a lot of performers long to be big in America but, in truth, I'd never given it much thought. But now, suddenly, America was calling me.

*And when America calls you, you pick up.*

While I was still touring Quebec, Claude started getting phone calls asking me to fly to New York to go on *The Ed Sullivan Show*. This was *the* entertainment show in America, but I don't think Claude realised exactly what a big deal it was.

'That *Ed Sullivan Show* has called again,' he would tut. 'They won't stop ringing me.'

'Er, I think it's quite important, Claude?' I'd say.

'We cannot get there,' Claude would reply. 'We have too much on. We are too busy.'

Claude was certainly right that we were busy. After Canada, we only had a couple of days in Paris before we had to go to Italy for the Sanremo Music Festival. And what a curious event that turned out to be.

The festival was, and still is, a song contest. There were all sorts of stars appearing – Gene Pitney, Dusty Springfield, Kiki

Dee, Connie Francis and Fred Bongusto – but the judges were marking the songs, not the singers. The festival was big news in Italy and the whole country stopped to watch it.

I shared a dressing room with Dusty Springfield. The odd thing was that I didn't know her all that well because shows never booked us together. If they wanted a female singer, they would book *either* me *or* Dusty. So, it was nice to get to hang out with her in private … even if it wasn't quite as private as we thought.

They put us in a temporary dressing room: a kind of screened-off area, with no ceiling. Dusty and I were in our undies, changing into our stage clothes, when I heard clicking. I looked up to see a gang of paparazzi feverishly taking photos over the screens. I often wonder what happened to those photographs. Nothing, I hope.

I sang a lovely song called '*Invece no*'. The song was melodramatic, but I guess it had to be for an Italian song contest. A great Italian musical director, Ezio Leoni (whom I knew as he used to produce my Italian records), was conducting the orchestra.

The middle section of the song was complex, with some difficult high notes. When I hit them, people in the audience stood up. They were talking and shouting. I thought there must be an emergency in the theatre. I stopped singing and stared at the musical director. He mouthed at me: 'Go on! Carry on!' I finished the song to a standing ovation.

Backstage, I collared Ezio, the MD: 'What was *that* about?' He explained that they loved how I'd hit the high notes, and Italian audiences *get involved* in shows: people like to show off that they know a performance is good. At operas, they'll jump up and demand an aria is sung again. That's Italians for you. They love music and they love singers.

* * *

The phone calls from America kept coming. Warner Bros wanted a quick follow-up to 'Downtown'. Luckily, we had one. Tony Hatch had come up with a very good pop tune with a great hook: 'I Know a Place'.* We recorded it in London, it hit number three in the US ... and we finally arranged to go on *The Ed Sullivan Show*.

It was still tough to sort out. The show was broadcast live from New York – to 50 million Americans – on Sunday nights. We were to appear on 14 March. The producers said we had to do a full-day rehearsal the day before, but I was doing a benefit for a Paris school that night. I didn't want to cancel *that*, so we said we'd fly in on the morning of the show.

Well, that was our plan. The reality was different. Our Sunday-morning plane from Paris to New York was cancelled. We had no choice but to get an afternoon flight, which was cutting it very fine. I arrived at the CBS TV Theatre on Broadway jet-lagged and not quite sure where the hell I was, two hours before I was due to perform.

The producers were relieved to see me: 'Oh, thank God, she's here!' They were very kind. They put a little bed in my dressing room to give me the chance to try to grab some sleep. I stumbled along to the pre-show dress rehearsal, arriving on set to find the orchestra playing the introduction to 'Downtown' way too fast.

---

* After 'I Know a Place' was a hit, I recorded an album of the same name in London. One of the session guitarists on it was Jimmy Page.

I walked onto the stage in a demure little black dress and the audience just stood up and cheered. *What?* It was a spine-tingling moment. It seemed that New Yorkers had adopted 'Downtown' as their city's song. It had become their anthem. And, in a way, it still is.

I had arrived with a song that everybody loved, and they all wanted to see the girl that sang it. It was my first time in New York as a performer and it started a love affair that's never ended. I sang 'Downtown' and 'I Know A Place' on the live show, it went really well, and, suddenly, America exploded for me.

Americans began calling the big, shining production that Tony Hatch was putting on my records 'the London Sound'.* My voice and his orchestration were definitely a winning combination and America fell for it. And, in no time, I found myself getting bracketed with what was being called the 'British Invasion'.

I could see why. It was only a year since Beatlemania had broken out in America and The Rolling Stones, Dusty Springfield, The Kinks, The Dave Clark Five and a lot more British names had all had hits. And it wasn't just music: America was hooked on the whole idea of 'Swinging London'. They couldn't get enough of it.

How did I feel about being lumped in with it? Mixed feelings. I'd sometimes try to tell interviewers that I'd lived in France for the last five years, but they really weren't all that

---

* About eighteen months later, I recorded my 'Colour My World' single in New York with a brilliant US session drummer, Allan Schwartzberg, whom I'd worked with many times. During the session, he was looking nervous. When I asked what the problem was, he said, 'I'm scared I won't be able to get that London Sound!'

bothered. In any case, because I'd been going back and forth from Paris to 'Swinging' London to record, I knew what had been going on there.

I'd seen the rise (if you'll excuse the pun) of Mary Quant and her miniskirt, which had been mirrored in Paris by André Courrèges. Like everybody in the world, I knew all about The Beatles, who'd first played Paris in 1964, supporting Sylvie Vartan at the Olympia. I liked the clever way they played American music with their own original twist.

Sylvie, by the way, was later to marry Johnny Hallyday. She was lovely and I liked her a lot. At the end of 1964, I hosted a TV special and sang a trio with Sylvie and Françoise Hardy. We were the three biggest female singers in France at the time, so it was big news. We all really enjoyed doing it.

I'd met The Rolling Stones at the Golden Rose TV festival in Montreux the same year. Mick Jagger was a smart, well-spoken, well-educated guy who you could really have a good conversation with. He was nothing like the image you see onstage, but he could switch between the two so easily.

I once stood with Mick in the wings just before a Stones gig at the Olympia in Paris. We were chatting away, then he said, 'Right, watch *this*!' The lights went down, he leapt onstage and turned into *Mick Jagger*: this wild, incredible, hypnotic performer. Over the years, so many singers have tried to imitate him, but there's only one Mick.

So, in 1965, when I got sucked into the whole American-media thing, and was even called the First Lady of the British Invasion, I didn't mind. I just figured, *OK, I live in France, but I'm still British.* And, let's face it, it was an exciting thing to be a part of.

I still had my European commitments, including upcoming tours of France, Switzerland and Belgium, so I went back home to Paris. And Claude and I moved out of our family home on the Bois de Boulogne. We wanted the girls to have a garden to play in, and bought a house in an area called La Celle-Saint-Cloud, ten miles from the city.

I adored that house. It felt like home from the very first day. It was big but not pretentious and I had some of my happiest times there. I moved my baby-grand piano into a lovely garden outhouse and wrote a lot of songs sitting at it. I'd come to enjoy the art of songwriting almost as much as singing.

I was to co-write at that piano with some great lyricists, including Pierre Delanoë, a very poetic writer who translated all of Bob Dylan's lyrics into French – no easy task! Pierre wrote for my English accent in songs such as '*Que fais-tu là, Petula?*' – 'What Are You Doing There, Petula?' People would jokingly stop me and say it in the street.

Despite all of this, it was increasingly clear that America was about to play a very big role in my life and career. That became even more apparent in April 1965 when I won a Grammy.

I didn't go to the ceremony as I was playing the Paris Olympia that night, but they gave me a Grammy for 'Best rock and roll recording' for 'Downtown'. Now, as I said earlier, I've never seen awards as all that important, but even I had to confess that a Grammy was prestigious.*

I was flying in and out to do more American TV shows such as *Shindig!* and *Hullabaloo* and would meet some memorable

---

* I got a second one the following year, for 'I Know A Place'. The Grammys are the only ones of all my awards that I have on display in my living room. I think they're quite cute. Although bits of them keep falling off.

fellow guests. I did *Hullabaloo* with the great Marvin Gaye, and in May I was back on *The Ed Sullivan Show* with a pair of legendary co-stars: Rudolf Nureyev and Margot Fonteyn.

I stood by the stage as they rehearsed. They were divine, of course, yet the amazing thing when you see ballet up close is how strenuous it is. Normally, the exertion is covered up with music and lights. But I could hear Nureyev grunting as he lifted Fonteyn. Ballet is beautiful, yet really hard work.

Their rehearsal was hilarious. They were dancing a *pas de deux* from *Swan Lake*. Nureyev was wearing a hairnet and Fonteyn a coronet, which got caught in his hairnet. Rather than stop dancing, they thought, *Sod it!* and turned it into a comedy routine. Everybody was falling about.

Doing television shows was all very well, but it definitely felt like time to start singing live in front of American audiences. By now, I had an American agent called Bert Block, who decided that I was a 'sophisticated' singer. So, he booked me in for two weeks at the Copacabana in New York.

The 'Copa' was a legendary venue. I'd seen it in one or two movies, and in the pages of magazines, and it looked the epitome of glamour: the place to be. Artists such as Frank Sinatra and Sammy Davis Jr played there all the time. And now it was to be my turn.

We had to solve one issue first. American unions ruled the roost in those days and Bert Block told me I'd have to hire an American musical director. So, we hired a rehearsal studio and I did a day of auditions.

The auditionees were three Black guys. The first two were very good but the third was so much more. He was a good-looking guy named Frank Owens, and he already knew all my songs. He just walked in without any sheet music, sat at the piano and played my stuff off the bat, with an edge and with soul. And that was it. He was hired.

* * *

I'd like to take a short detour here to talk about Frank, who was my musical director for twelve years and a big part of my story. He was classically trained and a superb pianist and orchestrator. A lot of my best arrangements were by Frank. I loved him and he became a close family friend. He was also funny … and eccentric.

Timing is crucial in music but in normal life, Frank's time-keeping was dreadful. If we stayed in hotels we had been to before, Frank might ask for the same room he'd been in previously, because he knew that it was the closest to the elevator so he could wait until the last second to leave to get to work. That was Frank for you.

In the days of segregation in the Deep South, he didn't want to come to Birmingham, Alabama. Well, I wasn't going to be dictated to by racism. I told him, 'Look, you're my musical director – you're coming!' When we got there, I told the theatre owners: 'If you want me, *here* is my MD. End of story. Take it or leave it.' Of course, they took it.

Frank was even warier about going to South Africa. At our first rehearsal there, he turned up to find an all-white orchestra. A Black guy, he had to tell them all what to do. Luckily, after two songs, they were putty in his hands.

Then, that evening, he turned up for the show in a tuxedo with his trousers held up with string instead of a belt. Someone as stylish as Fred Astaire might have got away with that look.

Frank? *Not quite!* But he was a wonderful musician who went on to be MD on *The David Letterman Show*, win loads of awards for his work on Broadway and release his own albums. He died in 2023, and I feel privileged to have known him for nearly sixty years. I miss him.

* * *

But back to those Copacabana shows. Once Frank was in place, I was keen to have a look at that legendary club. But, when I did, it wasn't quite the glittering nexus of glamour and showbiz that I was anticipating.

Seen in the daytime, lit only by bare light bulbs, the Copa was pretty grotty. It wasn't very clean, there were cigarette holes all over the place: it was *tacky*. The world-famous Copa Girls had just finished their rehearsal. They were scruffy, with holes in their pantyhose, chewing gum and, frankly, not all that beautiful.

The Copa's manager then told me that I had to go to the police station to have my fingerprints taken. That was a rule for entertainers in New York at that time, for some reason. So, I had to trot off to the local cop shop. But we had a big orchestra and Frank had them brilliantly rehearsed. I felt ready for the shows.

They were an eye-opener. The Copacabana didn't even have a dressing room, so I had to get changed in a room in the hotel next door. Every night, I got the elevator up there with 'working girls' who were clearly in a different line of work from me! These ladies of the night would look at me curiously, but they were very nice and we got quite friendly.

The Copa shows were all sold out and the opening night was crazily jammed. Talk about intimate cabaret! I was nose-to-nose with the people at the front of the audience. I could have reached out and touched them. And behind them, sitting at tables, were some very striking-looking guys. The Copa was a big Mob hang-out and these guys looked like caricatures, in their slick Italian suits and dark glasses, puffing away on Cuban cigars with their molls by their side. In a simple white Parisian crepe suit, I looked as if I came from a different planet.

But the Mob guys, like everyone there, seemed to know all of my songs, and every one of the Copacabana shows was an amazing experience. It was the first time I'd come across the high energy levels of American showbiz and American audiences, and it was a fantastic thing to feed off.

In fact, performing in America felt like the start of a new chapter in my life. When I'd moved to France, the French hadn't been interested in my English career as a child star, and now the Americans weren't bothered about my success in France and Europe. The only thing they cared about was right here, right now. I loved this fresh start. I was singing in English again, and, in fact, I was almost *learning to sing again* in America because, let's face it, they're *good*. Pop and rock is their music. It was another education, and I soaked it up.

And it has to be said that New York was at my feet. They loved 'Downtown' and, having adopted it as their anthem, they set about adopting me. I was being treated as a huge star, even though, a few months earlier, hardly anybody in America had heard of me.

From New York, I went to Los Angeles. Now, LA isn't a visually spectacular city that blows you away, like New York, but it has its own unique energy. And one of the first things I did there was to head for a huge club, the Moulin Rouge on Sunset Strip, to appear in a concert film called *The Big T.N.T. Show*.

This was a cinema film starring a host of big music names performing their hits. It had quite the star-studded cast. The musical director was Phil Spector. Ray Charles was there, as were Bo Diddley, Joan Baez, The Lovin' Spoonful, The Byrds, Roger Miller, The Ronettes, Donovan and Ike and Tina Turner.

Joan Baez was lovely. She was a quiet, reserved person, quite similar to me, I suppose, and we had a great conversation. And Tina Turner was extraordinary. She must have been going through a difficult time in her life, but what a talent! She was incredible to watch. I was a big fan of Tina right to the end.

The band on *The Big T.N.T. Show* was fantastic, and Phil Spector directing them had to be seen to be believed. Phil was clearly driven and an utter perfectionist. He was leaping and bouncing around like some kind of mad elf, but he got a performance from that band that only he could get.

I have to say that I was not remotely prepared for the reception I got in Los Angeles. Fans were stopping me in the street to tell me that they loved my music. I even had extraordinary encounters with stars. I'll never forget the day I walked out of a restaurant where Steve McQueen was sitting near the door. When he saw me, he leapt to his feet.

*It's Steve McQueen!* I thought.

'Petula Clark! I love you!' he said.

I was the new star, and LA loves a new star. I went into Warner Bros to see Joe Smith. As I walked past the offices, heads turned and I heard whispered voices: 'Wow, is *Petula* here? Is that really *her*?' And Warner bumped me right to the top of their artist priority list. That included putting me straight into the legendary Western Studios on Sunset Boulevard with their top session musicians, including The Wrecking Crew, who were an amazing rhythm section. If ever you walked into a studio and saw The Wrecking Crew waiting, you knew you were working with the very best.

It was time to record a new single, and Tony Hatch had flown in from London to join me. We recorded three songs in that LA session. One of them was 'Where Am I Going', which I had written. Another was 'The Thirty-First of June', which I loved. And the third was 'My Love'.

Tony had written 'My Love' on the flight from London. He'd had a song ready for me, 'The Life and Soul of the Party', but got chatting to a fellow passenger who told him that that phrase means nothing in America. Tony therefore realised it wouldn't work as a single (it ended up as an album track) so he wrote 'My Love' there and then.

And, I have to confess, I didn't much like it. I'd loved all of Tony's previous compositions for me but I found this one flat, and not very interesting. Joe Smith, the A&R man from Warner Bros, had come in to watch the recording session and decide on my next single, and I went over to have a word with him before I left.

'Joe, I'll leave it to you to decide which song to release,' I said. 'But don't you *dare* put out "My Love"!' As I've already said, Joe was a short guy, no taller than me, so I grabbed both of his lapels for effect. 'Promise me you won't do that?' I said.

Joe laughed. 'Trust me, baby!' he said.

So, what do you know – and, more to the point, what do *I* know? Warner Bros ignored me and put out 'My Love' in America and it became my biggest hit since 'Downtown'. Up the *Billboard* chart it went, until it became my second US number one, as well as topping the charts in Canada. I still didn't like it that much. But the people had spoken.*

Tony Hatch was still a dear friend, his songwriting was on a roll and our professional relationship was going from strength to strength, but he'd had some recent upheaval in his personal life. He'd divorced his wife, Jean. I was quite upset about this as I liked her.

Tony had now got together with a singer, Jackie Trent, whose records he was producing in London. In fact, they'd just co-written, and he'd produced, a UK number-one single for her, 'Where Are You Now'. But I must admit that when I first met Jackie, she and I did not get along *at all*.

We were so very different. We didn't have a single thing in common. I was – and am – a reserved, guarded person, and Jackie was the total opposite. She was a bit pushy and touchy-feely – things that I'm not, and never will be. She was too full-on for my liking and I found her hard to be around.

Jackie was a good singer and a talented lyricist but I couldn't see any way we would ever be close. I warmed to her a little, over time, as I grew more used to her. You'd never call us best friends but, in all fairness, Jackie was to co-write some fine songs for me with Tony over the next few years. The first hit they co-wrote for me, 'I Couldn't Live Without Your Love', was about how they had first got together. It's still one of my favourites.

One of the last solo Tony compositions for me was 'A Sign of the Times'. I recorded it at the end of 1965 at the Pye

---

* Has 'My Love' grown on me, over the years? Well, yes and no. It's still not my favourite, but it would disappoint too many people if I didn't sing it live. So, I sometimes disguise it as a country-and-western song.

Records studio on a flying trip to London, then sang it at the start of 1966 on *The Ed Sullivan Show*, the studio orchestra again playing it too fast. It was a hit in America, as I was once more touring snowy Canada in the winter.

Late 1965 also found me in New York recording a New Year's Eve special for French TV, *Soirée Révellion*. A French crew came over and filmed me singing with Peter, Paul and Mary, duetting with Charles Aznavour and talking to Sammy Davis Jnr. Unfortunately, the recording hit a snag.

We filmed some of the programme on the set of *The Ed Sullivan Show*. American union rules barred the French crew from working and the producers couldn't afford to pay for US technicians. We couldn't even use the dressing rooms: on a freezing winter's day, I had to change in a side street by the theatre. It was surreal, and very memorable.

\* \* \*

In addition to Bert Block in New York, by now I also had a Los Angeles agent, a lovely guy called Ed Leffler. He lined me up some concerts that were truly special. In the spring of 1966, I was to do two weeks at the kookily spelled Cocoanut Grove, a big, classy, beautiful venue in the Ambassador Hotel in LA. It was to make news headlines worldwide two years later when it was the site of the assassination of Bobby Kennedy.

My reputation in America had gone through the roof and the first night at the Cocoanut was a hot ticket. I hadn't realised quite *how* hot. On the opening night, a little nervous back-stage, I made the rookie error of creeping onto the stage to have a quick peep at the audience through the stage curtains. I instantly wished that I hadn't.

The first person I spotted in the auditorium was Rock Hudson. The second was Natalie Wood. At which point, I stopped peering through the curtains! Backstage, there were rumours flying around of who was out there: Sinatra. Astaire. Sammy Davis Jnr. Lucille Ball. Jack Warner, who was one of the Warner Bros. *Oh. My. Word.*

It was nerve-wracking. It helped a little that the show's compère was Anthony Newley, my old crush from London, but my heart was still beating fast as the lights went down. Yet I walked onstage to a deafening ovation. Everyone was up on their feet. They made me feel like a star. And, you know what? That helped me to perform like one.

Every night at the Cocoanut Grove was a joy. The LA showbiz royalty came out to see me and I gave them all the best show I could. I had clearly impressed the Warner Bros boss, Jack Warner, because, soon afterwards, he came to me with a very enticing offer. But I'll come to this shortly …

\* \* \*

I never got to sing with Sinatra. Pity. But I got to meet him several times. While I was at the Cocoanut Grove, Frank was making his *Strangers in the Night* album in Hollywood. I had covered 'Strangers in the Night', so Frank got a message to me to invite me to call in and watch him record his version of 'Downtown'. He always liked to record in front of a small, personally invited audience.

Frank was charm itself when Claude and I got to the studio. He had given 'Downtown' to his long-term arranger, Nelson Riddle, to rework and try to give it more of a swing feel. It didn't work out too well but Frank's voice, of course, was perfect, and when he was done, he invited us out to dinner with him and his wife, Mia Farrow.

The four of us went to The Bistro, a chic restaurant in Beverly Hills, and then on to the 'in' disco club of the time, The Daisy. Frank didn't like the disco and soon led us through to a back room that was very quiet. Tony Bennett dropped by and said hello.

We were all sitting chatting when a few guys came in. We didn't know who they were but they looked heavy. The mood in the room changed. Frank reached for a pistol from the inside pocket of his jacket and put it on the table in front of him. Mia didn't seem at all fazed by this. I got the impression she'd seen it before.

Claude glanced at me. I glanced at him.

'Maybe … we should be leaving?' he whispered.

'Yes!' I said. And we did.

Less than eighteen months earlier, I'd been a complete unknown in America. Now, here I was, entertaining LA's A-listers every night, and watching Frank Sinatra pull out a gun in a VIP room at one of Hollywood's most exclusive clubs. Luckily, there's a phrase that exactly sums up that kind of craziness: *that's showbiz!*

# CHAPTER 8

# OH, GERMAINE!

Sometimes, it's nice to go home. Being so busy in Europe, then Canada and the US meant I'd been spending far less time in Britain. It hadn't been a deliberate policy, but I'd hardly done any shows in the UK for three or four years. That all changed in June 1966 when I did a month-long residency at the Savoy Hotel in London.

I had a great time there. In the very centre of town, slap bang on The Strand, the Savoy is unique, a lovely place both to stay and to play. They gave us a luxurious suite and, just to ensure that our every requirement was catered for, a butler.

This chap was certainly attentive. One morning, while we were having breakfast, he glided across the polished floor to me. 'Excuse me, Miss Clark, but I've noticed that you haven't been eating your bacon,' he murmured. 'So, I have taken the liberty of changing the bacon for you.'

The shows were in the summer, and it was a hot one. The Savoy didn't as yet have air conditioning, so they left all the doors and windows to the theatre open while I was performing. I guess some of its upmarket guests weren't into pop music, because there were complaints to the management that my concerts were too loud.

The Savoy's gentleman who booked the shows, who was impossibly posh, came to see me. 'Miss Clark, would it be possible for you to … reduce the volume?' he enquired.

'No, not really,' I replied.

'Ah,' he said. 'I suppose you are more of a *winter* artist.' By which he meant that he would only ever book me again if the doors and windows could be firmly closed.

During my month in London, the singer Richard Anthony, a close friend and a huge star in France, happened to be in town. He'd rented a Ferrari and, knowing that I love sports cars, he called me up.

'Petula, would you like to go out to the countryside for a few hours?' he asked.

'Of course!' I replied. 'Let's go!'

Richard and I had a great summer's drive. In the early evening, we got back to the Savoy, which had its big main front doors flung open to the heat, and Richard actually drove the Ferrari into the reception area of the hotel. A doorman strolled across the carpet and opened the passenger door for me.

'Good evening, Miss Clark.' He smiled. 'Did you have a nice day?'*

While I was in London, I also took on another project. As with the live shows, I hadn't done much British television in recent years. This was about to change. The BBC got in touch, asking if I'd host a weekly variety show they wanted to call *This Is Petula Clark*.

---

* Strange as it sounds, this was so bizarre that I convinced myself it must have been a dream – until I bumped into Richard again many years later. 'No, Petula, it really happened!' he assured me.

I would have probably done it anyway, but a big attraction for me was that the series was to be directed by Yvonne Littlewood. I'd known Yvonne and worked with her, on and off, ever since the days of *Pet's Parlour*, so I knew she was the very best at what she did.

This didn't mean that she was easy to work with. Yvonne was a total perfectionist who always had a precise visual script for every camera. Every show that Yvonne directed was beautifully photographed. She was relentlessly fussy and the frazzled cameramen would be tearing their hair out. It also meant that rehearsals could be very, very long.

Yvonne had no idea of time. We would spend all day in a windowless basement rehearsal studio at Television Centre, often just me, her and a long-suffering pianist. She was a very musical person and, again, wanted everything *just so*. Well, so did I, but by 7pm, I'd be flagging.

'Yvonne, can we call it a day?' I'd ask.

'No, Petula, we haven't finished yet.'

'But this poor guy has been here for ten hours and he's got a family to go home to,' I'd say, gesturing towards the piano player. 'And *I'm* kind of hungry too ...'

But to her credit, Yvonne being such a perfectionist brought great results. Whenever Tony Bennett came to the BBC, he always insisted on working with her.

*This Is Petula Clark* had music, comedy sketches and special guests. For the latter, I invited on a few European singers: the French Claude François; Raphael, from Spain; the Italian Fred Bongusto; Conny Froboess from Germany. They were all successful in their own countries and I hoped British viewers would find it interesting to see them.

After so long away, it was nice to be active in Britain again, but after I'd finished the television series, we headed back to France to enjoy the end of the summer. And Claude and I made a major life decision.

Claude had decided that he'd like us to leave Paris and raise the children somewhere more tranquil and less frenetic, and with great schools. He liked the idea of us living in Switzerland, and on a visit to the country, he spotted a wonderful piece of land in Cologny, overlooking Lake Geneva.

Cologny is a very beautiful little village on the edge of Geneva. Geneva has a great International School, which we realised would be perfect for Bara and Kate when they were a little older. For my part, I still loved our house in Paris but could certainly see that Switzerland could be an ideal place to raise our family. OK, we decided. *Let's do it!*

We bought the land and hired an architect, who got to work. The house was to take two years to build. During that time, whenever I wasn't in America or touring the world, we divided our time between our house in France and Le Richemond hotel in Geneva, from where we could keep an eye on the building work.

No sooner was our Swiss house commissioned than, inevitably, America was calling me again. By October 1966, I was back for another two weeks at the Copa in New York. I was happy to see that the cigarette burns in the seats and the holes in the Copa Girls' pantyhose were still in place. A kind of tradition.

On a flying visit to LA, I was a guest on *The Andy Williams Show* on ABC. I was to go on Andy's show a lot over the years and it was always fun because he and I adored singing together. On this first appearance, we duetted on 'I Will Wait for You'.

We had to sit together in a little love seat and stare deep into each other's eyes.

All of this was in front of a full orchestra and a live audience, and we got the giggles. We couldn't get through the song. Andy and I did three takes and collapsed in fits of laughter each time. By now the orchestra also had the giggles, which didn't help.

Claude had a helicopter waiting to whisk us to LA Airport to catch a flight, so he was at the side of the studio tapping his watch and gesticulating wildly at me to hurry up. Naturally, that made me giggle even more. Andy and I had to switch angles to sing without looking at one another (or at Claude) in order to finish the song.

Then I did *The Danny Kaye Show*. Danny took Claude and me back to his house afterwards. He had two kitchens: a French gourmet kitchen and a Chinese kitchen, with a little Chinese lady who seemed to spend all her time chopping things up. Danny made us a marvellous Chinese meal. He was an excellent cook.

My life was a whirlwind in these days but it's strange how some moments still stand out and live so vividly in my memory. By now I was good friends with Bert Block, my New York agent, and after I'd done the Copa shows he invited me, Claude and the girls out to his house in Connecticut for Halloween.

It was the first full-on American Halloween that Bara and Kate had ever seen, and they were the right ages to love it. But while we were there, I heard that a friend, the singer Alma Cogan, had died in London from ovarian cancer. She was just thirty-four years old – a few weeks older than me.

I knew Alma well. Back in the day, some people saw us as musical rivals, but I never did. She was a great girl with a terrific sense of humour, and her death was a terrible shock. Bert's family house had a beautiful forest next to it, and I wandered through that wood with a rather surprising sense of loss. She was much too young to have died.

I went to Washington DC for a week of shows. It wasn't without mishap. One morning, my ever-mercurial musical director, Frank Owens, announced he had to pop up to New York. His return flight was delayed and we had to do that evening's show without him.

*Gulp!* It's difficult to do a performance without your musical director. Luckily, the orchestra were great and had already played my show a couple of times, so we were able to get through it. And, as ever, I forgave Frank. It was impossible to stay angry with him.

From there, it was time to make my debut at a holy temple, a Mecca, of American entertainment – Las Vegas. And what an eye-opener it was.

Las Vegas in 1966 wasn't yet the crazy riot of neon, casinos and skyscraper hotels that it is today, but it was still spectacular. The Strip was developing quickly and I was to do three weeks at the Circus Maximus at Caesars Palace, which had only just opened. I would be the third act to play there, after Andy Williams and Tony Bennett.

Is Vegas sublime or ridiculous? A bit of both. The twenty-four-hour coffee shop at Caesars was called the Noshorium. The Japanese steak house was Ah So. There were no clocks at Caesars Palace (except backstage). Why? Because the management didn't want customers to see how late it was, stop drinking and gambling, and go to bed. *Keep going! Ker-ching!*

Vegas treats its performers supremely well. Caesars Palace asked in advance: 'What do you want, Miss Clark? What size orchestra do you need?' They gave me all I asked for and the musicians were wonderful. Claude, Bara, Kate and I were given a suite that went on forever and the dressing rooms, lighting and sound were all perfection.

On the bill with me was Woody Allen, who wasn't yet the huge movie star and director he was to become. He was a sharp, up-and-coming stand-up comic from New York. I got on very well with Woody. When he wasn't up in his hotel room writing, he'd hang out and chat to Bara and Kate.

Well, he'd chat to them – and, primarily, encourage them in mischief. Not that they ever needed too much encouragement in that area. He told the girls, 'Never listen to your parents,' and, 'Never go to bed before 3am.' *Thanks, Woody!*

During my first Vegas week with Woody, there was a doctors' convention in town. They were quite a sophisticated bunch, and when Woody came onstage in his flannel pants and tweed jacket, *very New York*, they loved him. He was making these clever, witty jokes and getting laughs every night.

The second week was a different story. The doctors had left and now there was a farmers' conference going on. The Caesars Palace management put a bull in the foyer to make them feel at home. The farmers didn't appear to follow a word that Woody was saying, or relate to him, and he died the death every night. Credit to him, he didn't seem too bothered.

Woody got on particularly well with Claude. They bonded over their love of jazz – Woody played jazz clarinet, and Claude told him all about his time working with Sidney Bechet. I didn't see Woody for years after Vegas, but the first time we happened to run into each other again, his opening question to me was, 'How's Claude?'

* * *

After those Vegas shows, I did the short trip to Reno to finish the year with some dates at Harold's Club, another casino venue. I liked Reno. It was surrounded by beautiful country-side … and, while I was there, a very peculiar chain of events began to unfold.

A music publisher from London called Cyril Simons, whom I was very fond of, called and said he had a song for me called 'This Is My Song'. He sent me a demo and I thought, *No. Not for me.* It was a bit boring. But Claude quite liked it and sent it to be orchestrated in Paris to see if it would sound better

In Reno, we were staying at a house supplied by the casino, and a courier arrived with a huge reel-to-reel tape of this orches-tration. *So, how am I supposed to listen to this?* We had to go to the local radio station to hear it on their equipment. *Nope.* Still didn't like it. Then, a few days later, there was another knock on our door. And it was Ernie Freeman.

Ernie was a big-name orchestrator who'd that year arranged 'That's Life' for Sinatra. He was an unusual-looking Black guy with long hair: you could mistake him for a Native American. I'd worked with Ernie a few times before, and I really liked him, but as soon as I set eyes on him on our doorstep in Reno, it was clear that he was falling-down drunk.

'Ernie! What are *you* doing here?' I asked.

'Well, P-P-Petula, I, I gotta work on the ssshong …'

'*What* song? Oh, well, come in!'

Ernie virtually fell into the house. He was plastered. Bara and Kate had never seen anyone drunk before and they found it very entertaining. I led Ernie to the piano and, as best as he could, he played me his take on 'This Is My Song'. His drunken rendition had a few duff notes but I had to admit it sounded a lot better.

Later, Claude and I poured Ernie into a taxi to the airport for his flight back to LA. As it pulled away, I called Joe Smith at Warner Bros. 'I've just had Ernie Freeman here, and he was sozzled!' I said. 'What's that all about?'

'Yeah, sorry, but we had to get Ernie drunk or he wouldn't get on the plane!' Joe laughed. 'He's terrified of flying! When you're back in LA, we'll record "This Is My Song".'

'Hmm. Maybe,' I said, still very wary.

When I got to Western Studios in Los Angeles a week later, I was told some very surprising news about 'This Is My Song'. It had, in fact, been written by, of all people, Charlie Chaplin. As it happened, Charlie was by then living near Geneva, but we'd never met him.

It seemed Charlie had penned the song for a movie he'd written and was directing called *A Countess from Hong Kong* (which turned out to be the last film he ever made). He had initially wanted Al Jolson to record it and, on being informed that Al was dead, had refused to believe it. Charlie had even insisted on being shown a photograph of Al Jolson's gravestone before he reluctantly accepted that he had shuffled off this mortal coil. At which point, with his original choice terminally out of action, he had come up with the idea of me (being still alive!) as a possible replacement. Goodness knows why.

Not only that, but there was a dream team awaiting me in the studio. Ernie was back to his usual sober, charming self, and his orchestration of 'This Is My Song', played by a full orchestra and The Wrecking Crew, was sounding perfect. Plus, the session was to be produced by the legendary Sonny Burke, Sinatra's go-to producer.

'Well, I guess we'd better do this, then,' I said.

At first, I was only going to record the song in French, Italian and German. I didn't want to do it in English: I felt that Charlie Chaplin's lyrics, which he wouldn't allow us to change, were kind of old-fashioned. But at the end of the session, against my better judgement, Sonny talked me into it.

Afterwards, I felt I probably shouldn't have done it. Luckily, I had a special occasion to take my mind off it. My old friend, Charles Aznavour, was making his Vegas debut at the Flamingo Las Vegas Hotel and Casino. When he saw that I was also in town, he asked me to be a witness at his wedding.

So, on 11 January 1967, I was matron of honour as Charles married Swedish model Ulla Thorsell at the Flamingo. Charles's best man was Sammy Davis Jr (I knew Sammy quite well by then, from various encounters: he was always great fun to be with), the wedding was joyful and the party afterwards was splendid.

I still didn't want 'This Is My Song' released as a single in English. In fact, I forbade Joe Smith from doing so. But two weeks after I recorded it, I reluctantly agreed to sing it when I appeared on an NBC TV show, *The Hollywood Palace*, hosted by Fred Astaire (I remember his other guest that day was Mickey Rooney).

Well, I sang 'This Is My Song' on *The Hollywood Palace*, in front of a live studio audience, and they went crazy for it. They absolutely loved it. I couldn't believe the strength of their reaction. It made it clear that I was fighting the inevitable. Warner Bros put out 'This Is My Song' as my new single.

It was the second time I'd butted heads with Joe Smith over the choice of a single ... and the second time he was dead right. 'This Is My Song' was a major hit all over the world. It shot up the US *Cashbox* charts into the top three and, to my surprise, was a number one in Britain: my first since 'Sailor', six years earlier.

So, I'll ask again – *what did I know?*

There is a lovely postscript to this story. When Claude and I got back to Geneva with the girls, there were two notes waiting for us from Charlie Chaplin, inviting us to go over and take tea with him at his house. *Tea with Charlie Chaplin? You bet!*

I guess I was nervous when we got to his lakeside mansion, but as soon as he opened the door – *there he was! Charlie Chaplin!* – he put us at ease. He was over the moon about the success of the song. We talked about his great days in Hollywood for hours, then Charlie asked me to play piano while he danced around his living room.

He was a wonderful man and the perfect host. Four o'clock teatime came, and his wife, Oona, came in to join us with some of their eight children. It was an enchanting experience, being in his family home and seeing his delight at the success we'd managed to have together. I never met him again, but I'll never forget my afternoon with Charlie Chaplin.

I'd done a little skiing in Switzerland (I was never exactly a natural, but I'd give it a good go) and Claude and I built a large chalet in the Alpine ski resort of Megève, just over the border in France. Sacha Distel and his wife, Francine, also had a chalet there. We were often there at the same time, and Claude and I would meet up with them on the piste.

Francine had been an Olympic skier and Sacha also skied very well. I'd try to keep up with them but I had no chance. I fell over so many times that Sacha made regular use of a new nickname he'd recently given me.

The two of us had done a comedy sketch on *Le Sacha Show* about a guy trying to pick up a girl. We were dancing and his character was being flirtatious and trying to guess my name. When I told him 'Germaine' – which, if I'm honest, isn't the prettiest name in the world – everybody laughed. It became our private joke.

Skiing in Megève, Sacha knew that if he said, 'Oh, Petula!' people would hear him, heads would turn, and I'd become a reluctant centre of attention. So, whenever he saw me sprawled in the snow yet again, he'd laugh and say, 'Oh, *Germaine*!' And this was to be Sacha Distel's nickname for me for many years to come.

\* \* \*

At the start of 1967, I was back on *The Ed Sullivan Show*, along with The Rolling Stones. The Stones were made to change the lyric of 'Let's Spend the Night Together' to 'Let's spend some time together', which, of course, Mick wasn't too happy about.

As well as *The Andy Williams Show* and *The Danny Kaye Show*, I was a regular on *The Tonight Show* with Johnny Carson. Later, I'd go on *The Pat Boone Show*, *The Carol Burnett Show*, *Rowan & Martin's Laugh-In* and *The Smothers Brothers Comedy Hour*. And I made my debut on one of my absolute favourites: *The Dean Martin Show*.

I adored Dean Martin. He was naturally funny and such a star. When he had split from his performing partner, Jerry

Lewis, a few years earlier, people had assumed Dean's career would be over, but the opposite had happened. He had gone from strength to strength. I got on really, really well with Dean. We clicked from day one.

In fact, Dean and I got on *so* well, and there was such chemistry between us, that some people thought we were having an affair. There were rumours in the gossip rags. There never *was* anything like that going on between us: we were both very careful about that. But he was so charming and hilarious that he was pretty irresistible.

*When he was there, that was.* The producers on *The Dean Martin Show* rarely gave Dean anything he'd need to learn, or rehearse, because he hardly ever came to rehearsals. He didn't like to work. He liked to play golf, so that was what he did. His guests would rehearse for a week before the show while Dean was out on the golf course.

The show's director, Greg Garrison, would stand in for Dean in rehearsals. I recall one week when I was a guest with Orson Welles and Dean didn't turn up once. Orson and I spent the week together: he was hysterically funny and somewhat amused that Dean couldn't be bothered to turn up because he was playing golf.

The guests and the orchestra would all be perfectly rehearsed and then, if his golf game didn't run on too long, Dean would turn up for the dress rehearsal right before the show was taped late on Saturday afternoons. He'd watch a bit of it on a screen in his dressing room, so he'd have some idea of what was going on. But not very much.

When we came to tape the actual show, in front of a studio audience, Dean would walk on set and have everything on what they call, rather rudely, idiot cards. Not just everything he had to say: there'd also be arrows on the cards telling him which way to walk. He looked as if he didn't know what was going on, because he didn't.

Due to the way he drawled and slurred, Dean used to look drunk on the show, but he wasn't. If he *was* a bit out of it, it wasn't booze. He would just read his lines and ad-lib through a show that he knew virtually nothing about, and he did it so brilliantly, and with such charm, that he got away with it every time.

Because Dean liked to play golf, and not rehearse, he never wanted to learn any new songs. I used to duet with him, and we did a couple of medleys together – one had originally been written for Peggy Lee and one for Lena Horne. Luckily, I happened to sing in the same key as them, *so hey-ho*.

After I'd been on the programme a couple of times, the producers realised I was a quick learner and didn't have to go to every rehearsal. They had my measurements, so they'd make my costumes without me having to go to fittings. I must confess, I also arrived under-rehearsed and had my own idiot cards once or twice.

Dean Martin didn't like to work, yet he was a delight to work *with*. He was a true one-off. Whenever I think about Dean, I always have one prevalent memory of being with him: laughing non-stop. I loved him.

Really, my life in America at this time was such a roller-coaster that it was hard to catch my breath. I just went along with it and raced from one extraordinary situation to another. And in April 1967, I found myself in Washington DC at the Sheraton-Park Hotel, performing as a guest of honour at the annual White House Correspondents' Dinner.

It was a very formal occasion, as these political events tend to be, but I talked to some interesting people and I felt flattered to be there. Apparently, the President, Lyndon B. Johnson, had personally requested that I be invited, but I didn't meet him. I *did* get waylaid by the vice president, Hubert Humphrey. He seemed to be spending most of his time peering down my bodice.

\* \* \*

At this point, I was spending far more time in America than in Britain or France. In March 1967, I co-hosted a tribute show on US TV to Rodgers and Hart with Bobby Darin. The Supremes and The Mamas & The Papas were on, and Quincy Jones was musical director of the Count Basie Band, hugely augmented with strings and percussion.\* They were playing the songs with The Wrecking Crew.

Everybody was in place except for The Wrecking Crew's bass player, without whom we couldn't start rehearsals. Ten minutes late, the doors swung open and in came the missing musician: Carole Kaye. Carole scurried in, very apologetic. A demure, little blonde lady in glasses, she plugged in her bass ... *and that was it.* The music instantly came alive. The orchestra took off. *Wow*, she could play.

That spring, Tony Hatch and Jackie Trent came up with one of my favourites of their compositions for me: 'Don't Sleep in the Subway'. As with all of Tony's work, it was musically

---

\* I loved Basie's band but when I once played a couple of live shows with them, it was tricky. They were essentially a swing band and, as Sinatra had discovered, for all of their merits, Tony Hatch's songs don't swing.

sophisticated and beautifully constructed, a truly great song, and I adored it from the second that I heard it.

I've always loved Tamla Motown, and while Tony's music wasn't influenced by Motown, I think there was a kinship. Frank Owens would play Tony's arrangements on piano and ask me, smiling: 'It's not too *Black* for you, is it, Petula?' American radio loved 'Don't Sleep in the Subway' and it was another US top-five hit.

By now, though, I was deeply involved in a major, time-consuming project which was to prove one of the most engaging and enjoyable things I had ever done.

I was making a Hollywood movie.

# CHAPTER 9

# DANCING IN COW DUNG

Jack Warner from Warner Bros must have been *very* impressed with my show at the Cocoanut Grove in Los Angeles. Because, off the back of it, he had got in touch with my movie agent, Jerry Steiner, to offer me the female lead role in a musical film that the studio were set to shoot called *Finian's Rainbow*.

The movie was a kind of fairy story, based on a hit 1947 Broadway play about an Irishman who steals a pot of gold from a leprechaun and emigrates to America with his daughter to try to make their fortune. I was asked to play the girl, Sharon, and the role of the father, Finian, had already gone to Fred Astaire.

This was pretty big news. My music career had taken over my life so much that I hadn't made a proper movie for more than a decade. The idea of filming in Hollywood, with the mighty Fred Astaire, sounded almost dreamlike. I've never been the kind of showbiz person who meticulously plots their career step by step: I've just always said yes, or no, when things are offered to me, and this felt like an exciting new project.

I had such a wonderful time making *Finian's Rainbow*. Thinking back over my very long career, I think it was one of the happiest times of my life. And one of the main reasons for that was its brilliant young director.

Jack Warner was taking a bit of a chance on Francis Ford Coppola. He wasn't yet thirty and was just starting out. He'd had some recent success with a left-field comedy called *You're a Big Boy Now*, which he'd originally shot as his college thesis project, but a big Hollywood musical was quite a leap, to say the least.

I adored Francis from the moment I met him. He was very off the wall, with his scruffy mop of hair and big beard, and very un-Hollywood. There again, so was his assistant, an even younger guy called George Lucas. They were almost a pair of hippies: it's amazing to think what they both went on to achieve.

Fred Astaire was the polar opposite. Fred was true Hollywood royalty, of course, and by now nearing seventy, but he took the movie extremely seriously. He was incredibly dedicated and professional. Yet Fred was also a lot of fun and he and I got on very well, not least because, like me, he loved pop music. We did a lot of singing together.

The other big name in the movie was Tommy Steele, who played a leprechaun called Og. Tommy was very talented and had just had big success in Britain in *Half a Sixpence*, but I must confess that I thought he was rather strange casting. I'm not sure that a six-foot-plus Cockney is anybody's idea of a leprechaun.

We did most of the work on the movie in the summer of 1967. Francis gave us five weeks of rehearsals before filming even began and Warner Bros transformed about 9 acres of their back lot into the village of Rainbow Valley, where the film was set. They built houses, barns, shops, a school, a post office … the works.

Just before we started filming, we had to do make-up tests, and Francis wanted me to sing 'How Are Things in Glocca Morra?' Which I did. And Quincy Jones orchestrated it for me. Not bad at all!

While I was making the film, Claude, the girls and I lived on San Ysidro Drive in Beverly Hills. We did a house swap with our friend Leslie Bricusse – the composer and Anthony Newley's co-writer – who went to stay in our house in Vallauris. Leslie's place was a bit of a party house, and this tendency carried on while we were there.

We had a gathering one night, and Fred Astaire came over after we'd finished filming. He was playing pool with Sammy Davis Jr. Fred looked so elegant, as if even his pool-playing was choreographed, but Sammy was leaping around, waving his cue in excitement: 'Look at me! Can you believe it? I'm playing pool with Fred Astaire!'*

The composer and arranger Michel Legrand, whom we knew well from France, came to stay with us. Michel had not yet made a name for himself in Hollywood, and was searching for somewhere to live in LA, so he lodged with us for a while. When I came home from shooting, we spent some wonderful evenings with him talking about music.

Michel didn't much like pop music and thought that The Beatles were rubbish. We had a few lively arguments about *that*. But it was always fun having him around – and he was such a superb musician. He very quickly became successful doing the

---

* That pool table saw some big-name action. I recently went to dinner with a dear old friend, the songwriter Don Black. Don said: 'Yeah, I remember that house. I had dinner there once and ended up playing pool with Steve McQueen.'

music for movies like *The Thomas Crown Affair, Summer of '42* and *Yentl*.

I've always enjoyed driving fast, and I used to love driving myself from the house to the studio in Burbank each morning. The route was a winding road through Laurel Canyon. There was no traffic around that early in the day, so I'd stick on some great music like The Beach Boys and go for it.

Until one day, when I got there a bit late. An assistant had phoned Claude at the house to ask where I was. 'Ah, she left ten minutes ago,' said Claude. At which point, I screeched into the back lot. The assistant was gobsmacked. 'She's just arrived!' he told Claude. 'How the hell did she get here in ten minutes?'

'Yes, that is the way Petula drives,' Claude confirmed.

I wasn't allowed to drive to the studio after that. There had apparently been a spate of crazy fans throwing themselves in front of famous people's cars to get insurance money off them. So, Warner Bros began sending a limo for me every day. That was no fun: I missed my early-morning vrooms through the Valley.

It was an unbelievably hot summer as we made *Finian's Rainbow*. We were shooting outdoors the whole time, so there were no air-conditioned dressing rooms to retreat to. We had to take salt pills.

We were all given bikes, and we used to cycle from the back lot to the commissary in the main Warner Bros studio every day to have lunch. One lunchtime, I was cycling past a sound studio when a huge door opened and out walked Ella Fitzgerald. I was so shocked that I fell off my bike. Ella always had problems with her eyes and she was dazzled by the sunlight. She blinked down at me, literally lying at her feet. 'Petula Clark!' she said. 'My God, is that you?'

'Yep,' I confessed. I was tangled up in my costume and my bike but Ella bent down and helped to extricate me. She was saying such lovely things: 'I adore your singing. I love the way you *phrase*.' We were overjoyed to meet. She helped me back onto my bike and, as I cycled off, she shouted after me.

'Hey, Petula! Write me a song!'

Of course, I did no such thing. I mean, how would I even go about trying to write a song for Ella Fitzgerald? *Come on!*

Filming with Francis Ford Coppola was terrific. As I said, *Finian's Rainbow* is basically a fairy tale but Francis wanted somehow to make it more *real*. He shot some of the scenes himself with a camera on his shoulder, Claude Lelouch-style: unheard of at the time in Hollywood, where you always had to have a full unit of camera crew, lighting and grips.

Jack Warner mainly left us to it but, because we were filming on Warner Bros lot, he occasionally wandered down to the set. I think he was quite wary: *what the hell is going on here?* I don't know if he noticed all the pot-smoking. I've never been that partial, but I dabbled. Some people did a lot more.

We did some filming on location in the gorgeous Napa Valley, near where Francis lived. One day, we all met up in a place called, of all things, Petaluma. We arrived to find limos, Warner Bros trucks, lighting rigs, technicians, make-up and catering all waiting for us. It was like the circus coming to town.

But Francis didn't want all that. He just wanted to film Fred and me out in a field somewhere. 'If we take a Warner Bros truck, we'll have to get permission to film,' he said. 'Forget that! Fred, Petula, come with me.' The three of us jumped into a limo with a driver and sped off in a cloud of dust, leaving everyone else behind.

As I say, this was totally unheard of. In those unionised days, you didn't film anything in Hollywood without a camera crew. Fred wasn't at all sure about what was going on. He was old school, and used to doing things *correctly*, and Francis was this wild new boy making it all up as he went along.

The three of us were having a great time in the car, meandering through the beautiful countryside. Fred and I were singing, as usual. Francis was looking out for locations. 'That's a great-looking field!' he suddenly said. 'Let's stop here.' The driver pulled over and Francis, Fred and I got out. Francis was carrying his camera.

'OK, let's climb over this fence into the field,' he said.

Fred was horrified. '*What?*' he said. 'Look here, I'm not climbing over a fence to break into somebody's field. We don't have permission!' Laughing, Francis and I managed to persuade him to do it. Francis raised his camera to his shoulder.

'Right,' he told the two of us. 'Now dance across the field.'

Fred looked even more aghast. '*Dance across the field?*' he repeated, incredulously. 'But there are rabbit holes! And cow dung! And ...' But, again, we talked Fred into doing it. The three of us had so much fun that day.

I had the best time making *Finian's Rainbow*, but I can't pretend it was a perfect movie. Our Irish accents, to say the least, were erratic. I'm normally OK at accents but my brogue bounced between Dublin and Belfast. Fred sounded Scottish, and I don't know how to describe the sounds Tommy Steele was making. There wasn't a decent Irish accent in the movie.

The 1947 storyline was also dated. In 1967, we were in the middle of the civil rights era, yet central to the film's plot was a racist senator, played by Keenan Wynn, walking around in blackface after I cast a magic spell and turned him Black. It's a bit odd, and I'm sure some people watching it today might raise an eyebrow.

Well, as they say, it was a different time.

If I had one small fear going into making *Finian's Rainbow*, it was that I had to dance with Fred. Well, let's be honest – I mean, *dance with Fred Astaire*? In truth, I'm not one of life's natural dancers. I'm certainly no Ginger Rogers. Fred knew I was worried about it, so in the rehearsal studio he gave me his choreographer, Hermes Pan.

Hermes was great. He even looked a bit like Fred. He taught me the routine, made it seem simple, and, in the end, I had a wonderful time dancing with Fred. He was so good that he made it feel easy. And the funny thing was that Fred later confessed he'd been just as nervous about singing with me.

From my personal perspective, there was only one big downside while I was making *Finian's Rainbow*. It was that Claude, the girls and I had to keep leaving the country. It was a visa thing: we were only allowed to spend so many days at a time, per year, in America. So, we had to leave the country every weekend – and the closest place was Mexico.

That sounds great, right? *Wrong!* Every Friday night, the rest of the team would head off to lounge around their swimming pools and air-conditioned homes (except for Fred, who was so dedicated that he'd stay in the studio and work). And Claude, Bara, Kate and I would set off on a journey from hell.

I'd leave the set with my make-up still on and we'd get a flight from the local airport, Burbank, to San Diego. We'd rent a car and drive to the Mexican border, where there'd be queues of Mexicans, who worked in California doing jobs like peach-picking, going home for the weekend.

They just wanted to get home quickly, and the Mexican customs would wave them across the border. It was a different story for us: the whole point was to get the stamps in our passports that confirmed we'd left the US. So, Claude and I would have to go and badger the customs officials.

They weren't interested and would try to shoo us away. We spoke no Spanish, they had little English and *zero* French, so the conversations went in circles and were exhausting. Then, when we finally got our precious stamps, we would drive through Tijuana (an experience in itself!) and on to Rosarito beach.

Rosarito beach sounds idyllic? Don't be fooled! I believe it's quite nice, and even hip, nowadays, but back then it really wasn't. It was a complete dump: a place where American guys would take their girlfriends, or whatever, for a dirty weekend. And when I say dirty, I mean *dirty*.

Our hotel (the 'best' in town) was grubby, to say the least. The mattresses had plastic covers on them. You'd shower with your mouth and eyes firmly shut because the water came out of the pipes brown. The food was dreadful. The beach itself was covered in what the French call *caca* from the donkeys. It was downright awful.

We'd spend a miserable weekend there, then have to leave on Monday morning at the crack of dawn for me to get back to the movie set. We'd be going back across the border at 6am with the peach-pickers, and this time it would be the American customs who couldn't be bothered to stamp our passports, until we begged them.

*Honestly. What a palaver.*

I've always been good at making the best of things, but it was hard to find an upside to our awful Mexican weekends. Yet even they couldn't sully the pure joy of making *Finian's Rainbow*. I'll never forget what a fun, free time I had on that movie. It was truly one of the happiest moments in my life.

# CHAPTER 10

# CHIPS AND PICKLED ONIONS

When we had wrapped up *Finian's Rainbow*, it was time to get back to music, for a short while at least. I went on a college tour of the American heartland. And I absolutely loved it.

By now, I was getting quite used to New York, Chicago, LA and Las Vegas. I hadn't seen much else of America, but now I ventured right into the heart of the US, to places such as Oregon, and Idaho, and Montana, and North Carolina. I guess they're areas of the States that most Brits rarely get to see. And I found them fascinating.

In the same way that I'd enjoyed journeying up and down Britain, and doing shows in all corners of France, I loved going to Middle American towns that I'd never even heard of. And what struck me the most was that even the smallest towns had a 'downtown' area. So, who knows? Maybe that's why that song was so big!

I also got very busy in the studio. I'd recorded a new single, 'The Other Man's Grass Is Always Greener' with Tony Hatch in London, and had gone back into Western Studios in LA to record an album of the same name with Sonny Burke. It included a cover of 'Black Coffee', one of my favourite songs of all time when sung by Peggy Lee.

Then, in no time at all, I got another big movie offer. Executives at MGM had seen some of the early rushes of *Finian's Rainbow* and must have thought I was halfway decent, because they got in touch with me and asked if I'd play the female lead in a musical adaptation of the well-known novel and movie, *Goodbye, Mr. Chips.*

I liked the idea. I'd seen the famous 1939 film version starring Robert Donat and thought it was brilliant. Even so, I have to confess that, initially, I couldn't see why, or how, MGM thought they could make it into a musical. Happily, those doubts were quickly dispelled when they sent me over the script. It had been written by Terence Rattigan, the noted dramatist and screenwriter. Terence was a lovely man and he'd done a wonderful job: as I read the pages, the scenes came to life in my mind. *OK*, I told the studio. *I'm in!*

It seemed the casting had been a bit of a kerfuffle. Lee Remick had originally been lined up to play Katherine – the glitzy singer and 'soubrette' who falls in love with, and marries, a fusty old public-school ancient-languages teacher – until they decided they wanted me instead. Who knows why? Lee was a brilliant actress. I'm sure she'd have been great.

Apparently, Richard Burton had been pencilled in for the lead role of the teacher, Arthur Chipping, aka Mr Chips, but had since dropped out and been replaced by Peter O'Toole. I didn't know until years later that Richard hadn't wanted to act with me because he 'didn't want to play opposite a pop star'. *Huh!* Cheeky Welshman!*

---

* Peter later told me that he'd asked his friend, Katharine Hepburn, what she thought of me playing the part. She'd told him, 'Oh, yes, Petula will be marvellous!'

MGM suggested that I meet Peter O'Toole to see if we got on, which seemed a good idea, so I flew over to Ireland. Peter was over there finishing off making *The Lion in Winter*, so he and I went out for a quiet dinner in Dublin. Well, that was our plan.

Peter liked a drink, and I didn't mind joining in. After a couple of glasses of wine over dinner, we went to a nearby pub. Of course, the two of us in a pub in Dublin quickly got noticed and in no time we had a whole gang of new Irish best friends. By the end of a somewhat tiddly evening, there was no doubt Peter O'Toole and I would get on very well indeed.

While I was waiting for filming to begin, I made my first American television special … which, somehow, turned into an international news story.

NBC had invited me to host a one-off special simply called *Petula*. I was happy to accept. The director, Steve Binder, was wonderful – he was later to direct the famous Elvis Presley comeback special – but I also asked Yvonne Littlewood to fly over and help. I always felt better with Yvonne in my corner.

Things didn't get off to a great start when I broke my ankle skiing in France three weeks before rehearsals started. I didn't even do one of my 'Germaine' tumbles – I was standing up on my skis when I heard it *snap*. The ankle swelled up on my flight back to the States but *what can you do?* I just had to get on with it.

NBC asked if I wanted a special guest on the show and I said, 'Yes – Harry Belafonte!' I'd never met Harry but I admired him as a person and loved his singing. Duetting with him would be a dream. I didn't imagine he'd accept my invitation, so I was delighted when NBC told me that he had.

We rehearsed for three weeks so I spent a lot of time with Harry. We really got to know one another and we liked each other a lot. We were to duet on an anti-war song I'd co-written, 'On the Path of Glory'. I felt very emotional about it: it seemed the perfect song for us to sing together.

We did three takes but the first one was the best. Harry sang his own song, 'While I Got Time', before I entered upstage in a long, flowing white dress – trying not to limp on my dodgy ankle – and we segued into 'On the Path of Glory'. Our duet sounded lovely and, in a spontaneous gesture of affection, I rested my hand on Harry's forearm.

'That's great, Harry and Petula!' said Steve Binder. 'Really good.'

Yet a few minutes later, an assistant came over to us. 'Can we do another take or two?' he asked. 'It's a technical issue. Harry, can you stand *here*?' Then he pointed to a spot about 5 feet away. 'And Petula, can you go *there*?' We did a couple more takes with the two of us standing well apart, but they didn't feel as good or as natural.

I was puzzled – but the issue soon became clear. Apparently, an on-set representative of the show's sponsor, Plymouth Motors (part of Chrysler), had objected to me putting my hand on Harry's arm. The awful truth was that he didn't want his company to be associated with a white woman touching a Black man.

I didn't yet know this but Claude, who was an executive producer on the show, *did*. He ran up to me. 'Come with me,' he said. Our lawyer, Pete Pryor, was also there, and the three of us scuttled off the set and down some stairs to a technicians' room where we found a startled engineer scoffing a sandwich as he recorded the show on videotape.

Pete Pryor spoke to the guy. 'You have to erase all the takes of that song except for the first one,' he told him.

'I can't do that!' the engineer said. 'I have to keep all the takes in case we need them.'

'Do it *now*!' said Claude. 'This is an order!'

The hapless technician pushed a few buttons and deleted all the other takes. It left NBC no choice but to use the sole remaining recording, where I touched Harry. Not that they minded – Steve Binder and the network were right behind us. The only objection had come from the sponsor's rep, who I believe rapidly lost his job.

The story leaked into the press and caused a bit of a hoo-ha. Chrysler put out a press statement apologising and blaming the incident on 'one individual'. That individual then phoned Harry and tried to say sorry. Harry wasn't having any of it.

'Apologies in this situation mean nothing,' he said in a statement. 'They change neither that man's heart nor my skin. Inside, he feels the same way because of how I look on the outside.'

Harry was very emotional about what had happened. He later thanked Claude and me for our support – *but what else would we have done?* I'd never given a single thought in my entire life to whether someone was Black or white. What was the big deal about one person touching another? The whole fuss was ridiculous.

But those were racially troubled times in America. Segregation was still going on in parts of the South, and two days after NBC broadcast *Petula*, Dr Martin Luther King, the civil rights leader and a close friend of Harry Belafonte, was shot dead at a hotel in Memphis. So, little battles like the one we had just won *mattered*.

\* \* \*

It was time to begin work on *Goodbye, Mr. Chips*. Claude and I were still living in France while we waited for the house in Geneva to be completed, so MGM decided to do the pre-filming rehearsals in Paris. Peter O'Toole was pleased about this because he loved the city. He said he'd spent a lot of time there when he was making *Lawrence of Arabia*.

We started rehearsing the dance routines and other bits in Paris at the beginning of May 1968. And then Paris exploded.

It was the famous riots that swept through France for weeks. Students were protesting about inequality in French society, and against capitalism, and occupied the Sorbonne campus at the University of Paris. When police cracked down heavily on the students, trade unions came out in support of the protesters and called a general strike.

The protests spread throughout the country and France came to a virtual standstill. It got really hairy in Paris. Protesters erected barricades in the streets and ripped up paving stones and cobblestones to hurl at riot police. There were running battles in the Latin Quarter. It felt like we were in the middle of a revolution.

It got very violent, very quickly. I obviously felt concerned but Claude was really, really worried. I think it instinctively re-triggered in him the fear and insecurity he'd felt as a Jewish boy wearing the yellow star in Nazi-occupied Paris. It made him even more fixated on us quitting Paris for the peace and safety of Switzerland.

MGM also felt it was too dangerous for us to carry on rehearsing in Paris, so the cast of *Goodbye, Mr. Chips* fled the city in a fleet of limousines to Geneva. I must admit, it looked serene and idyllic by comparison. We moved back into Le Richemond hotel, rehearsed, and enjoyed the scenery and sunshine.

After a few weeks, we switched to London and began filming at MGM Elstree Studios. And I realised just how charming and generous Peter O'Toole was, both as an actor and a human being.

Peter had a reputation as a hellraiser but I didn't see too much of that. I think he had calmed down a little, and he got very into his character as the serious academic, Mr Chips. And, of course, his smart Welsh wife, Siân Phillips, was also in the film, playing the socialite Ursula Mossbank. So maybe she kept him in check.

Mind you, we had our moments. One evening, Peter and I went out to a restaurant near his home on Hampstead Heath. The night ended with him giving me a piggyback down Hampstead High Street with both of us singing at the tops of our voices, doubtless annoying everyone who was trying to sleep.

'Keep it down!' a few people shouted. I wonder if they'd have been as miffed if they'd known it was Peter and me? Yes, I think they probably would!

Peter was a very *gallant* individual. There used to be a nice pub near Elstree Studios and we'd go there for lunch more days than not. The food was terrific, and they used to sell gorgeous cockles and my own personal weakness, my Achilles heel when it comes to food – pickled onions.

Ever since I was a toddler, I've loved pickled onions. As a kid, I used to get up in the night and sneak into the kitchen to scoff them. They have to be firm, not soggy, but when they're just right, I can't resist them. And this pub used to sell excellent pickled onions. *Delicious!*

Peter knew about my craving, so he'd order them for me. He also knew that I'd feel awful if we had to do any close scenes, or kissing scenes, that afternoon and my breath was a bit whiffy – because, let's face it, pickled onions pong! So he'd gulp down one or two himself, even though he didn't like them that much, to save my feelings.

I had a fine time making *Goodbye, Mr. Chips* with Peter and Siân and Michael Redgrave, but I had reservations about the direction of the film. I think, somewhere along the line, MGM lost their nerve with it. They began having doubts about making it into a musical and they bottled it.

The director was a nice man called Herb Ross but, instead of having us perform the songs or do big dance routines, he'd play the music over beautifully shot footage of views and landscapes. It was poetic, in parts, but I must admit that I missed the wild, wayward genius and unconventionality of Francis Ford Coppola.

Still, the script was tremendous, and I had some wonderful times filming on location. We shot the public-school scenes at Sherborne School in Dorset. The producers gave us a gorgeous house to stay in, with a croquet lawn. Believe me, playing croquet with Peter O'Toole, after a few drinks, isn't an experience you forget in a hurry.

I hadn't lived in England for so long, and I felt as if I was *finding* the country again. I indulged my love of the countryside by going for long walks on my own. One day, in a field, I got chased by a herd of young heifers. I had to hurl myself into a hedge and got covered in scratches. Flashbacks to being butted by a goat in *Trouble at Townsend*!

Making *Goodbye, Mr. Chips*, I had the same issue as *Finian's Rainbow* in that I could only spend so many days per year working in Britain. Thankfully, this time we had a far nicer solution than iffy Mexican motels. Claude and I rented a place in Deauville, in Normandy, to spend the weekends.

It was a very simple, very quick flight. We'd fly in and out of Hurn Airport, an old RAF base. It was mostly made from corrugated iron and had one guy with a ledger checking the passports. The producers arranged a cute little private plane for us and gave us a friendly pilot, John, who flew us to and fro.* It was a nice routine and we got used to it.

One Friday, Claude and I got to Hurn Airport to find a different plane and pilot waiting for us. We took off, but during the flight all the instruments packed up and the poor pilot had to admit we were flying blind. It was pretty scary, but thankfully, Claude and I knew the approach to Deauville well by now and were able to show him where to land.

In the script for *Goodbye, Mr. Chips*, Katherine bumped into Mr Chips by chance, a few months after their first meeting, when they coincidentally both happened to be visiting the ruins at Pompeii. This gave me my other great highlight of making the film – a trip to Italy with Peter O'Toole.

He and I had the *best* time in Pompeii. While we were filming, they closed the ruins to the public and we had them to ourselves. Peter loved archaeology and it's a real passion of mine. If I could have chosen any life, and career, other than the one I've had, I'd have loved to have been an archaeologist.

---

* Sadly, the lovely John died in a crash in that same plane a few years later.

Wandering around the ancient city together, we were in heaven. Peter saw an artefact he loved, in a little barred cage. Every time we passed it, he'd surreptitiously nudge it nearer to the bars with his walking stick to try to swipe it. 'Um, I don't think you ought to nick it, Peter?' I advised him. Happily, in the end, he didn't.

Peter got on well with Claude. They shared a love of antiques, and a few times the two of them took off in our Rolls-Royce on a mission to buy some choice items. They easily saw through a few local chancers who buried pots in the ground for a few weeks to make them dirty and then produced them with a flourish, claiming they were antiques.

Claude and Peter certainly weren't falling for that scam, but they did come across some genuine treasures. One afternoon, they returned triumphant with a fine haul of Etruscan pots and artefacts that they had acquired, stashed in our boot. That evening, the two of them did a little boozing to celebrate.

Peter was coming to Geneva with us for the weekend, so we set off the next morning. Claude was driving and I was sitting in the back. Peter was in the front passenger seat, hungover and a tad the worse for wear. I don't think he'd had his Fernet-Branca.* He was fast asleep as we got to the border.

The customs official asked for our passports. Claude and I showed him ours. 'And *'im?'* the guy asked, gesturing towards Peter. He was spark out. We didn't want to wake him.

'Oh, that's Peter O'Toole,' said Claude.

The customs guy was clearly no movie buff. '*Oo?*' he asked.

---

* Peter used to drink this thick, black, herbal pick-me-up every single morning. I tried it once, out of interest. It was foul.

'Peter O'Toole! Lawrence of Arabia!' said Claude. Which totally threw the official. In truth, Peter didn't look very dashing, passed out in the front seat. He was more … crumpled. The customs guy rolled his eyes and waved us through.

Peter was like Francis and like Quincy. *When you work with great people, something rubs off on you.* His genius lifted my own performance. I had a tremendous time making *Goodbye, Mr. Chips,* but my primary memory of the movie will forever be the chemistry that we had between us, and the friendship we formed.

Many years later, I went to see Peter in a brilliant London stage production of *Man and Superman.* He was simply incredible. I went backstage afterwards, and he and I sat opposite one another, on two chairs, held hands and wept. A wave of emotion just swept over us. 'Oh, God, it was so great to work with you!' we told each other.

What were we crying about? It's hard to explain, really. The intense memories of our time together. Our love for each other. The passage of time. *Les neiges d'antan.* I will never, ever forget Peter O'Toole. He was extraordinary.

Especially when it came to pickled onions.

# CHAPTER 11

# I'M SORRY, ELVIS, BUT WE HAVE TO GO …

By the time we finished filming *Goodbye, Mr. Chips*, our house in Switzerland was finally finished and all of our stuff had been moved in. Claude and I flew back to Geneva with the girls, and *there we were*. This was our home now.

I have to say, the architect and builders had done a tremendous job. Lots of rooms, which we filled with our beloved antique furniture, and a swimming pool. Due to a bizarre Swiss law, we were obliged to include an atom shelter capable of withstanding an atomic bomb. Claude and I felt this was rather sinister, so we mostly used it as a wine cellar. The local authorities would come and inspect it every now and then, so we had to also keep rice and water in there to satisfy them.

The house was certainly beautiful but I didn't like it nearly as much as the one in Paris. It may sound odd, but it didn't feel like home. It was the second time that I'd uprooted my life and moved to a new country, but this switch to Switzerland didn't feel as natural or as successful to me.

I had loved living in La Celle-Saint-Cloud, with the life and energy of Paris just down the road. Although I'm not really a showbiz person, I'd also adored the many months we'd stayed in Los Angeles, where there was always something to do, with interesting and talented people, and exciting things happening. You felt like you were at the centre of things.

The nature around Geneva is truly beautiful. The country-side around the city is stunning. The Alps, of course, are always impressive in any season. There are the Jura mountains, softer and more gentle. The sweeping vineyards, and fields and fields of sunflowers.

Just an hour away lay Montreux, famed for its jazz festival and loved by Freddie Mercury.* Plus, the Swiss people were all so nice and friendly. But everything felt … subdued. It was like snuggling into a warm blanket. Even as we settled into what was an undeniably attractive home, I had severe misgivings about how happy I would be there.

I was still travelling far and wide. In October 1968, I attended the New York premiere of *Finian's Rainbow* at the Penthouse Theater on Broadway and, the very next day, the London opening at the Odeon in Marble Arch. And, back in London a month later, I performed at a very illustrious occasion.

I appeared at a Royal Variety Performance at the London Palladium with Diana Ross and The Supremes, Engelbert Humperdinck, my good friend Sacha Distel and two old faces from my past: Arthur Askey and Frankie Howerd. I wore a Nina Ricci dress and coat in a hand-embroidered brocade. It weighed a ton. I never wore it again.

As was the tradition, we met the Queen after the show when she walked down a line of performers, being introduced

---

* There's even a statue of Freddie there.

and saying hello. I encountered Her Majesty a few times at Royal Command-type performances and also when she hosted cocktail parties at the Royal Academy. Those were great because they were a little more casual.

I'd occasionally overhear some very strange royal conversations at those gatherings. At one of them, I was talking to Brian May. Eric Clapton was standing nearby, and the Queen wandered over to our part of the room, glass in hand, an equerry by her side. 'This is Eric Clapton, ma'am,' the courtier murmured to her.

'Oh, hello,' she said, in that impeccable cut-glass accent. 'And what do *you* do?'

'I play guitar, ma'am,' he told her.

'Do you? How nice.'

At another cocktail bash, I was in a corner chatting to Shirley Bassey and Elaine Paige when Prince Philip came marching up to us. 'So, what are you girls talking about?' he demanded, brusquely. 'Money, I suppose?'

I didn't know what to say to that. 'No, not really,' we assured him.

Philip said, 'Ah!' and made a little small talk. Then, as he was leaving, he paused. 'I don't suppose one of you could lend me a tenner, could you?' he asked, then strode off, leaving us a bit bemused.

\* \* \*

In the spring of 1969, NBC invited me to present my second US TV special, this time titled *Portrait of Petula*. My guests were my friends Sacha Distel and Andy Williams, and Ron Moody, who had just won a Golden Globe for *Oliver!*

Around the same time, I had a hit in America with 'Happy Heart', which was co-written by James Last and Jackie Rae and produced by Claude, and then played a handful of dates in Mississippi and the Midwest. I was fortunate enough to do two or three of those shows with the great drummer Buddy Rich.

Buddy's reputation went before him. I'd heard all the stories, that he could be a bit of a bastard, but he was OK with me. And he was a genius. He had a fantastic young band who were all fresh out of music school and desperate to play with him. And Buddy was a hard taskmaster.

When he played his set, I'd stand side-stage to watch him, and marvel to myself: *How does he do that?* Then I'd be getting ready in my dressing room and hear him onstage doing his solo on 'West Side Story'. I mean, *wow*. Buddy Rich is the only drummer to ever make me cry.

It was a busy summer. I did two weeks of shows in Canada, including the ill-fated night in Montreal that sent me sobbing to John and Yoko. By July, I was back in Vegas, doing three weeks at Caesars Palace.* Bara and Kate were out of school for the summer by now, so Claude and I could take them with us.

After Vegas, I played my first ever dates at Lake Tahoe, one of the most beautiful places I've ever been to. Surrounded by mountains, it sits between Nevada and California: the border runs down the middle of a tiny town called Stateline. Gambling is legal in Nevada but not in California, so there are casinos on one side of the street but not on the other.

---

* I spent so much time in Vegas that I feel lucky I've never had any interest in gambling. A lot of performers gamble there, and it gets them into trouble, but I'd walk through the casinos utterly oblivious. I might as well have been walking across a field.

I was playing a Tahoe casino club in Stateline called Harrah's, which was owned by a guy called Bill Harrah. Bill really looked after us, giving us a house on the lake, with a chef, a Rolls-Royce and a chauffeur. Later that year, Bill married Bobbie Gentry (although the marriage was to last less than four months).

No matter how busy my schedule was, Claude and I always tried to make time for our family holidays. At the end of that summer, we went to Morocco with a friend, Maurice Siegel, the news manager of Europe n° 1 radio station, and stayed in a lovely hotel in beautiful Marrakech.

Claude and I got introduced to Prince Moulay Abdallah from the country's royal family. One night, the prince happened to be in the same restaurant as us. We'd just finished a long day of sightseeing and Kate, who was then seven, was very tired. She spent most of our meal dozing at the table.

The next morning, as we left our hotel, we bumped into the prince again. After greeting us, he nodded at Kate. 'Hello! I saw you asleep in the restaurant last night,' he told her.

Kate raised one eyebrow. 'Did you have nothing better to do than to look at me?' she asked, witheringly.

Prince Moulay merely smiled and took his leave. After he'd gone, Claude and I told Kate that the man she had just been rather rude to was the Prince of Morocco. Our daughter was blithely unconcerned. 'How was I supposed to know?' she retorted. 'He wasn't wearing his crown …'

* * *

In September 1969, I got an offer out of the blue to make an album that would take me a long way out of my comfort zone. I was invited to go to Memphis, Tennessee, to record a new album with a noted music producer, Chips Moman, in his American Sound Studio.

Chips had a spectacular musical track record. He'd worked with Aretha Franklin, Bobby Womack and Wilson Pickett, and had just produced the big comeback album for Elvis Presley, *From Elvis in Memphis*. It was an enticing offer, so I headed off for two weeks in Memphis in October.

Chips was unlike any producer I'd ever worked with. He was incredibly laid-back, quite literally: he would usually be leaning back in his seat with his cowboy boots up on the control panel, crumbs scattered all over the place. And I quickly learned that Memphis musicians are unique.

The guys in the American Sound Studio didn't even read music. Chips would play them a demo tape, and they'd listen and scribble down what looked to me like some kind of code. Then they'd sit down and play, and it sounded like no other music I'd heard in a studio before.

This was all new to me, but I loved it. On the *Memphis* album, I sang differently. I wasn't aware that I was doing it but, if you listen to the record, you can hear it in my voice. It wasn't a conscious effort, it just happened: the music, and Chip, drew it out of me. A sign of what a great producer he was.

I covered The Box Tops' 'Neon Rainbow' and Curtis Mayfield's magnificent civil rights anthem, 'People Get Ready'. I also wrote a song myself for the record, called 'Right On', although a lot of people probably didn't realise that it was my own handiwork as I had penned it under a pseudonym, Al Grant.*

---

* Over the years, I've written many songs as 'Al Grant'. People have asked me why, but it's quite a boring answer: it was Claude's idea, as an easy way around a contractual issue.

One Sunday, I went to Al Green's church, which was in the woods outside Memphis. He'd given up showbiz completely at that point. Al knew that I was in the congregation but at that point in his life he didn't see anybody at all outside of the Church.

I had met Al once before, though. A few years earlier, I'd gone to see one of his shows in Los Angeles. I'd gone backstage to say hello, and he'd said to me, 'I've got a plane waiting for me. Why don't you come with me? Let's go away together!' I'd had to politely decline his offer.

I have been back to the city of Memphis so many times since that first visit, and I absolutely adore it. I even wrote my own special tribute song to the city: 'To Memphis'. For me, it's truly a very special place.

Experiences like Memphis were great, but when I went home, it re-emphasised to me how sedate Geneva was. Everything felt so placid. I very quickly understood that I was going to find it impossible to have any creative ideas, or work on music, there. I had nobody to bounce ideas off.

Of course, Geneva was gorgeous, but a big part of me was still back in the States. I had been singing a lot better because I was working with great people. I'd been at my happiest and doing some of the best work that I'd ever done. I'd been fearless and sure of myself.

I'd had all those early years in England, not knowing who the hell I was. Then I'd moved to France and never really quite been myself: I'd been France's idea of who I should be. But in America, I'd been singing the kinds of songs that I wanted to sing, in the way I wanted to sing them. And people had loved it.

After a while in the new house, I tried to explain all of this to Claude but it wasn't easy. He was very happy with our new life in

Geneva. I knew exactly what he was thinking: *What's wrong with her? She's got everything she could ask for! We've got a wonderful house, two lovely children, a Rolls-Royce, a chauffeur, a cook, even a dog! Everything here is perfect. What does she want, exactly?*

I felt a bit like a fish out of water. Claude didn't understand. I'd try to explain and we'd go back and forth about it. It was tough. For the first time, strains and tensions crept into our relationship. Because, no matter how much two people may love one another, if they can't agree on where to live, that is a major hurdle to overcome.

* * *

At the end of October 1969, I flew back to England to make history, in a funny little way. The BBC were moving beyond black-and-white TV and launching a full-colour service, and the launch broadcast was to be a recording of a concert that I was playing at the Royal Albert Hall.

It was quite a big deal, but I was no more nervous about it than before any other show. I've never suffered *too* badly from stage fright. In any case, I think pre-show nerves are a sign of good health. It's like a dog having a wet nose. If you haven't got any nerves, *that's* when there's something wrong.

Plus, of course, I love the Albert Hall. It's one of my favourite venues of all time. It's such an extraordinary place. If you stand and gaze around it when it's empty, it seems massive and intimidating, yet as soon as the orchestra and audience are in, it somehow feels intimate and welcoming. I've no idea why, but it's the truth.

A week later, I was in LA for the US premiere of *Goodbye, Mr. Chips* at the beautiful, art deco Fox Wilshire Theater. It was

as glitzy and fun as these things usually are and, after the showing, MGM laid on a lavish meal for the attendees (rather nicely
including Robert Powell, the headmaster of Sherborne School
where we'd done the filming).

I was enjoying my meal when I heard live music starting up
in a corner of the room. Now, I'm no fan of dinner music: it's
either bad and that puts me off my food, or it's so good that it
puts me off my food. But as I listened, there was no question
that this music was *really* good. I got up from the table and
went to have a look.

There was a young guy sitting at a piano, playing warm,
clever harmonies, and a pretty girl playing drums and singing
like an angel. Close up, they sounded wonderful and I stood,
transfixed, and watched them. The girl noticed me, and when
the duo took a break, she came over to me.

'Excuse me, aren't you Petula Clark?' she asked.

'Yes,' I said. 'I think you're absolutely marvellous.'

Her eyes widened in delight. *'Oh, man!'* She smiled.

She told me a little about them. She was only nineteen years
old. Her name was Karen, the pianist was her older brother,
Richard, and they performed under their family name: The
Carpenters. They were just starting out, really.

I walked back to my table. Herb Alpert, the highly successful trumpet player who had co-founded and now ran A&M
Records, was sitting at the next table. Herb was a smart, handsome guy: I must admit that I used to have a bit of a secret
crush on him. I went over to have a quick word.

'Herb, you have to listen to those musicians over there,'
I said. 'They're terrific!' Well, Herb didn't need telling twice

and headed over to them. He was evidently just as impressed as me, because he immediately signed them up to A&M.

Two weeks later, it was London's turn for a grand opening for *Goodbye, Mr. Chips* – and time for another of my occasional royal encounters. We had a full royal premiere, in the presence of the Queen, at the Empire, Leicester Square. For what it's worth, I remember that I wore a white Dior pantsuit.

Claude and I were given very prestigious seats to view the film, right behind Her Majesty (I was glad she wasn't wearing a crown). So, it was deeply unfortunate that, as soon as the lights went down, and the movie began, Claude promptly fell asleep and started snoring. Quite loudly. Jetlag, I suppose.

I nudged him, hard, in the ribs. 'Claude!' I whispered. 'Wake up! You're snoring! You'll disturb the Queen!'

Claude winced, opened his eyes, and stared at me a little balefully. 'Eet's not my fault,' he said. 'I've seen it before.'

I don't think the Queen heard Claude's snoring and, if she did, she didn't mind, because she was very nice when we met her after the screening. She even talked to Claude for a while in French. I was impressed: she wasn't without accent, but she was pretty fluent.

My last big engagement of the sixties saw me doing two weeks at the Empire Room at the Waldorf-Astoria Hotel on Park Lane in New York. It's a fantastic venue, a small theatre in a luxury hotel, and it was wonderful to be back in Manhattan, playing in the city that had taken me to its heart.

\* \* \*

At the start of 1970, I was back in New York to host a show called *Kraft Music Hall Presents Petula Clark* on NBC. My special guest was Anthony Newley. Tony and I did sketches, bantered, and became a mock music-hall duo, The Lovebirds, to duet on songs like 'What Kind of Fool Am I?'

Herb Alpert had wasted no time. After I'd put him on to The Carpenters at the *Goodbye, Mr. Chips* launch party, he'd signed them, and put them straight into the studio. By the time I was back in Las Vegas at Caesars Palace, in the summer of 1970, they'd had a US number one with 'Close to You' and become international superstars.

I'd kept in touch with Karen, on and off, and was delighted when she turned up in Vegas while I was there. I had a night off, so I suggested we have a girls' night out. But what should we do? We scoured the Vegas listings, and one show jumped out at me.

Elvis Presley had a residency at the International Hotel as part of his hugely successful comeback. I'd never seen Elvis, and nor had Karen, so off we went. When we turned up at the International, we were instantly recognised – we were both huge stars right then – and the management, of course, gave us the best seats in the house.

Word had clearly also got to Elvis that Karen and I were there, because just after the show started, the lights were trained on us. '*Laydeez'n'gennelmun*, ah'm delighted to have Miss Petula Clark and Miss Karen Carpenter here tonight!' drawled the King. We stood and acknowledged the applause.

Now, I wasn't a massive Elvis fan, but I have to say that he was marvellous that night. He still looked great, and his voice sounded fantastic. *And what a showman he was.* At the end of the show, one of his people came over to us: 'Miss Clark, Miss Carpenter, Elvis would like to invite you to his dressing room.'

Vegas dressing rooms have a big entertaining area, and an inner sanctum where the artist gets dressed and ready for the show. There were a load of guys from Nashville in the main room, so Karen and I waited in a corner until Elvis emerged from his private space. He looked amazing.

Elvis couldn't have been more charming. 'Wow!' he said. 'Thank you so much for coming. I can't believe you two ladies are here. Can I get you a glass of wine?' We chatted, and he was a real Southern gentleman. It was as if Karen and I were the only people in the room.

After a while, I realised … *we were*. The Nashville guys had vanished, it was just the three of us, and Elvis was coming on to us pretty heavily. The penny dropped: *Uh-oh, he's got plans for us here!* By now, I was pretty worldly-wise but Karen was still innocent and a bit naïve – still a country girl, really. Suddenly, I felt very protective towards her.

'Well, Elvis,' I said. 'Thank you for a lovely evening but we have to go.'

The King looked disappointed. 'Oh, no! Really?' he replied.

'Yes, we have to get our beauty sleep,' I said.

'Hey, we don't need beauty sleep,' said Elvis. 'We're beautiful – all three of us!'

'You have *that thing* tomorrow morning, Karen, remember?' I said. Karen looked at me, perplexed, as if to say, *what thing?* Because, let's face it, *nobody* in Vegas does anything in the mornings. But I persisted – 'Come on, let's go!' – and steered her out of there.

Elvis looked disconsolate. As Karen and I walked down the corridor, I looked behind us to see him standing in his dressing-room door, watching us go. He gave me a knowing smile that said one thing, and one thing only: *OK, I'll get you next time!*

But he never did.*

From Vegas, I was back at Harrah's in Tahoe, where I had a curious experience. Sammy Davis Jr had a place there and asked if I'd go to Reno to play a late-afternoon charity event with him. Reno was only a forty-minute drive away, and my Tahoe concert wasn't until the evening, so I agreed.

The chauffeur drove me down to Reno in Bill Harrah's Rolls-Royce. The charity show was fun, and on the way back to Tahoe, I saw a Dairy Queen ice-cream place. Now, when it comes to food, soft ice cream is nearly as big a weakness for me as pickled onions, so I asked the driver to pull over.

I'd been vaguely aware of a black limousine following us up the mountain road from Reno. It had had a couple of chances to overtake but it hadn't done so: it had just tailed us. When we stopped at the Dairy Queen, the limo stopped as well. When we started off again, there it was, still right behind us.

I was a bit perturbed, because I'd heard about the Mafia being active in that area, so I spoke to the chauffeur. 'Do you know that a car is following us?' I asked him. 'Oh, yeah,' he replied, sounding not in the slightest concerned.

'Who is it?' I asked.

'Well, Mr Harrah knew you were doing a show with Mr Davis this afternoon,' the driver explained. 'And he doesn't

---

* I was to meet Elvis just once more, also in Vegas. It was very sad. He'd put on so much weight, he could hardly sing: his backing singers did all the work. Backstage, he seemed out of it: not there anymore. Everyone was saying, 'You're great, Elvis!' but he wasn't. I didn't know what to say. I just kissed him on the cheek and said goodbye.

want you to miss your show at his place tonight. This is your dinghy.' So, if my Rolls-Royce had happened to break down (unlikely!), I would have had a big black limo on hand to whisk me back to Harrah's. Only in America.

That trip had a funny ending. With his rotten timekeeping, Frank Owens rarely comprehended that planes are supposed to leave on time. When we flew out of Tahoe, the air crew had to hold the plane for him. When my musical director finally turned up, his sole hand luggage was an enormous bottle of Lake Tahoe water. Why, I'll never know. Souvenir?

* * *

In the autumn of 1970, I flew to Miami to make an album, *Warm and Tender*, with the renowned producer Arif Mardin at Criteria Studios. Arif had worked with all sorts of huge stars, such as Aretha Franklin, but he didn't look like a rock-and-roll person at all. He was a very dapper, polite little Turkish guy.

I arrived on a Sunday with a terrible cold and sore throat, totally unable to sing. Arif set about finding me a doctor. Let me tell you, that isn't easy on a Sunday in Miami: they're all out playing golf. The only doc he could locate for me was Ferdie Pacheco, a Cuban medic who worked with Muhammad Ali and his team.

Ferdie was a funny, lively, intense guy, and he produced a needle and gave me a shot of vitamin B12. And when I say a shot, I mean *a shot*! It made me so up and hyper that I could hardly sleep for three days. It turned out that Ferdie had given me the kind of dose that he usually dispensed to heavyweight boxers.

Claude and I got very friendly with Ferdie. We kept in touch and shortly afterwards, in October, he invited us to

Muhammad Ali's trainer Angelo Dundee's gym in Miami, where Ali was training for a big comeback fight after being banned from boxing for three years for refusing to fight in the war in Vietnam.

I was excited by the prospect of meeting Muhammad Ali. My dad was a boxing fan and I'd seen a few of his fights, when he was still called Cassius Clay, on TV. But our first sighting of him, outside the Miami gym, was somewhat odd. He was trying to get into a locked car (his, I assume!) with a coat-hanger.

Meeting Ali was a joy. He was quite the character: funny, charming, and every bit as charismatic as he always was on TV. He was getting ready to fight a boxer called Jerry Quarry, and Claude and I stood by the boxing ring and watched him sparring. Claude was filming it with a Super 8 camera.

Ali was magnificent to watch, just so powerful and graceful, but then he let his guard drop for a second and his sparring partner hit him hard in the ribs. Ali fell to his knees, got straight up and, a few seconds later, said that he was in pain. Ferdie Pacheco took him off for an X-ray and they found he had broken a rib.*

This was major bad news, right before Ali's big comeback fight. How had he let it happen? Ferdie had an explanation: 'Ah, it's because you're here!' he said. 'He was showing off to you!' But it took more than a fractured rib to stop the great Muhammad Ali. Two days later, he beat Jerry Quarry in three rounds. Amazing.

---

* There was a BBC TV crew filming the sparring. They were changing their film as Ali got hurt and missed the fateful blow. They asked Claude if they might borrow his Super 8 footage and the BBC broadcast it.

At the end of 1970, I did my third NBC US TV special, this time just called *Petula*. I had a fabulous array of mostly American guests, and yet the strange thing was that we recorded most of the show at Elstree Studios, because it was an ATV production.

I'd been on Dean Martin's show so often by now that he returned the favour and guested on mine. It was a memorable recording. We managed to clamber onto a horse together – it took Dean a few attempts – to duet on a medley including 'Hey, Good Lookin'' and 'I Walk the Line'. I'll tell you, it's hard to sing when you're laughing. Try it!

I also sang with The Everly Brothers. It was a joy to blend in with their golden harmonies. I'd heard that, although they always sounded immaculate together, Phil and Don didn't get on well, but they certainly didn't show any signs of that around me. They were all sweetness and light.

David Frost was another guest on that show. We had a good chat and did a funny little *Romeo and Juliet*-themed sketch together. I loved David: he was intelligent, knowledgeable and, most of all, *funny*. Yet this time around, the guest that I was the most excited about was Peggy Lee.

As I've said, I adored Peggy. I knew every single breath on her *Black Coffee* album off by heart. By now, she wasn't at all well and needed oxygen in her dressing room. No one was allowed to go in there, or even walk down the corridor outside. Had someone lit a cigarette, it could have caused an explosion.

Singing 'Wedding Bell Blues' with Peggy was pure joy for me. *For both of us.* We loved how our voices sounded together. Meeting her was yet another highlight in a working life that seemed to always be full of such memorable moments. Sadly, my personal life right now was not quite so happy.

# CHAPTER 12

# WHERE'S THE FRENCHMAN?

As we moved into the 1970s, it's a sad fact that Claude and I were not getting on very well. Day by day, the strains and tensions in our relationship were increasing, and they still had the same, inescapable root cause: that Claude adored living in Geneva, and I didn't.

We had our amazing house, plus our plush skiing chalet up in the mountains. We'd made quite a lot of money by now, our life was extremely comfortable, and Claude felt that *we'd made it*. He was beginning to lose his interest in show business, and was content to lead a quiet life in Geneva.

The problem was ... I didn't think like that. It just wasn't me. No matter how much success I have, I've never had an 'OK, I've made it' attitude. For me, singing, and performing, isn't something I can dip in and out of. It's a huge part of my life. *It's who I am.*

The most truthful way to explain it is that I was bored in Switzerland. Bored in paradise. I had no proper friends in Geneva, *nobody* to hang out with and chat to about music and show business ... with one major exception.

Geneva is the European headquarters of the United Nations and of their humanitarian and charity wing, UNICEF, dedicated to improving the lives of children worldwide. When UNICEF heard I was now living locally, they asked me if I'd get involved with fundraising and charity events both for them and for UNHCR, their agency dedicated to helping refugees.

I was delighted to do so because they are hugely laudable organisations, and it also gave me something worthwhile to do in Geneva. A tremendous bonus was that it brought me back into regular contact with a valued friend from the beginning of my career, who was by now also a local resident – Peter Ustinov.

Spending time with Peter again reminded me (not that I'd forgotten!) how much I adored the man. He'd achieved so much in the interim, including winning an Oscar for his 1960 role in *Spartacus*, yet he was still, essentially, the same hilarious, mischievous, anarchic soul who'd directed me in *Vice Versa* back in 1948.

Peter and I would attend UNICEF and UNHCR events together, then go for dinner. I tell you, those dinners went on for *hours*! Peter was a true Renaissance man: he'd been everywhere, could speak every language going, and had a deep knowledge of music. He was a godsend, and magnificent company.

It still felt like I was always on planes between Switzerland, America and the UK. In December 1970, I was back at Elstree Studios to co-star in a TV special, *This Is Tom Jones*. The theme was relationships, so Tom and I duetted on songs including The Partridge Family's recent hit, 'I Think I Love You' and Bacharach and David's 'This Guy's in Love With You'.

I loved hanging out with Tom. Being from the Valleys, he knew my grandparents' village, and we chatted about our beloved Wales. He'd certainly held on to his Welsh accent. I liked the fact that international fame and success hadn't changed Tom at all. It's just as true today.

Duetting with Tom, I sensed that he was an even better singer than we were hearing, if that makes sense. He could do even more with his voice. I suggested to him, probably a bit cheekily, that he could try edgier material? He didn't seem interested. Tom was extremely happy with how his career was going, and who could blame him?

Back in America, I made a guest appearance on NBC's *The Bob Hope Special*, singing the old standard 'Tea for Two' with Bob, and a repeat appearance on *The Dean Martin Show*. Then, in April, I headed to the Dorothy Chandler Pavilion in Los Angeles for the glitziest event I'd ever attended.

Being asked to perform at the 43rd Academy Awards was quite a thrill. It's nigh on impossible to describe how glamorous an Oscars night is. *You just have to be there* ... and my presence there was largely down to my new friends, The Carpenters.

They had had a big hit with their recording of 'For All We Know', a lovely, gentle tune from the soundtrack of a movie, *Lovers and Other Strangers*. The song was up for an Oscar but they weren't allowed to perform it as they'd never appeared in a film, so Karen and Richard asked the Academy if I could replace them.

When I got to the theatre, the marvellous, if rather scary, dress designer Edith Head was there. A legendary figure, Edith was, over the years, to win no fewer than eight Academy Awards for her costume design. 'What are you wearing tonight, Petula?' she enquired.

'Um, one of my own dresses?' I replied.

'I'll have to have a look at it,' Edith declared. She followed me into my dressing room and looked my garment up and down. 'Hmm, very nice,' she decided. So, that was a good start to the evening.

It's a cliché to say that the Academy Awards are star-studded, but do you know the thing about clichés? They're mostly true. Backstage, anyone you could think of in Hollywood was there. Gregory Peck. Walter Matthau. Goldie Hawn. Steve McQueen. Ryan O'Neal. Jack Nicholson. John Mills. Angie Dickinson. Shirley Jones. George Segal. And everyone getting on well, just happy to be there.

It was too much to take in. I bumped into old friends and colleagues. Harry Belafonte was presenting an award. I got to catch up with Francis Ford Coppola, who was winning his first Oscar, for best writing and screenplay, for the epic war film *Patton*. It picked up seven awards at the ceremony.*

Just before I went on, I received a telegram from Karen Carpenter. 'Hi, Petula,' it said. 'Sing the song pretty for me tonight.'

As well as performing 'For All We Know', with Quincy conducting, I presented the award for Best Art Direction (to the designers behind *Patton*) and sang 'Thank You Very Much' (co-written by Anthony Newley), from the soundtrack to *Scrooge*, with Sally Kellerman, Burt Lancaster and Mexican actor Ricardo Montalbán.

It was a night that I will never forget.

\* \* \*

---

\* One was for best actor for George C. Scott, who declined his Oscar, sneering that the Academy Awards were no more than 'a two-hour meat parade'. Ouch.

Far away in Geneva, I had to juggle my work commitments, still overwhelmingly in America, with *being a mum*. Bara and Kate were settled in the International School, and happy there, but it was a huge wrench for me every time I had to leave them and fly to the US.

Don't get me wrong, we had some wonderful family times in Switzerland. We all loved the mountains in the summer probably even more than in the winter. Yet I'd be home for a few weeks, and the phone would start ringing: 'Hey, Claude, when can Petula get back over here? We need her ASAP!'

Saying goodbye to the girls was hard for all of us. I'd try to make a joke of it: '*Well, here we go again!*' But they sensed my pain beneath my smile. And, like any kids, they wanted their mum at home.

Claude and I tried to take the girls with us as often as possible. This meant we had to work around their school holidays. The easiest way to do this was for me to take two- or three-week summer residencies in Vegas or Tahoe. Fortunately, I had plenty of chances to do that.

Vegas was always considerate. They wanted me, so they'd book me when the schools were out. They'd give us terrific accommodation, and we'd try to treat the trips like family holidays (a bit harder for me, as I'd usually be doing two shows a night: an evening show and a midnight performance).

So, we were back in Tahoe in August 1971. Kate was getting into horses, and Bill Harrah arranged for her to ride with some friendly local cowboys. I'd wave her goodbye as Bill's chauffeur drove her off in his Rolls-Royce. Kate looked like a little peanut in the back of the enormous car.

When we couldn't take the girls out of school, things were trickier. To maximise my time with them, I'd delay my departure to America until as late as I could. Instead of having a week to rehearse a show, I'd get to Vegas the day before and literally have twenty-four hours to prepare for it. Not ideal.

This was where Frank Owens really came into his own. I'd phone him from Geneva and describe the style of arrangement I wanted on a song. Then I'd arrive just before the show and find that my musical director had all the music prepared – and it was perfect. Thank God for Frank. I couldn't have done it without him.

But it wasn't easy. I'd have to fly into America just before my shows, or television appearances, and leave immediately afterwards. People said, 'Hey, Petula! You're never around anymore! You always rush off! You never hang out!' And it was true. I felt that I was missing out on all the fun; that I wasn't able to enjoy my success.

I resented being stuck in Geneva, and Claude resented that I was unhappy in what he thought was our dream home. We'd have the occasional blow-up but mostly we'd just bicker. And then, we did what so many couples over the years have done, in an attempt to mend – or save – a troubled marriage.

We had another child.

I was pregnant again by spring 1972, when I was back in Vegas for two more weeks at Caesars Palace. This was a fun trip. The support act this time were The Osmonds, who were just becoming enormous global stars, especially Donny, who was a true teen heartthrob.

The Osmonds were five singing brothers from Utah. They were Mormons and polite, respectful and well-mannered. They

weren't the sort of act who drew high-rollers to the Vegas casinos, like Sinatra did, and maybe I did, but the audiences loved
them and I got really friendly with them.

The brothers invited me to one of their own shows. I took
Bara and Kate along. The audience was thousands of scream-
ing, hyperventilating girls. Bara and Kate quite enjoyed it but
the music wasn't really their thing. They were little French girls,
after all, and pretty sophisticated for their age.

After the show, I took the girls backstage. They were like
two little princesses: they'd even curtsey when they met someone. I introduced them to Donny.

'Hey, Bara!' he said. 'Hey, Kate! Did you enjoy the show?'

'Yes, thank you,' they replied, politely.

The Osmonds famously wore peaked caps onstage. Donny
still had his on. He took if off and offered it to Bara.

'Would you like my cap?' He smiled.

'No, thank you,' she replied, sweetly.

Donny looked quite taken aback. I had to explain to him
that it was nothing personal: it just wasn't their thing. But it was
a cute moment.

From Vegas, I went on to Tahoe, where I experienced a
very curious onstage incident. The previous year, I had released
'I Don't Know How to Love Him', Mary Magdalene's song
from *Jesus Christ Superstar*, as a single. When I sang it at Tahoe,
we had a blackout at the end of the song for dramatic effect.

One particular night, when the lights came back on, a
guy with long hair had appeared onstage next to me. He
looked at me.

'You're not Mary Magdalene,' he told me.

'And you're not Jesus,' I replied.

'Oh yes I am!'

The audience were sitting there watching this, apparently thinking it was all part of the show. I heard noises from the wings: '*What the hell is going on?*' Then the stage manager appeared and, in a very matter-of-fact manner, said, 'Come with me, young man.' And Jesus got escorted off the stage.

After the show, I collared the stage manager. 'What happened to him?' I asked. 'Where is he? Is he OK?'

'Do you want to see?' he asked me. He led me to the door to the casino, opened it, and pointed. And there was Jesus, in the casino, playing craps.

On that same States trip, I also recorded a CBS TV show, *Here's Lucy*. It was a sitcom starring Lucille Ball and was a follow-up to her long-running, very successful, *I Love Lucy* and *The Lucy Show*. And Lucille Ball was an amazing woman: slightly crazy, and a whirlwind force of nature.

Lucille was the absolute boss on that show. She ruled the roost and was in charge of every single shot. She had a cast on her leg, which she kept whipping on and off as she filmed. Not even that could slow her down. She was unstoppable.

My pregnancy was quite noticeable by this point, and Lucille reworked the script on the spot to accommodate this. And when she realised that not only did I have a French husband, but he was right there with me, she immediately demanded that he should be in the show, too.

Claude wanted nothing to do with this. He had no interest in being on a television screen. He did what he did every time we went to a TV studio: grabbed one of their telephones and talked on it non-stop. This didn't bother Lucille, who was determined that Claude was to be part of the action.

'Where's the Frenchman?' Lucille would yell when it came to his part.

'He's on the phone,' the reply would come. And the technicians would roll their eyes, put down their equipment and go for a coffee while they waited for Claude to finish his call. Which could take forever.

'He doesn't want to do it,' I told Lucille. 'Can't you use some other Frenchman?'

But she was having none of it: 'No way! It's got to be Claude!' She was adamant.

Eventually, she got Claude in front of a camera and he mumbled a few lines. The moral of the tale? That you really didn't mess with Lucille Ball.

* * *

Before I had my third child, I went to London, to the wonderful Trident Studios in Soho, to record a new album, *Now*. It was to give me two US hits in 'Wedding Song (There Is Love)' and a cover of Smokey Robinson's 'My Guy' (which I'd recorded earlier in LA). All the way through recording it, I could feel the baby bouncing around inside of me.

Once I got back to Geneva, I called my very charming obstetrician, Professor William Geisendorf. 'How close am I to giving birth?' I asked.

'You are having the baby on Thursday,' he replied.

'How do you know it'll be Thursday?'

'Because I am going on holiday on Friday.'

So, on 7 September 1972, Professor Geisendorf induced me. It was painful and I quickly decided, *I don't want to go through this*. Somehow – and please don't ask me how I did this, because I don't know – I managed to hypnotise myself. I was floating around the room, watching it all happen from above, and I didn't feel a thing. It was great.

As was the moment when Professor Geisendorf handed me my baby and said: '*It's a boy.*'

Silly as it may sound, this threw me. Claude and I hadn't found out the sex of any of our children before they were born but, having had two girls, I guess I'd subconsciously assumed that I would have another. And now, here I was holding a beautiful little boy.\* And feeling incredibly happy.

Claude and I hadn't given the first thought to what we might call a boy, but suddenly there was a nurse hovering by the side of my bed, with a form and a pen. 'What's his name, please?' she inquired, briskly.

'Oh! I don't know,' I said. Then, off the top of my head: 'Er, Patrick?'

'Thank you. Second name?'

'Hmm. Philippe?'

And that was it. Patrick Philippe it was. Although we almost immediately started calling him Paddy, as I still do today.

Paddy's sex was unexpected but we were delighted to have a boy. Claude was totally overjoyed and, alongside my own elation, I loved seeing how happy it made him. I think a part of me thought: *We have a boy. He completes our family. Completes everything. Things are going to be OK now.*

Although, sadly, they weren't.

Initially, Bara and Kate weren't so pleased about Paddy's

---

\* I only found out later that bookmakers in Vegas had a book going on whether I'd have a boy or a girl. They made a lot of money on that one.

arrival. They enjoyed having Claude and me to themselves, and didn't regard a boy as being anything special. Their basic thinking was: *What's the big deal? So, he's got a little thing in between his legs – so what?* They were jealous of Paddy and teased him relentlessly until they got used to him.

Suddenly, I was thrust back into a world of nappies, dummies and sleepless nights. It was a different situation this time around. I'd had Bara and Kate when I was around thirty. Now, I was about to turn forty. But some things, you just never forget.

After Paddy was born, I slowed my work pace down a little. I focused on the UK, where I could fly to make an appearance and be back home the following day. In December 1972, I got to work with Michel Legrand again when we were both guests on the BBC's legendary Saturday-night TV talk show, *Parkinson*.

I've never really enjoyed interviews, but Parky was really good at doing them. I was to sing as well and, before the recording, as Michel and I were in a rehearsal room, running through the score on a grand piano, a woman was sitting in the corner, noting down any changes that Michel made.

*Hmm*, I thought. *That's odd!*

When we came to tape the show, with a big orchestra, we had one or two corrections and, again, this mysterious lady was heavily involved. *Eh?* So, when the recording was over and she'd left, I collared a floor manager. 'Who was that woman?' I asked. He looked at me and smiled.

'Oh, you don't know,' he said. 'You've been away, haven't you? That was Angela Morley. Who used to be Wally Stott.'

As soon as I heard the name, the years fell away. *Wally Stott!* The hugely famous former *Goon Show* musical director, whom I'd worked closely with, and whose wife and kids I'd met, more than twenty years ago. Dear Wally, who'd unbeknownst to me undergone gender transition and was now living publicly as a woman named Angela. *That* was a surprise!

*Well, good luck to her*, I thought. But the strange thing on that *Parkinson* show was that Wally – or, rather, Angela – never came over and said: 'Hi, Petula, remember me?' And I never said hello to her, for the very good reason that I had no idea who she was. It was a curious episode all round.

Still in Britain, I hosted a new six-part BBC TV music and variety series called *The Sound of Petula*. Yvonne Littlewood was my trusty producer again and each weekly show had a theme: 'Girls Who Make Music', or 'Songs of The Beatles', or 'The Bacharach & David Songbook'. Barbara Windsor was a guest on that last one.

Barbara was hilarious. I once shared a dressing room with her at a royal gala up north. As we were getting changed, she looked over at me and said, 'Ooh, you've got great tits!' Which, coming from Barbara Windsor, was quite a compliment. I mean, she was famous for hers.

At the start of 1973, I also did a week-long British tour, my first for years, and then Vegas was calling again. I was back at Caesars Palace in the girls' Easter school holidays, then again during their long summer break. At those later shows, my support was a very funny upcoming New York comic and TV star, Joan Rivers.

After those Vegas shows, I'd have a snack in the grandly named Noshorium coffee house. I'd often bump into Sonny and Cher, who were playing the Flamingo, across the street from Caesars. They were good fun. (Cher is great. I wish our paths crossed more often. The last time was when I bumped into her by chance on a Eurostar to Paris.)

In October, I made my first ever trip to Australia. I was invited to perform as part of the festivities to celebrate the opening of a spectacular new architectural, and cultural, landmark in Sydney Harbour: the Sydney Opera House. And getting there was a total nightmare.

Claude and I had to fly from Geneva to Rome and stay overnight, as there was a strike at Sydney Airport. Flights kept getting cancelled, then they flew us to Canberra, and we had to drive to Sydney. The whole kerfuffle took nearly three days and I arrived with just two hours to rehearse before the televised concert. Madness!

Strange as it is to recall now, there was a lot of opposition within Australia to the new building. A lot of very vocal Aussies were saying: 'Strewth, mate! What do we need a bloody opera house for?' Of course, it is absolutely iconic now, and it's impossible to imagine Sydney without it.

And yet I found the Opera House cold and sterile, as many 'modern' venues tend to be. I've always preferred playing old theatres with history and character. I've never been back to the Opera House. I have played the lovely old Sydney State Theatre many times instead. On that first trip, Claude and I only spent two days in Australia. But Sydney was spectacular: it felt like a wonderful décor waiting for the play to begin. I've been to Australia many, many times since, and I'm mad about the place.

But these were really my Las Vegas years. At the end of 1973, I was back in Sin City yet again for my third residency of the year, doing two weeks over Christmas and New Year. Now, spending Christmas in Vegas presented its own kind of challenges, especially when it came to festive décor.

Everything was fake in Vegas and that extended to the Christmas trees. Claude and I always had a real Christmas tree but we couldn't find one for love nor money. They were all plastic, or tinsel, or pink, or coated in something weird. We had to drive out of the city into the countryside to finally locate a real one.

I was to go to Vegas three times again in 1974, alongside some very interesting other activities. I began the year with a tour of South Africa, which was magnificent, then headed over to Britain, where I appeared on a BBC children's show called *Clunk-Click* that was hosted by Jimmy Savile.

I'd encountered Savile a few times over the years and always found him repellent. I had no idea what he was up to, but he was an unpleasant man. My fellow guest on his show was Olivia Newton-John. I'd never met her before but she was charming. She knocked on my dressing-room door and very sweetly asked me for some advice.

'I've just been asked to go to America,' she said. 'Do you think I should go?'

'Yes, *of course* you should go!' I replied. They will absolutely love you over there.' And, as they say, the rest is history.

I was in London mainly to play a Valentine's Day concert at the Royal Albert Hall. It was a truly wonderful night: Frank Owens and the orchestra were impeccable, and I adored the entire night, including singing a tribute-to-London medley including 'London Is London' from *Goodbye, Mr. Chips* and 'A Nightingale Sang in Berkeley Square'.\*

Over the years, I'd made a few TV and radio commercials, including for Coca-Cola, and in 1974, I did an interesting new one. Burlington Industries, a big US manufacturing company who made fabrics and textiles, asked me to film an advert to promote their clothing range.

I didn't want to schlep from Geneva to America just to make an ad, so they agreed to film it in Paris. Burlington took it very seriously. They flew a whole production crew over, hired a proper movie studio and recruited French dancers to film an all-singing, all-dancing number.

The ad had quite a catchy jingle, which I'd pre-recorded in London: 'It's the Burlington look / It's the Burlington air …' But the filming soon hit problems. A Burlington executive decided that the tights that one of the dancing girls was wearing weren't exactly the right colour.

'OK, let's go out and buy another pair of tights,' someone said.

'No, it has to be *Burlington* tights!' the exec said.

They weren't available in Paris at that time, so we had to stop work to wait for a pair of tights to be especially flown in from America. It was like a sitcom. The French can be cynical about Americans, so you can imagine what the locals in the studio made of *that*.

---

\* The BBC broadcast the concert over two nights. Nearly fifty years later, in 2020, a friend and producer, David Hadzis, found the recordings, restored them and released a CD through the United Music Foundation, a Geneva non-profit organisation.

August came around, the schools were out and I was back in Vegas for some extremely special shows at Caesars Palace with a friend – and ex-crush – whom I'd known, and loved, since the start of my career. I did three weeks of double-header shows with Anthony Newley.

Tony's career had been going from strength to strength. After winning a Grammy for 'What Kind of Fool Am I?' and co-writing the theme to a James Bond film, *Goldfinger*, he'd directed a movie called *Summertree*, starring a young Michael Douglas. He'd also become a Vegas star in his own right.

Our shows were a joy. We showed a short clip on a screen of *Vice Versa*, the 1948 movie we'd made together, opened with a duet, then I'd do my set and Anthony would do his. I always closed with a wonderful Frank Owens arrangement of The Beatles' 'Fool on the Hill'. The audience would be up on their feet, the place would go wild and, as Tony came on for his set, he'd whisper in my ear: 'Petula, how do you *do* that?'

We would duet again at the end of the night. They were really emotional shows, for both of us. I have such wonderful memories of them.

\* \* \*

Back in Geneva, one strange development was that Claude was given an official UN role representing the country of Chad. He had never even been to that central African nation but suddenly was a sort of ambassador. He had to go to the UN every now and then, and we even had diplomatic-corps car numberplates. I never understood why.

Claude was given a huge portrait of the President of Chad to hang in our house. It was not really a work of art so we hid it, respectfully, behind the sofa. It was there when my father and Annie made a rare trip to Geneva to see us. My dad and I weren't as close as we had been, but it was good to see them. I still have photos of the visit.

On a Sunday afternoon, I had to pop out, so my dad and Annie were hanging out in the garden with the children. A Black man appeared at our gate, got buzzed in, and headed down the drive. There were very few Black people in Geneva in those days, so Bara had one reaction: *it must be to do with Chad!*

Bara ran into the house, hung the portrait back up and arranged for our guest to be served caviar and Champagne in the garden. The man spent a nice afternoon talking to my family then, when he had to go, left me a message. It turned out he was an orphan from Josephine Baker's children's home, with no connection to Chad whatsoever.

At the end of 1974, I reprised my BBC *The Sound of Petula* series. My guests this time around included Peter Ustinov, Telly Savalas, Susan Hampshire, Frankie Howerd and David Essex, who was just enjoying – or, rather, enduring – a level of pop hysteria that the papers were calling Essexmania.

On an episode called 'Tale of a Scorpio', I was reunited with Diana Dors. It was marvellous to see her again. She was still the same Diana that I'd first met in the Huggetts films, but by now she had left all of the silly 'sex-bomb' hype behind and become known simply as a very fine actress.

Yet my highlight of the series was the mighty Canadian jazz pianist and composer Oscar Peterson coming on a show with the theme of '... And All That Jazz'. I'd always found his music sublime, and singing 'When I Fall in Love' with Oscar and his group was a memorable experience.

Yet, at this point, I was taking stock of my career and my life. I looked at the day-to-day situation I was in, and realised … *I don't think I can do this much longer.*

Claude and I sold the house in Cologny. I'd never been happy there: it was Claude's dream home, not mine. We still had our chalet in Megève and it seemed mad for us to have two big houses. So, we moved to a nice, comfortable top-floor apartment on the outskirts of the city.*

By now, though, I'd spent years living in Geneva and performing mostly in America. And it wasn't working. When I was in Switzerland, I felt cut off from my work. When I was in the US, I felt cut off from my family, missed my kids and felt guilty. Plus, my agent kept telling me: 'Petula! You've got to be in the States!'

It was making me stressed, and unhappy. Claude could see how frustrated I was and, eventually, he conceded and said that, OK, we will have a go at living in the US. And, by the start of 1975, *it was on.* We were moving to America.

It was not to end well.

_____

* Nana Mouskouri was a neighbour. She lived in the same building.

## CHAPTER 13

# WE'RE GOING TO WIPE OUT EVERYBODY IN THE HOUSE

We moved to California early in 1975 and rented a charming house in Brentwood, in western Los Angeles, from a well-known actress. I loved that place. We lived next door to Helen Reddy, the Australian-American singer who'd had US number-one hits with 'I Am Woman' and 'Angie Baby'.

I got on well with Helen and befriended her. Bara and Kate would usually take a shortcut through our garden fence to play with her daughter, Traci. Helen had quite a few parties in the evenings. She'd invite Claude and me: we'd walk in and feel like we were getting high from passive dope-smoking. Not that that was ever my thing.

We put the girls into Le Lycée Français de Los Angeles. A lot of people thought that had snob value because it was seen as 'posh' to go to a French school in LA. Bara and Kate didn't get that at all: *what was so posh about speaking French? They'd been doing it since they were toddlers!* And they weren't mad about the place.*

---

* One of Bara and Kate's classmates was Jodie Foster (who had just finished filming *Taxi Driver*). Consequently, Jodie speaks perfect French.

209

That February, I was back in Vegas for two more weeks. By now, I'd moved from Caesars Palace to the Riviera. They treated their performers equally well, the musicians there were just as good and as for the audiences? Well, they remained exactly the same.

Las Vegas audiences are fantastic but they're not sophisticated. They tend to be Middle America on holiday, and they know exactly what they like and what they want. If you're not big in Middle America, you don't get booked into Vegas. But the crowds are always appreciative and fun to play for.

And, while I was in Vegas, we had a dramatic family emergency.

Bara and Kate were in school, so they hadn't come on this jaunt. My sister, Babs, was staying in the LA house and helping the nanny look after them. Before one of my shows, Babs called me and said that Bara had been rushed to hospital and had to have her appendix out.

I had to play the show, but I wanted – *I needed* – to race to Bara's side. I spoke to the promoters, and they made a few calls. Fortunately, Sinatra's private jet happened to be in Vegas at the time. They spoke to Frank, and he gave me the use of his plane to fly back to LA right after the show. Luckily, the operation went smoothly and Bara was fine.

Rather than take on my usual punishing schedule of work as soon as we moved to America, Claude and I had decided that, initially, we should just settle in, take it easy and enjoy LA life. We went to a few of the slightly infamous parties that music promoter Ben Shapiro used to throw in his house looking down on Sunset Strip. They were also very 'smoky' gatherings, and you'd spot Miles Davis, Marlon Brando or Bob Dylan holding forth or sitting quietly in a corner.

Claude and I got invited to the famous Playboy Mansion in Los Angeles. Hugh Hefner was a fabulous host and the house was truly extraordinary, with tasteful décor and jaw-dropping artwork. It was full of interesting, sophisticated people – artists, poets, sports and movie stars – and, of course, scantily clad young women.

I was standing with a glass in my hand when a very pretty girl wandered over to me. 'Hi!' she said, before inquiring, very seriously, 'Are you *happy*?' (a question that rather a lot of stoned young Californians used to go around asking back then).

'Yes,' I said. 'I'm happy.'

'What's your name?'

'I'm Petula.'

'Oh, that's pretty,' she informed me. 'I'm Tracey. What do you do?'

'I'm a singer. And what do *you* do, Tracey?'

She stared at me, earnestly. 'I'm going to be a Playmate.'

'Oh! Right. But what do you *do*?'

'I exercise my body.'

'Ah, yes, but what do you *do*?' I persisted.

She stared at me rather vacantly, then raised her arms over her head. 'I do *this* …' she explained. Then she mimed stretching her calves. 'And I do *that* …' I often wonder what happened to Tracey. Claude and I left around midnight. Which, we sensed, was when the mood was changing and a different kind of party was about to begin.

Bara and Kate took well to life in Los Angeles. The house had a lovely garden with a pool, of course, and the girls loved to swim in the California sunshine. We'd take them to the beach or to see the sights, or sometimes they'd come to watch me work in the recording studio or play live. They were certainly having a far better time of it than Claude.

Claude had never liked LA. Why? Well, it sounds silly now, but it was quite backward in those days, compared to Paris or London. There were not many good restaurants or stores. Claude would hang out with French friends, playing tennis with Michel Legrand or spending time with the great Michel Colombier, but he never truly got to grips with the city.*

The summer passed very pleasantly. And we got to know a remarkable Hollywood individual whom Claude and I had decided to bring into my working life: Allan Carr.

Allan was quite a character. He was very flamboyant, very funny, very camp and – although he hadn't come out, as such – very gay. Having made his name in the entertainment business in his native Chicago, he'd moved to LA and begun managing such A-listers as Tony Curtis, Peter Sellers, Ann-Margret, Joan Rivers and Peggy Lee.†

After a meeting, Allan agreed to begin co-managing me, alongside Claude. And he had some *very* interesting ideas about what I should be doing next. He felt my stage show should have a more glamorous presentation and set about devising an extremely razzmatazz production for my next Vegas booking in the autumn.

---

* Michel Colombier had been my musical director and was starting to make a name for himself in Los Angeles. He was to score more than thirty movies, including co-scoring *Purple Rain* with Prince.

† Allan famously invented the story that 'Mama' Cass Elliot, from The Mamas & The Papas, died from choking on a ham sandwich. He went on to be the marketing genius behind the successes of *Saturday Night Fever* and *Grease*.

Allan hired me four fantastic male backing singer–dancers called Friends. They were young, handsome Californians and very talented. We really *did* become friends, on- and offstage. My act with them was energetic, forensically choreographed and, shall we say, very varied. A whole new wardrobe was designed for me by the great Bob Mackie. Very glamorous and beautifully made.

Supported by The Righteous Brothers, I debuted this production at the Riviera in August. The audience loved it and so did we. From there, I took the show to Harrah's in Reno, which Bill Harrah had run since even before he opened his Tahoe casino.

Allan was producing this show, alongside Claude, and my musical director was Harold Wheeler. If I'm honest, I was probably far more on Harold's wavelength than Allan's. He was a very clever, sensitive man who just *got* me musically and who knew how my mind worked. We were close. I was very glad to have him in my corner.

* * *

Having loved recording my *Memphis* record with Chips Moman, six years earlier, I was delighted to get the chance in the late summer of 1975 to go back down south and make another album with him – this time at his new American Studios (later to become Legends) in Nashville.

I jumped at the opportunity. I fell in love with Nashville, and the trip was made even better by Chips and his wife, Toni Wine, inviting me to stay with them while I was there. Toni was both a terrific singer (she'd actually sung back-up vocals on

213

*Memphis*) and a great songwriter and I liked her a lot.\* The two of them made me really welcome.

Chips's new Nashville studio was very funky. It was in an old house, and the sound engineer doubled up as the chef. Every day, this guy would cook tasty Southern food such as ham hocks and black-eyed peas, so there would always be tantalising cooking aromas swirling out of the kitchen and around the studio.

Chips had his cowboy boots up on the mixing desk, as always, and the vibe was so relaxed that the street doors to the studio were always flung open. People would wander in and out. It was a creative atmosphere to record songs like 'It's Midnight (Do You Know Where Your Baby Is?)' and the album's title track, 'Blue Lady'.†

At the end of September, as the leaves were falling, I took a break from making the album to reprise my glitzy, glamorous new show in a very special residency. I returned to New York for another two weeks at the Empire Room in the Waldorf-Astoria. And they were wonderful.

Having focused on the West Coast casino towns in recent years, I hadn't played a run of shows in New York for six years. But I still adored the city, and I always will: the place, the vibe, the people, every single thing. And the feeling was still mutual. The demand for tickets smashed all records for the venue.

A lot of international diplomats used to stay at the Waldorf, so the security there was very tight. My orchestra had three

---

\* Believe it or not, Toni sang the female vocals for the cartoon pop group The Archies on their number-one single, 'Sugar Sugar'.

† *Blue Lady* was due to be released in 1976 but was shelved due to changes at the record company. It finally saw the light of day nearly twenty years later, in 1995, titled *Blue Lady: The Nashville Sessions*.

trumpet players, but one night I went on, glanced up and noticed that a fourth 'trumpeter' had appeared. It was a security guard, pretending to play a trumpet but instead keeping an eye on everything.

Another night, I'd finished my set and was about to go back onstage for my encore when two guys grabbed me. 'We're security and you're coming with us,' they told me. There had been a bomb scare and they were clearing the hotel out. Still, I adored the Waldorf-Astoria. It was a grand place to play.

I went back to Nashville to finish the *Blue Lady* album. I couldn't help noticing that things had changed. It felt … *different*. The doors to Chips Moman's studio were no longer flung open to the world. Nobody was dropping in. At home, Chips and Toni no longer had newspapers lying around, and never put the TV news on.

It felt odd, like something weird was going on, but I didn't pay it much attention – I had an album to finish, and all my focus was on that. And a couple of days after I got back from New York, I got invited to a major event: the annual Country Music Awards (CMA) at the Grand Ole Opry House in Nashville.

I was delighted about this, as it would be a chance to see all the big country stars. 'Great, let's go,' I said to Chips, who'd obviously been invited as well.

But he didn't seem very keen.

'I don't know, Petula,' he said.

'Oh, come on,' I said. 'It will be an amazing evening.'

'Well, I guess we've got our own box to watch them from,' he said. 'We can just keep ourselves to ourselves.'

Again, a strange comment, but I let it pass.

The CMA were as fascinating as I'd hoped. There were huge country stars winning awards and being nominated: Glen Campbell, Willie Nelson, Waylon Jennings, Loretta Lynn, Conway Twitty, Dolly Parton. A lot of them performed. During the show, a few people in the audience looked up and spotted me.

They were waving and shouting – 'Hi, Petula!' – and seemed to be attempting to tell me something. I couldn't hear them, so I told Chips I was going to go down to talk to them. Chips looked worried.

'No, I don't think so,' he said.

I was baffled. 'Chips, I want to say hello!' I said. 'I know one or two of them.' And I made my way out of our box and down to where they were standing. They all crowded around me – and began saying the weirdest things.

'Petula, we're so sorry to hear what's happened!'

'Oh, my God, it must be awful for you – is everyone OK?'

'We've been so worried about you!'

I was completely flummoxed. Chips had followed me down from our seats and, before I could ask the people what they were talking about, he grabbed me and steered me out of the building. We stood outside the Grand Ole Opry House in the pouring Nashville rain.

'Chips, what's going on?' I asked him.

'Claude told me he didn't want you to know,' he replied.

'Didn't want me to know what? What are you talking about?'

Chips took a deep breath. 'There's been a death threat to your house in LA and the place is surrounded by police,' he said. 'It's been all over the television and the radio and the newspapers, and Claude didn't want you to worry about it.'

Rehearsing with Harry Belafonte on the set of my first US TV special for what became an unforgettable moment, 1968.

Cor Blimey! Andy Williams and me doing a Cockney routine on his TV show. Such great memories, 1969.

A silly comedy sketch (one of many!) with dishy Sacha Distel for French television, Paris 1970.

What a joy to sing with Peggy Lee and have her as a guest on my TV special, Elstree Studios, 1970.

Very proud – having just been presented with the Medal of the City of Paris, 1970.

With Bara during rehearsals of a Josephine Baker benefit in Lausanne, 1970.

At home in Geneva with Claude, Bara and Kate, circa 1970.

I love this picture of Annie and my father with Bara and Kate (plus Wimpy the dog!) in Geneva, 1970.

Claude and me, young and foolish, circa 1972.

Young Paddy with Claude, circa 1980.

This is just one of my many marvelous duets with Dean Martin on my TV show, 1970.

'Where's the Frenchman?' asked Lucille Ball! Here he is, always on the phone! Circa 1972.

With my wonderful American musical director Frank Owens in *The Sound of Petula* TV series, 1973. He was an inspiration.

Micky the Moose, me, and the Muppet gang, 1977.

On stage in Montreal with Michel Legrand, 1977.

Playing backgammon with Bara in St Tropez after her accident, 1979.

Wedding scene in *The Sound of Music* at the Apollo Victoria Theatre, London, 1981.

With the real Maria von Trapp, 1981.

With Jonathan Morris in
*Candida* by George Bernard
Shaw at the Yvonne Arnaud
Theatre, Guildford, 1983.

With Stéphane Grappelli, one
of my favourite people and a
great musician, circa 1985.

All smiles with David Cassidy,
my co-partner in the New
York production of *Blood
Brothers*, 1993.

Me as Mrs Johnstone singing
'Tell Me It's Not True' from *Blood
Brothers* during my one-woman show
in Montreal, 2000.

Yes folks, this is me in *Sunset Boulevard*! Adelphi Theatre, London, 1995.

Claude and me, proud grandparents at the baptism of Sébastien in New York, 1996.

With Sébastien.

Bara, Paddy and me holding my CBE outside Buckingham Palace, London, 1998.

With Liza Minelli at a party in New York, circa 2001.

Somewhere in the sun with my beloved half-brother Chris.

Taking a bow with Cameron Mackintosh after a *Mary Poppins* performance, Prince Edward Theatre, London 2021.

Claude with our splendid grandchildren Sébastien and Anabelle.

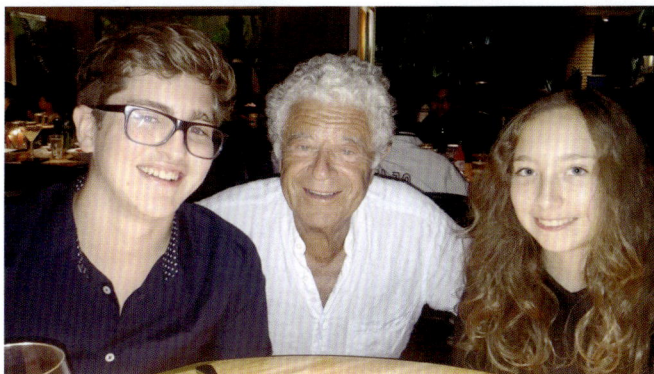

One of my favourite shots of the family – Roger, Claude, Bara, Sébastien and Anabelle.

My sister Babs with my daughter Kate, two lovely blondes.

Paddy and his wife Olivia.

In Barcelona with my longtime musical director Grant Sturiale.

Very VERY longtime musical director and friend Kenny Clayton

Bara and her husband Roger.

Matron of honour at David Hadzis and Yves de Matteis's wedding, Geneva Town Hall, 2016. (Oh, happy day!)

My blood ran cold. *What?* Needless to say, I found a telephone in the Opry and called the house straight away. And Claude told me everything that had happened.

It seemed that the well-known actress we were renting the house from had links with the Mafia. Or maybe she didn't have *enough* links, because something had gone badly wrong, and a Mob boss had phoned her and said, 'OK, we're going to go to your house right now and we're going to wipe out everybody who's in there.'

Somehow, a telephone operator had overheard and called the police. They took it very seriously: after all, it was only six years since the Manson murders. LAPD police cars raced to our house, sirens wailing, and locked it down. There'd been armed cops swarming all over the place, plus armies of TV reporters and cameras outside, for the last three days.

*Oh. My. God.* I didn't know what to say. No idea how to react. All I could think was how terrifying it must have been for Claude and the children when the police came bursting in. After a sleepless night in Nashville, I caught the first flight back to LA in the morning.

As I got to Brentwood, there were still two police cars on the drive. One cop was staying in the house overnight, for security, but he said the police's job was over now and if we wanted any more protection, we'd have to pay for it. And Claude and I had very intense and serious conversations.

For Claude, this was the last straw when it came to living in America. 'I don't want to be here,' he said. 'We're out of here!' He said there was no way we could raise Bara, Kate and Paddy in a place as dangerous as this. We had to take them home to the safety and security of Switzerland.

What could I say? I didn't blame Claude. It felt impossible for me to argue. There were a few upcoming bookings to honour: I had ten days of concerts in San Francisco, I had to fly back to Nashville to finish off the album and there was a week at Caesars Palace. But, a few weeks later, we were off back to Geneva.

As we flew out of Los Angeles, I knew we'd never be back there to live. I felt like it was the end of an era. I knew I was leaving that side of my career behind. And it was a lot to lose.

# CHAPTER 14

# IS IT A MOOSE
# OR A MOUSE?

It was the start of 1976. We were in the new apartment in Geneva. Kate and Bara were at the International School again. I had to do some US shows we'd lined up before we knew we were quitting: I sang at the Golden Globes, went on a Perry Como TV show in Hawaii and played shows at Miami's renowned, and beautiful, Fontainebleau hotel.

I tried to settle back into life in Geneva … but things were not good between Claude and me. The problems we had had before we left for LA had not disappeared: they had multiplied. We had tried to reignite our marriage by having Paddy, and *my God* am I glad that we did, but it hadn't worked. We were simply drifting apart.

Claude was coming on fewer of my work trips with me, and even when we were both in Geneva, we were spending less time together. Claude would spend hours in his study playing a solo dice game, play tennis and vanish to the local bistro with his mates. I was finding myself spending a lot of time alone.

The atmosphere at home wasn't helped by the fact that Bara and Kate weren't getting on terribly well. They were teenagers by now and, while they were both wonderful girls, they were very different. Everybody knows how powerful sibling rivalry can be, and I'd have to calm down some pretty full-on arguments.

While this was all going on, of course, I was still working in the States. I spent a week in Philadelphia co-hosting a syndicated TV variety programme that I had appeared on before, *The Mike Douglas Show*. This was an interesting experience.

One day, there was an item on the show about the benefits of eating insects: they have a lot of protein, apparently. So, they made up little caviar toasts from ants and bees and I was required to eat them. I can't say it was my favourite moment on TV. The darn things were stuck between my teeth for days.

After another two weeks at the Waldorf in New York, it was over to England for a week at the London Palladium, which is always a joy, then dates in Manchester and Birmingham. And early the following year, I had a very exotic appointment.

In March 1977, I was asked to sing at a grand gala evening in Iran. My family came with me and we were invited to a splendid dinner in Tehran. We were informed that, as the youngest girl at the gathering, Kate, who was then thirteen, had the honour of curtseying to Tadj ol-Molouk, the mother of the Shah of Iran, and handing her a bouquet of flowers.*

In our hotel suite, before the banquet, I had Kate practise her curtsey twenty or thirty times. By the end, she had it down pretty well. But our rehearsal overlooked two crucial factors:

---

* This was two years before Iran's Islamic Revolution. By 1979, the Ayatollah Khomeini was in charge, and highly unlikely to invite me to any grand galas.

that Kate would be wearing heels, for the first time, and doing the presentation on a marble floor.

At the big moment, disaster struck. As Kate curtseyed, one of her heels slipped on the sheer marble. She tripped, shoved the flowers in the Shah's mother's face, instinctively grabbed her arm and the two of them tumbled to the ground. Perfectly gracious, the royal Iranian matriarch got up, smiled, and acted as if nothing had happened.

Back in England, I made a TV advert. It was for the Chrysler Sunbeam, and I had to sing a jaunty little ditty for the occasion: 'Put a Chrysler Sunbeam in your life / And it'll put a smile on your face.'* Like all the best advertising jingles, it was stupidly catchy.

Chrysler spent a fortune on that ad. We drove to Sussex to film it like an MGM *Ben Hur* production team: a convoy of coaches full of the crew and Chrysler executives, and two trucks transporting the brand-new Sunbeams. It also had a big-name director: Richard Lester, of The Beatles' *A Hard Day's Night* and *Help!* fame.

Chrysler's big budget ran to lovely hotels and we were down there for two or three days. The filming was going well enough but Dick Lester, a charming man, thought it was all a bit boring. He suddenly had a brainwave. 'I know!' he exclaimed. 'Why don't we put an elephant in the car?'

The busload of young Chrysler execs looked horrified. There was a lot of tutting, and shaking of heads. I lost it with

---

* It was released the following year as a single: 'Put a Little Sunbeam in Your Life'. Unfortunately, it got banned by the BBC for being too closely linked to an ad. I had to re-record it as 'Put a Little Sunshine in Your Life' before they would consider playing it.

them. 'Look,' I said. 'You've got one of the greatest film direct-ors going here – *listen* to him! Let's at least do something interesting!' But they were far too scared to try anything adven-turous. The elephant got the elbow.

One fine consequence of that ad was that Chrysler gave me a Sunbeam. As a US car, it was a left-hand drive, which made overtaking in England death-defying, but, if I say so myself, I'm a very good driver. Eventually, my insurers insisted that I switched to a right-hand drive. I did so very reluctantly. I loved that little car.

One thing I have learned over the years is that family life will always be full of ups and downs. And I suffered a far more serious heartache in October 1977 when my father died.

My dad had never been ill. He didn't have a healthy lifestyle – he was very much a beef-and-roast-potatoes man, who never touched fruit or veg – but he was a naturally very fit guy. He and I hadn't seen as much of each other in recent years as we might have done … but, sadly, his health issues developed after he came to see me.

He'd flown over to see one of my shows in America. After he got home, my dad had a terrible time with jetlag. He didn't seem able to shake it off and started taking pills to help him sleep. Things started going downhill from there. He got very ill and the doctors thought it was likely to be terminal.

Annie told me the name of the medication he'd been prescribed and I spoke to our friend Bernard, the brilliant heart specialist from Paris. He sadly shook his head. 'Yes, that is the right medicine for him to take,' he said. 'But, eventually, it will kill him.' And I think that was exactly what happened.

I was in Geneva when my father died, on 5 October 1977. His funeral in Chichester was low-key. Annie, of course, was heartbroken. And how did I feel? Sad ... but also full of so many conflicting emotions which, if I am honest, I don't want to go into in detail. Not even for this book. *Especially* for this book.

\* \* \*

Sometimes, after tragic events in your life, such as the death of a parent, it may help to lift your spirits to do something unashamedly fun and silly. And I certainly did that at the end of 1977 when I appeared on *The Muppet Show*.

We used to get *The Muppet Show* in French in Geneva and we all loved watching it, especially Paddy, who was by now just the right age for it. I'd once been in a studio in Paris and, in the next-door studio, seen big-name actors such as Roger Carel and Micheline Dax dubbing it into French.

I had such fun filming the Muppets. They made the show at Elstree Studios and I went along to a script meeting with loads of people sitting around a conference table. They were writing and all talking in the funny character voices: Kermit, Miss Piggy, Fozzie Bear, the lot. I sat and laughed from start to finish.

When I came to shoot my scenes, the puppeteers were crouched on the floor behind screens doing their thing, and I obviously had to play to the puppets. I bantered with Scooter and Kermit then sang a song with Rowlf the Dog, which involved me pulling a fish out of his piano ('That's the piano tuna!' said Rowlf).

I also had a scene where I had to chat to a moose called Mickey Moose. Unfortunately, I messed up and called him 'Mickey Mouse' (it's an easy mistake to make!). 'Cut!' said the director, and we had to wait as the crew readied themselves to do another take.

'Well, that was pretty stupid, Petula,' Mickey Moose admonished me.

'I'm sorry, it just slipped out,' I replied. Before realising that I was apologising to a puppet.

Claude and I made an unlikely new acquaintance around this time. I think Claude met him first in London. It was a famous young man called Roddy Llewellyn, who ran a horticultural company, played guitar, and longed to be a singer. But he wasn't famous for any of those things. He was famous because he was Princess Margaret's boyfriend.

Roddy was very well-mannered and charming and we became quite friendly. He was so politely enthusiastic about making a record that Claude agreed to help him put together an album of covers.* At which point, Roddy invited us to Kensington Palace to have lunch with him and Princess Margaret.

It was a curious afternoon, but it was fun. Margaret was rather different from her sister. She loved music, and you could tell that she was a party girl. She sat at the piano and sang us a few songs. She wasn't too bad: I remember she sang 'La Marseillaise' in Claude's honour. I have to say, I liked her.

Yet I was scaling my work back at this point. I was, deliberately, the least busy I'd been in my career. In 1978, I appeared on television shows across Europe, but I played virtually no concerts. I didn't go to America once. Really, to all intents and purposes, I was living a quiet life in Geneva.

---

* Roddy's album was ... OK. Claude helped to produce it. Not that anybody ever really heard it. So, Roddy went back to horticulture.

Why? Well, I was tired of traipsing back and forth to the US, but the main reason was that I wanted to have some family time and to be there as Paddy grew up. I'd always felt guilty about racing off to the States so often when Bara and Kate were toddlers and, while I missed playing shows now, I figured at least I was being a good full-time mum.

But I can't pretend that this family time was terribly happy. Because Claude and I were drifting further apart than ever. And he had begun having affairs.

I was upset when I found out and yet, at the same time, not surprised. When I'd first met Claude, he'd been a sophisticated Parisian man about town. He still was. Claude was still an extremely attractive man. *Why wouldn't he be doing that?*

Claude was going to Paris and St Tropez a lot: who knew what he was doing there? And I got the feeling his friends knew what was going on. Knew he had girlfriends. He'd go to our chalet in Megève and host big parties with a lot of people that I didn't even know. I'd turn up, and sense that people were whispering, '*Uh-oh – SHE'S here!*'

We were married, yet Claude seemed to be living the life of a single man. I'd try to talk to him, but he never seemed to be around, and he and I weren't doing a lot of talking. My priority was the children, so I guess I resigned myself to what was going on. As I said, a lot earlier in this book, I've often had to pretend things are OK when they're not.

But it was incredibly painful, and made worse by the British newspapers latching on to us. The tabloids began running stories about how Claude and I were always apart, and asking, 'Is Petula's marriage over?' We naturally issued denials, but the papers were like a dog with a bone. They thought they were on to something.

*And, sadly, they were.*

It was a strained situation that was driving me slightly crazy, so I welcomed a chance to get back to work. Grace Kelly, whom I'd met once, had a connection with Chichester, my father's hometown. When she got in touch to ask me to play a special one-off concert at the cathedral, I jumped at the chance.

By now, I had realised that Allan Carr's flamboyant showbiz style wasn't really 'me'. I wanted to get back to the one-woman show. I was more comfortable with that formula. So, I had to say a fond farewell to the glitz and glamour and get back to the real me.

My former musical director Kenny Clayton played the Chichester show with me. Three years before, I'd hooked up with him again when I'd seen him playing with Charles Aznavour at the London Palladium. Kenny helped me to put a band together and we began playing British dates in 1979.

The timing was good. Given my fraught situation in Geneva, I felt as if I needed to spend more time in my home country. I would fly over from Switzerland for just a few days at a time, to rehearse and play concerts. We started off with a short run of shows in London. My new-boy support act was Roddy Llewellyn.

It was a chance to get back in touch with England and what was going on. The previous year, I'd been extremely impressed by Kate Bush's debut single – and number-one hit – 'Wuthering Heights'. So, when I realised that she was doing a run of London Palladium shows, I went to see her.

She totally blew me away. Her voice was incredible and her show was mesmerising: so theatrical, and spectacular, with dancers, clowns, illusionists and countless costume changes.

It was so magnificent that I left feeling depressed: *How can anyone compete with that?* I sent Kate flowers and a note. I never heard back.

Britain was going through a lot of changes, and none bigger than in May 1979, when it elected its first female prime minister. I've never been political, and I didn't know much – probably not enough – about Margaret Thatcher and what she was all about. But I liked the idea of a woman in charge, for once, and sent her a congratulatory telegram.

I was to meet Mrs Thatcher at an event a couple of years later. I couldn't help but ask her, 'Are you *really* going to close down all the coal mines?' She smiled and said, 'Oh yes, dear. I said that I was going to do it, so I *am* going to do it.' And she certainly did. I hate to think what my dear grandad would have made of that, and of her.

I may not be a political animal, but some causes are close to my heart, and that summer I found one to feel strongly about. I was the host at the Theatre Royal Drury Lane of a televised event called Eurogala, celebrating the thirtieth anniversary of the European Community, which Britain had belatedly joined in 1973.

I instinctively loved the concept of a unified Europe. It felt like a wonderful notion. I also felt particularly well placed to expound on this lofty idea, as someone who had been born and raised in Britain, lived in France and worked all over Europe for many years, and was now resident in Switzerland.

At the same time, I knew that some people harboured fears of losing their own national identities within a greater Europe, so I gave a little pep talk (Pet talk?). 'No matter *where* we are, or *what* we do, we shall remain ourselves,' I said. 'And no European

Parliament is going to change that for any of us. Our national character shall remain unaffected.'*

I introduced a friend to perform at the gala, the marvellous French singer Mireille Mathieu, who had a voice like Piaf with a lot of vibrato, and was a huge star both in France and Germany. And yet my most memorable moment of the event came in my dressing room during the show.

There was a gentle knock at my door, and I opened it to find Yehudi Menuhin, whom I'd briefly met before, standing there holding his violin. He was extremely polite and quietly spoken. 'Petula, I'm sorry to bother you, but could I please use your dressing room to tune up?' he asked. 'It's so noisy out here.'

'Of course! Please, come in.'

So, for ten minutes, I had the pleasure of my own private Yehudi Menuhin concert as he warmed up for his performance. It was a completely unexpected, totally wonderful moment that I'll never forget.

* * *

While I was doing all these things in England, I was, of course, primarily still living in Geneva and looking after the children. That summer of 1979, Claude and I took them to St Tropez for a family holiday. And it was an unmitigated disaster.

We had rented a villa, but there were a few people with us in St Tropez who were friends of Claude and whom I didn't like too much. They would all sit around our swimming pool drinking, smoking and playing backgammon.

---

* Nearly forty years on, of course, it was disheartening to see the result of the Brexit vote which led to Britain leaving the EU. I don't have much to say about it except that maybe people didn't understand what they were voting for.

One day, Paddy was playing in the pool with a friend and accidentally splashed the backgammon table. A guy snarled at him: 'Oi! Get out of it!' and pushed his head under the water. I was furious, and let the guy know it.

We hired motorbikes, the best way to get around St Tropez in the summer. One Sunday, Bara got on her bike to go to the 55 Club on the beach. I remember seeing her walk downstairs and thinking, *What beautiful legs she has.* I decided to join her on the beach and followed on shortly afterwards by car. But when I arrived, Bara wasn't there.

Then somebody at the club told me, 'Bara has been in an accident. She's hurt.' *What?* It instantly threw me into a blind panic. I got back in the car, tore down the road, and saw *les pompiers* loading Bara into an ambulance to take her to the local clinic.

Bara had been turning right on her bike when a car hit her. It had ripped a huge gash in her leg, which was full of dirt and grit from the road. Her ligament was sliced open. Claude and I raced after the ambulance to the clinic … only to discover that it was a disaster zone.

It was like something out of *M\*A\*S\*H*. Because it was a Sunday, there were no doctors and hardly any nurses. The sole surgeon was apparently on an extended lunch hour and tanning on the beach. They had to send someone to find him and eventually he strolled in, sand still in his hair.

They thought that Bara might lose her leg. While we were there, paramedics brought in one poor guy who had got his leg caught in the propellor of his boat. It was a mangled mess and they sent him to Marseille to have it amputated. But the surgeon looked at me, realised Bara was my daughter, and got down to business.

The operation went on for more than three hours. The surgeon had to first of all remove the bits of road from Bara's leg and then work on what little muscle was left. It was truly a miracle that he managed to save it. It shouldn't be how things work, but as one of the nurses said later: 'If she hadn't been Petula Clark's daughter, we'd have amputated.'

It was an absolute nightmare. It felt both all too real and like none of it was happening. I returned to our holiday house utterly distraught. That night, I had a fever dream about Lord Mountbatten, whom I'd recently met at the Eurogala. I woke up the next morning to the news that he'd been blown up and killed by the IRA. *Nothing made sense.*

Bara had to stay in the hospital for days as she recovered. She was in a lot of pain. Her room was on the ground floor, and security in the hospital was non-existent: people were climbing in through her window at night to steal her medication and anything else they could lay their hands on. I spent the nights in a chair by her bed, like a sentry.

The whole episode was incredibly traumatic. Bara got through it, Johnny Hallyday came to visit her in hospital and she totally healed, apart from the souvenir of a large scar on the back of her leg. It was definitely a holiday to forget … one of those where you feel as if you need a long holiday to recover from it.

A rather more positive adventure in 1979 was going to Brazil to host an HBO US TV special, *Carnival in Rio*. This was a fantastic experience right from the off. We flew from Paris on the French Concorde and halfway through the flight, the pilots kindly invited me onto the flight deck.*

Being on the flight deck was remarkable. There was absolute silence – no engine noise, nobody speaking – but they had classical music playing. Being in the tip of Concorde, listening to glorious classical music and arrowing through the sky at twice the speed of sound was a once-in-a-lifetime experience.

Rio de Janeiro at carnival time was wild. I had to record a song, and they gave Kenny Clayton and me a full orchestra and a rhythm section of ten exuberant Brazilian drummers, all playing like crazy. It wasn't exactly the sound we were looking for, but it was an interesting change.

The TV producers wanted me to perform two songs, including doing 'I Don't Know How to Love Him' from *Jesus Christ Superstar* beneath the statue of Christ the Redeemer which towers over Rio. This meant climbing up the steep steps of Mount Corcovado with a full HBO crew with equipment and cables. No easy task.

We rehearsed the song in daylight, but the producers wanted to film at night, beneath the brightly lit statue, because it would look more dramatic. So, there I was, beneath the statue in the gloaming, in my costume, surrounded by boom mikes, cameras and crew, set to sing … when all the lights on the statue and the hilltop went out. *Oh dear.*

It transpired that an HBO lighting technician had inadvertently pulled out a vital plug and plunged Jesus, and the top of

---

* I flew Concorde a few times over the years. It was always exciting. It felt like sitting in a tube, but the food was great and you got treated like royalty. And it was certainly fast. I never once saw Concorde's toilets because I was never on there long enough to need to go.

Mount Corcovado, into darkness. *Oops!* Our local guides were not pleased. It took a long forty minutes to fix the problem, then I sang my song and we quickly scarpered from the scene of the crime.

*Sorry, Jesus! Sorry, Rio!* Of course, we laughed about it later … and even this odd mishap couldn't mar a memorable trip.

## CHAPTER 15

# THE HILLS ARE ALIVE ...

As the 1980s dawned, I wanted more and more to be in England. By now, I'd been living away from Britain for twenty years, and I needed to get back in touch with my homeland. They say that home is where the heart is. I'm not sure that's *always* the case but I did know that I'd been away from the UK for too long.

Claude and I were living separate lives: besides being with the children, we did very little together. We were hardly a couple at all. I'd even broached the subject of divorce but he'd closed the topic down immediately. Claude was adamant that he didn't want to do that.

*If I'm honest, I don't think that I did, either.*

It was all change in my family. Bara and Kate were moving out. They were in their late teens by now and were finding Geneva too boring. They were, separately, both about to move to Paris to lead new lives. Kate had already got a job lined up as an assistant to the brilliant Japanese fashion designer Kenzo Takada.

So, Claude and I sold our big top-floor apartment. Claude bought two adjoining smaller flats in the same building and I got a London place, in Knightsbridge. I guess you'd call it a trial separation. I brought Paddy to England and, after much soul-searching, put him in a boarding school in Chichester, where we had family close by. Thank goodness, he loved it from day one.

There was one sure way to get to know Britain again. With Kenny Clayton firmly by my side, I spent the first part of 1980 doing shows up and down the land. I enjoyed being on tour as much as I always have done. And, while I was on the road, I received an unexpected offer.

I hadn't appeared in a stage play since *The Constant Nymph* (and its collapsing bed!) back in 1954 but a London theatre producer, Ross Taylor, got in touch. Ross was looking to stage a West End production of *The Sound of Music* the following year at the Apollo Victoria Theatre, and he wanted me to play the lead role of Maria Rainer.

And my instinctive reaction? *Absolutely not! No way!* Why? Well, there was one crucial reason. *The Sound of Music* was inextricably linked in people's minds with Julie Andrews. And I figured that the very last thing I wanted was to be seen to be following in Julie's footsteps.

*Petula Clark and Julie Andrews.* We'd always been talked about together. Ever since we were tiny kids, being taken on those night trains to sing to the troops in the war, we'd been compared to one another. It was nothing personal: Julie is great, and she's had a fantastic career. I just didn't want those tiresome comparisons yet again.

So, I said *no*.

Then I realised: I'd never actually *seen* the film of *The Sound of Music*. I was about to play a few shows with Kenny and the band in Abu Dhabi and Dubai, so I took a VHS tape of the movie with me. I sat and watched *The Sound of Music* in the desert. Julie was perfection in it … and I thought the story was tremendous.

So, I phoned Ross Taylor from the Middle East. 'Well, maybe,' I said. 'But Julie was wonderful. What do you want from *me*?'

'I want a different kind of Maria,' he answered.

'Well, I'd certainly be *that*,' I said.

But I still wasn't sure. Once I was back in London, I got cold feet and had to be talked back into doing the show by its elderly American director, John Fearnley. John had worked with the musical's composers, Rodgers and Hammerstein, for decades, even directing a 1960s Broadway production of *The Sound of Music*. He knew it inside out.

And I succumbed. *OK, then*, I said. *I'll do it.*

While I was waiting for rehearsals to begin, Claude and I took the family on a vacation with a difference. I'd always felt that it was important that our children saw more of the world than just Las Vegas, glitz and first-class travel and we, maybe, opened their eyes a little by going to Senegal, a magnificent French-speaking African country.

It was a very adventurous holiday. We hired a jeep and a driver – an amazing, larger-than-life character – and went off into the bush. One day we helped deliver medical supplies to people who were living off the beaten track. I recall that, for some reason, we were all singing UB40 songs every day.*

We all fell in love with the place. I remember one day, in a little village in the middle of nowhere, I was getting a watch repaired in the local market. I looked up to see Paddy playing

---

\* Or UB Quarante, as they called them in Senegal.

football barefoot with the local kids. They were all laughing, shouting and having a great time.

While they were playing, a very graceful woman walked through the middle of their game, balancing a tall pot on her head. Paddy and the other boys just carried on running about and playing football around her. It was an extraordinary little tableau. I can still picture it now.

Once I was back in London, I played more UK tour dates, including going over to Jersey and, once again, finishing off in Chichester. And then, I did another thing that I hadn't done in many years: I acted, in French, in a TV mini-series.

*Sans Famille* [*Without a Family*] was a serious, non-musical drama based on a famous, much-loved 1878 French novel of the same name by Hector Malot. We filmed it in a chateau just outside Paris and I enjoyed making it and being back in the French capital again.

I have a very quirky memory of filming *Sans Famille*. I was good friends with a couple in England who said that their daughter, who was about seventeen, would love to see a TV shoot. 'OK, she can come with me,' I said. This teenager came over and hung around in the studio, watching us work.

In the drama, I had a scene where I had to cry as I took care of my ill son. We had to do about three takes, and after the third one, I heard giggling. I looked up to see my friends' daughter staring at me and laughing.

'What's so funny?' I asked, puzzled.

'You're crying.'

'Yes, it's called *acting*,' I explained, carefully. 'Do you want to be an actress? Is that why you're here?'

'No, no, no!' she snorted, scornfully. 'I want to be a *star*!'

*Well, well, well ...*

The best thing about filming in Paris, of course, was that it allowed me to catch up with my two girls. Kate was having a whale of a time. A creative soul, she liked working at the Kenzo fashion house, and was also developing a keen interest in *trompe-l'oeil* (she was soon to utilise this talent by working on the glass pyramid at the Louvre).

Sadly, Bara was not doing as well. Unknown to Claude or me, she'd been dabbling in drugs in Switzerland. Ironic, really: we'd brought the girls back from America because Claude didn't want them exposed to the vices of LA, yet Bara had picked up a drug habit in sleepy Geneva. And she still had it in Paris.

It's every parent's worst fear. It was terrible news for me and Claude ... and, of course, mostly for Bara. I returned to London knowing she was going to need all the help, support and love I could give her – and that I was going to give it to her if it was the last thing I did.

\* \* \*

We went into rehearsals for *The Sound of Music*. Ross Taylor, the producer, had a vision for the production. He wanted it to be based on Rodgers and Hammerstein's original score and script, which had been written not for Julie Andrews but for the female lead of the first, 1959 production, Mary Martin.

This worked for me because I sing a lot more like Mary than I do Julie. Mary had a chest voice, like me, so Kenny Clayton redid some musical arrangements for my lower voice. Meanwhile, the American director, John Fearnley, didn't feel able to deliver the production that Ross Taylor wanted, and left. Ross took over. He did an excellent job.

The rehearsals were pretty enjoyable. I loved working with Michael Jayston, who played Captain von Trapp, although we used to make each other giggle onstage. I also adored Honor Blackman. Honor was very athletic and even managed to persuade me to do a charity run in Battersea Park with her.*

Yet it was impossible for me to fully enjoy it all because I was worried sick about Bara. I was speaking to her on the phone every day and managed to persuade her to come over to London. She agreed to go into a famous rehab clinic, Broadway Lodge, near Weston-super-Mare. She was in there for months.

At the same time, I was going down twice per week to see Paddy in his boarding school right next to the cathedral in Chichester. He still loved it there. I'd also drive down every Friday night, pick him up to bring him to London for the week-end, then drive him back down on Sunday night.

I adored those journeys with him. We used to listen to music in the car. On one trip, I was playing some blues and asked Paddy, 'Do you know what the blues is?' When he said, 'No,' I explained how the blues is structured, musically. He *got* it straight away. Paddy has a wonderful ear for music. A shame he never wanted to study it.

Paddy played football for the school. I'd drive down and watch him. Sometimes, I was the only parent watching the game in the rain. Still, he preferred that to when Claude went over to visit. Claude would be on the touchline, shouting instructions in French: '*Allez! Plus vite!*' Paddy didn't much like that.†

---

* I am *not* athletic. It was the first and last time that I ever did anything like that!
† Once, the school had a parents' cricket match. Claude insisted on playing. He looked splendid in his whites but, as a Frenchman, had no idea what was going on. It was hilarious.

As the opening neared, it came time to do promo for *The Sound of Music*. I went on the *Parkinson* show with the musical's original star, Mary Martin, and we duetted on 'My Favourite Things'. And I had a fascinating encounter with the lady whose memoir the entire musical was based on: the real-life, seventy-six-year-old Maria von Trapp.

As *The Sound of Music* told Maria's life story, it was obviously very important to her. She came along to one or two rehearsals and was extremely encouraging to me. Then she and I got dispatched to Birmingham in a chauffeur-driven car to appear on a lunchtime BBC show, *Pebble Mill at One*.

It was a highly entertaining journey. Maria was, let's say, rather eccentric. She was very set on the notion that I should do the entire show barefoot, which I managed to tactfully resist. When we got to the BBC, we sat side by side on a sofa, held hands and sang 'Edelweiss' together. I really liked her.

I hadn't known if I'd wanted to do *The Sound of Music* but there was clearly no doubt that people wanted to see it. To my amazement, when the tickets went on sale, they attracted the largest advance sale in the history of British theatre. Somehow, the Apollo Victoria Theatre was officially 101 per cent full every night. As I've said, maths is not my strong suit, but this always seemed odd to me.

The production opened on 17 August 1981 and was a joy. As I've said, I've never been a person who pays much attention to press reviews but I was told that it was going down well with the critics. And, more importantly, people just kept buying tickets. The planned half-year run was soon extended to thirteen months.

The cast were tremendous. One of the great joys of *The Sound of Music* was working with the children. There are a lot of legal restrictions on how often children can appear onstage, and for how long, so we had to change the kids pretty often. I'd walk onstage to be greeted by beaming little faces I'd never seen before.

Some stick in the mind. Every night, I had to pick up and carry one adorable little girl with a strong Northern accent. This could be tricky as she was somewhat overweight. There was also a very beautiful, dark-haired little girl. She only lasted two nights as she turned out to be allergic to the stage lights.

One bizarre thing was that I had a *Sound of Music* stalker. A young American woman sat in the front row every night. She didn't watch the show unfold: she just stared at me, very intently. She wrote me notes and left me gifts at the stage door, but I never met her face to face. She didn't seem to want to.*

One night, Karen Carpenter was in London and came to the show. I'd seen Karen in LA a year earlier and … things weren't right. She was so skinny. LA likes its women stick-thin, but that look just didn't suit her. And then her wish to lose weight turned into a sickness. A sickness called anorexia.

When she came to *The Sound of Music*, she was … skeletal. There was nothing to her. At the end of the night, as she was leaving my dressing room, I gave her a hug. I whispered in her ear: 'Karen, I don't know *what* you're doing, but you have to stop it. This is bad.'

Karen just smiled, and said, 'I'm fine, Petula. I'm fine.'

That was the last time I saw her.

---

* This same woman later turned up at one of my shows in Vegas. She wrote me a very disturbing letter. I showed it to the hotel security, who took it extremely seriously. They escorted her out of the hotel and she never came back.

My memories of *The Sound of Music* are all mixed up with how worried I was about Bara. I got so stressed about her that I lost my voice. I couldn't perform. The producer said I should see a specialist and sent me to a rather grand gentleman in striped trousers and a black jacket. He looked at me and asked, 'What seems to be the problem?'

I opened my mouth and tried to tell him, but nothing came out.

'Oh, I see,' he said. He looked down my throat at my vocal cords. 'There is absolutely nothing wrong with your cords,' he told me. 'But you are obviously very stressed and your cords are not meeting. And the cords meeting is what makes the sound.'

'Oh,' I croaked.

'Do you ever smoke pot?' he asked me.

'What? No!'

'Oh, that's a pity. Do you drink?'

'Not really,' I said. 'Maybe a drop of port before I go onstage. That's all.'

'How about brandy?'

The producer had clearly said to him, 'She's got to get back onstage. We'd rather have a diminished Petula than no Petula at all.' Because this doctor told me, 'Well, I suggest that tonight, before you go onstage …'

'*Tonight?* I'm not going onstage tonight!'

'… you get a bit tiddly.'

'That's impossible,' I said. Nevertheless, I followed his advice. Before that night's show, the theatre management made an announcement. 'We are afraid Petula Clark is unwell and will be unable to appear tonight.'

There was a huge groan from the 2,000 people in the audience.

The announcement continued: 'However, she has very courageously said she will do the show.'

'Hurray!' went the crowd.

I drank some brandy and staggered out onstage. I don't remember too much about it. By now, I knew the show backwards, of course. I got through it and got a tremendous ovation. I did that for three nights, before we had a couple of nights off and I could get a little rest and recover.

And that, folks, is what stress can do to you.

Through all this mayhem, some precious people helped me to keep my head together and my feet on the ground. My sister, Babs, had worked in the recording industry then at the Festival Theatre in Chichester. So, she knew what it takes to just *get up and do it*, come what may. She and our brother, Chris, were truly towers of strength.*

*The Sound of Music* was vastly successful but I never quite shook off the fear that the audiences left thinking, *Well, she's OK, but she's no Julie Andrews*. But I did love it when Maria von Trapp said that I was the best Maria she had ever seen. *That* meant a lot to me.

All the way through the run, Bara was never off my mind. She was in rehab for many months. She came out of Broadway Lodge in far better shape than she went in, then slipped again. I bought her a flat in my apartment block, but her life was still chaotic. They were terrible times for her. For all of us.

---

* And they are to this day.

Later, I would accompany Bara to AA and NA meetings. Not only were these a godsend for my precious daughter, but I also found myself learning so much about my own lack of understanding. These were hard lessons. Bara's addiction was a terrible thing to get through, but thank God, and her own strength, she came back to us.

When Bara was properly clean, she went to New York and met – and fell in love with – her now-husband, Roger de Cabrol. He'd had his own drug issues in the past but was now well over them and, together, they made a great new life. They've been clean ever since. They married in Manhattan and they have two splendid children.

And nothing in my life has ever made me happier than that.

## CHAPTER 16

# TELL THE UN
# TO FUCK OFF

When I came out of *The Sound of Music* in autumn 1982, I was still living in London and fetching Paddy home from boarding school each weekend. I was making trips, as often as I could, to see Bara and Roger in New York, to visit Kate in Paris and to see Claude in Geneva. And I was playing concerts in the UK.

It wasn't perfect, but it was a certain sort of life and, in a way, it suited me.

In February 1983, I did a big show at the Royal Albert Hall with the Royal Philharmonic Orchestra. It was billed as my 40th anniversary concert. This sounded a bit too grand for my liking, but it had, indeed, been forty years since I had dog-eared my comic backstage and skipped onstage to trill 'Ave Maria' and recite the 'Movie Mad' sketch in 1943.

*Forty years. How had THAT happened?*

It was a great evening but not without sadness. Karen Carpenter had died just two days earlier, and I came back on at the end, sat at the piano and performed 'For All We Know', the song she and Richard had asked me to sing for them at the Oscars. Before I sang, I said a few words for her, or, rather, *to* her:

*Karen, my sister, my friend*
*It's hard to believe this sad, tragic end*
*You were funny, and nice and a little naïve*
*And you lived for your music*
*And now, for you, I grieve.*

It was hard to sing without breaking down. I hadn't rehearsed it: I just winged it. It was extremely emotional, both for me and the audience. But I felt that it had to be done.

I suppose *The Sound of Music* must have whetted my appetite to do more stage work because, later in 1983, I took on another play. I took the lead role in a George Bernard Shaw comedy, *Candida*, at the Yvonne Arnaud Theatre in Guildford, a beautiful little playhouse that I am very fond of.

We rehearsed the production in London and then all moved down to Guildford to do what they call a technical rehearsal. We stayed overnight: I had a room in a nice little old coach house. But when I got to bed, I simply could not sleep. There was definitely someone in the room with me. Or some*thing. A presence.*

I was still wide awake at 4am and sick of it. So I sat up in bed, put the light on and gave the spirit, or whatever it was, a ticking-off.

'OK, I know you're here,' I told it. 'I don't know *why* you're here, but *I'm* here because I have to work in the morning. I need to sleep, so can you please just cool it?'

Eventually, I managed to drop off. The next morning, I went downstairs and saw the manager of the place in the breakfast room. 'Good morning, Miss Clark,' he greeted me. 'Did you sleep well?'

'No, not really,' I replied.

'Oh. Can I ask which room you were in?'

I told him. His face dropped. 'Oh, right,' he said.

'What do you mean, "Oh, right?"' I asked. 'Is there a ghost in there?'

'Well, yes,' the manager admitted. He told me it was the spirit of some kind of military figure from many centuries ago. I must say, it was a fascinating experience. I had never encountered anything like that before.

I loved doing *Candida*. I played a clergyman's wife who meets an idealistic, romantic young poet who falls in love with her and tries to steal her away from her staid partner. My husband was a very distinguished actor, Michael Craig, while the poet was played by Jonathon Morris, who was about to become famous in the BBC sitcom *Bread*.

Jonathon was wonderful and very funny, and used to drive me around in his fast sports car. But Michael disliked him because he felt Jonathon was all over the play, stealing the scenes and hogging the limelight. Which he probably was. That side of things was a tad difficult, but *Candida* was very enjoyable. For me, anyway.

\* \* \*

Life plays so many tricks. Sometimes, it throws so many things at you that you feel as if you can't cope. And one thing I have learned, in the course of my life, is that you never, ever know how somebody else is feeling and what they are going through.

In 1984, a year that I once again spent largely on tour in Britain, I made a relatively rare (by now) appearance on French TV on a big variety show called *Champs-Elysées*. And I found myself sharing a dressing room with an old friend, the French superstar whose covers of my songs had, indirectly, first brought me to Paris, way back in 1957: Dalida.

Dalida was extremely beautiful and absurdly attractive. Her Italo-Egyptian heritage had made her dark, exotic and alluring, and she still looked absolutely incredible. 'Dalida, you are so beautiful!' I told her. 'I would give anything to look like you.'

This goddess looked at me, incredulously. 'Are you kidding?' she asked.

'No, I'm not.'

'Well, I'd give anything to be *you*,' she said. 'You've got everything. A wonderful career, a husband … and children.'

Despite her beauty, and success, Dalida's life had been marred by tragedy. No fewer than three former partners had died by suicide (including her ex-husband, Lucien Morisse, long after they had divorced). An abortion had left her infertile, unable to have the children she craved. And, within three years of our chance meeting on that French TV show, she would also take her own life.

'*La vie m'est insupportable. Pardonnez-moi*,' her suicide note read. 'Life is unbearable for me. Forgive me.'

May she rest in peace.

\* \* \*

Of course, my own personal life was a long way from the domestic paradise that Dalida had imagined. I was not exactly at the heart of a traditional, close, loving, nuclear family. And yet, despite all that had gone on between us, shortly after that TV show, I moved back to Geneva to live with Claude again.

Why? I guess there were a few reasons. Bara and Kate had left home, but Paddy was still young, not quite into his teens, and loved his father. And Claude and I had grown apart, for sure, but I think I was still hanging on to the idea that there was something there that we could save. I'd never lost sight of the fact that we were still married.

That he was still my husband.

I kept my Knightsbridge flat, because I still wanted a UK base now that I was working so much more in Britain. But Claude and I bought a penthouse apartment, with views of the Alps on the horizon, on the outskirts of Geneva. That became our home. Forty years on, I still live there today.

In truth, Claude and I picked up where we had left off. Little had changed. We were still a couple, but not a couple: together, but leading separate lives. I was still travelling here, there and everywhere for work. And my next international trip was one of the most remarkable of any I'd done.

Now that I was back in Geneva, I started doing fund-raising work for UNICEF and the UNHCR again. And, early in 1985, UNHCR asked me if I would go to Vietnam as an international observer to help raise awareness of, and support for, the plight of the Vietnamese boat people.

At the end of the Vietnam War, violence and repression were still rife in that country. Some communities were victimised and oppressed by the Communist government, particularly the ethnic-Chinese Hoa people. And thousands of those people began fleeing Vietnam, often on small fishing boats.

The figures surrounding these so-called 'boat people' were horrific. Today, UNHCR estimates that as many as 400,000 had died at sea by 1985. The boats were being attacked by pirates and the refugees refused entry by neighbouring countries. The

UN had helped to set up refugee camps on uninhabited islands off their coasts.

Before I flew out, in March, I told Paddy that I was going to meet and try to help refugees, including children. His eyes lit up. His two much-older sisters had long since left home, and he was now living with just his middle-aged parents. So, he asked me, 'Can you bring me back a brother, please?'

'I don't think it works like that, Paddy,' I warned him.

We flew out from Geneva to Bangkok and then got a UN helicopter to one of the refugee islands. There were hundreds, probably thousands, of people of all ages on the island, many looking weak and desolate. It was harrowing. As soon as I set foot on land, a small boy of about Paddy's age took me by the hand.

He was a gorgeous little lad called Phat and he only spoke Chinese. We had a UN translator with us who helped out. The boy took me to meet the only relatives he had with him: an uncle and a cousin. They all appeared to be living in a cage. We spent the whole day on the island and Phat hardly left my side.

As we were leaving, I asked one of our UN escorts: 'Can I please stay in contact with this boy? I want to know what happens to him.'

The guy frowned. 'You're not really allowed to do that,' he said. 'And also, the problem is that he only speaks Chinese. He's with his uncle and a cousin, so a country has to take them all as a group, which makes it harder. But I'll try and find out what happens to him for you.'

In actual fact, I *did* keep in touch with Phat. I wrote to him via the UN and he replied, obviously through a translator. We exchanged a few letters and then they stopped. I was told by the

UN that Phat had left the refugee camp and been given asylum by Canada. Which was great news. I hope he did well there.

Later in 1985, I was at a big UN event in London to discuss possible future projects. Bob Geldof was also there. He'd already put out the Band Aid single to help fight famine in Ethiopia, and was building up to his huge Live Aid charity shows in London and Philadelphia that summer.

I knew Bob in the vaguest way possible. When I was staying in London, I'd sometimes go to an all-day breakfast café called Picasso on the King's Road. He was occasionally in there with his wife, Paula Yates, and their kids. We'd nod to each other, but that was it. We'd never actually spoken.

But the UN guys spotted Bob across the room at the event. 'Do you know him?' one of them asked me.

'Very, very slightly,' I replied. 'Why?'

'He's going to raise millions of pounds but the supplies will all be arriving at Ethiopian ports,' he said. 'It needs to be distributed from there. If he doesn't know what he's doing, it will be very chaotic and wasteful. The UN know how distribution works there and we're willing to do it for him. Will you tell him that?'

'What, *now*?' I asked, rather surprised.

'Yes, if you don't mind. It would really help.'

I took a deep breath and picked my way across the crowded room. Bob looked quite surprised to see me approaching. When I reached him, he listened carefully as I passed on the UN people's offer of assistance. And then he delivered his reply.

'Tell them to fuck off,' he said.

'Pardon?'

'This is our deal. It has nothing to do with the UN. Tell them to fuck off!'

I returned to the UN guys and relayed Bob's message. They were somewhat surprised and very disappointed. They thought they could have helped a lot. And, as it turned out, I believe some of the food donated by Live Aid *did* get misused and vanish onto the black market once it got to Ethiopia. But, there you go.

* * *

I'd been focused on Britain for five years, but now I was spending time in Geneva again, I took on more international engagements. I tried something new early in 1986: singing on a cruise ship, the SS *Norway*, as it sailed around the Caribbean to Miami. Stéphane Grappelli and Michel Legrand were also performing on board.

After a ten-day residency in Toronto, I went back to Las Vegas for the first time in nearly a decade. It had changed in my absence. There were more skyscrapers, more casinos, more hotels, more garish statues, more neon, more everything. *More more*. But the crowds were the same, and Caesars Palace was as welcoming as ever.

After singing at the opening night of the Proms at the Barbican in London, I returned to the US in the summer for a tour of the East Coast, then went back to Vegas to play shows with the comedian George Burns. George was ninety and a sharp, naturally funny man.* We even did a few duets together.

After a three-week tour of Australia, I was back in London towards the end of 1986 for a Royal Variety Performance at the Theatre Royal Drury Lane in front of the Queen Mother,

---

* But, I ask you – who would ever want to still be performing at ninety, ha ha?

who'd just recovered from illness. I was pleased to be on the bill with my good friend of nearly forty years standing, Peter Ustinov.

I was sharing a dressing room with two other people that I'd worked with before: Dame Vera Lynn and Margot Fonteyn. Feeling uncharacteristically apprehensive before I went on, I was about to take a mild tranquiliser pill to calm my nerves. Margot spotted me and gave me a bit of a talking-to.

'Don't you dare!' she said. 'It's better to be nervous and cope with it. That pill will take all the spark away from who you are and what you do.' Vera agreed with her and joined in. Which put me in the thoroughly novel position of being simultaneously scolded by Margot Fonteyn and Vera Lynn. But they were right and I didn't take the pill.

My work routine continued. In 1987, I made two trips to Caesars Palace. During the first, I was on the same bill as David Copperfield, the very slick American magician. I can still picture him strolling around the swimming pool in his long, black towelling gown, looking very pleased with himself.

Nobody was allowed to go backstage lest they found out how he did his spectacular tricks. It was a bit tiresome, and I didn't bother to watch his act too often: he wasn't my kind of thing at all. But at least he didn't get savaged by a tiger like Roy from Siegfried & Roy, Vegas's other resident illusionists.

That summer, I was at the Palladium for a Royal Gala for Birthright, a charity protecting women's rights in pregnancy. The very funny Cilla Black was the hostess and Princess Diana attended. I met Diana a few times, over the years. She was always absolutely charming, although very shy, which I recall made her blush a lot.

Sometimes, your past comes back from nowhere. One day in 1988, I got a big surprise. I was driving in my car when a cover of 'Downtown' came on the radio. It had been turned into a disco, or club, song. *Hmm, that's interesting*, I thought. *I wonder who's singing it?* I turned it up to find out, and it was … me!

They were calling it 'Downtown '88'. It was still my vocal but they'd removed the original orchestra and added an electronic *ticka-ticka-ticka* house music beat. They hadn't asked my permission. Not that I minded: I found it rather flattering, and quite amusing.

I can't pretend that I loved the new version but, hey, what did I know? It was in tune with what was going on musically and it was a hit. I even went on *Top of the Pops* for the first time in God knows how many years, to give it a little boost as it headed up the charts and into the top ten.

\* \* \*

While all this was going on, I'd been working, on and off, for years on a project that had become quite a labour of love. I was writing a musical expanding on an idea by an arguably rather surprising collaborator: Muhammad Ali's physician, Ferdie Pacheco.

Claude and I had kept in touch with Ferdie ever since he had given me that heavyweight-boxer-sized dose of vitamin B12 that kept me up for three days. Ferdie was quite the renaissance man. He was a very good artist and writer who was later to pen books, plays and screenplays. And when he talked about one of his passions, I was intrigued.

Ferdie knew a lot about the American Civil War, a period of history that's also always fascinated me. He and I came up with the idea of writing a musical set in West Virginia during the Reconstruction era, about thousands of people, including the Confederate soldiers, feeling displaced and demoralised after losing the war. We called it *Amen*.

Ferdie wrote a script in which I played a woman travelling through the post-Civil War South. I met a charismatic wandering preacher who got me to join his sect then got me hooked on laudanum and began controlling me. Then I had a passionate affair with a kind-hearted military man. I thought it was a quirky, original story based on historical reality.

I wrote the musical's songs with a lyricist and friend, Dee Shipman, whom I'd first met through Charles Aznavour. She wrote many songs with me over the years. We took the play to a producer, a nice man called Harold Fielding, whom I'd worked with many years earlier. Harold hired a director, Robin Midgley. Which was where the problems started.

Robin declared that he couldn't direct 'a show about sex and drugs' – *excuse me?* – and demanded a rewrite. Ferdie, Dee and I should have bailed at that point but we wanted the show to go on, so we didn't. Robin brought in a well-known writer, Fay Weldon, and he and Fay adapted *Amen* into a book called *Someone Like You*.

The problem was that it had a completely different plot which I found of no interest at all. It mangled and weakened our story. However, Dee and I were still very invested in the music, and proud of it, so I stayed in the lead role of this new show, now also retitled *Someone Like You*.

I did my best, as did my co-stars Dave Willetts and Clive Carter, but there was no getting around the fact that the new script was a mishmash. The musical opened in Cambridge on

25 October 1989 and toured the UK before arriving at the Strand Theatre in London in March 1990.

The reviews were iffy and it was a bit of a flop. Harold Fielding hit financial difficulties and liquidators got called in. The first I heard about it was on the news as I was in my car driving to the theatre. When I arrived, bailiffs gave me literally half an hour to clear my stuff out of the building.

It was a bruising and painful experience. I felt guilty, as if I'd let down the wonderful cast and crew working on the production. But I learned a valuable lesson from the debacle of *Someone Like You*. If you have a piece of work you believe in, don't compromise and let it get taken away from you. Never give up on your creative vision.

Because if you don't have that, honestly, what *do* you have?

# CHAPTER 17

# PETOO-LAH, YOUSE GOT THREE FRENCH NUNS!

As I licked my wounds and recovered from the failure of *Someone Like You* at the start of the 1990s, I suspect that I slightly lost my way career-wise. I played another three-week stint in Vegas, at the Desert Inn, but a number of my other work activities became a little haphazard.

Claude was taking far less interest in my career and had, a few years earlier, hired a guy called John Ashby to look after my day-to-day management. John was nice enough, but he and I were not at all alike, and on completely different wavelengths artistically and creatively. John just wanted me to take the jobs that paid the most.

He booked me to perform on two more cruise ships: the *Sovereign of the Sea* around the Caribbean, and then the *QEII*, first around South Africa, and then from Bermuda to New York. The *QEII* was certainly a splendid vessel but it didn't feel like the kind of work that I should be doing. Really, I was all at sea in more ways than one.

These spells on the ocean wave at least gave me a chance to spend time in Miami, where I used to have an apartment. I was there in 1991 when I happened to notice an ad for a play called *Once Upon a Song* at the local Coconut Grove Playhouse. It was written by, and starred, someone who by now was a local resident: Anthony Newley.

Of course, I went to see it. If I'm honest, I didn't think the play was all that great but, of course, Tony was. Afterwards, I said hello to him backstage. He and I headed off to an outdoor café, shared a bottle of wine and talked. He said he'd had some serious health issues. And we had a conversation like we'd never had before.

For the very first time, I told Anthony about my crush on him, all those years ago. And Tony astonished me by saying he'd felt the same about me. Yet he explained that when we were young, he'd found me daunting: so bright that I was an intimidating prospect for 'a nervous young man with pimples', as he was then.

Tony said he hadn't dared believe his feelings for me would be requited, so he'd never made a move on me. Instead, he'd resigned himself to us only ever being friends. I could hardly believe what I was hearing. I'm sure Anthony felt the same. If only one of us had ever dared to say how we felt – who knows what might have happened?

Tony and I sat in the Miami twilight, sipped wine, smiled, and reflected on just how different our lives could have been. How many years we might have spent together. *Ah, well. Life plays these tricks.* It was a strange, magical and very poignant evening.

\* \* \*

Back in Britain, I enjoyed doing an extensive tour of theatres late in 1992. As I've said, I'm never happier than when I'm on the road. But I also felt ready to commit to an involving new project with plenty of substance. Which was when another major theatrical production came along.

I'd known Bill Kenwright for many years. A renowned British theatre producer, he was a real Liverpudlian, a big pop music fan and a fun guy. Bill got in touch with me early in 1993 about a stage musical he was currently running in London and New York, called *Blood Brothers*. He wanted me to take over the lead female role in the Broadway production.

I didn't know anything about *Blood Brothers* apart from the song 'Tell Me It's Not True' by the excellent singer Barbara Dickson, who'd starred in the play in Liverpool and London. So, I went to see the West End production, which was playing at the Phoenix Theatre on Charing Cross Road (where it was to run for a total of twenty-one years).

The musical was written by Willy Russell when he was a high-school teacher in Liverpool and it has quite a dark story. It's about twin brothers separated at birth. One is raised in a rich family and the other in poverty. In later life, they both fall in love with the same girl. I'm trying to avoid spoilers here, but let's just say it doesn't end well.

Bill Kenwright wanted me to play the twins' mother, Mrs Johnstone. Stephanie Lawrence was excellent in the role when I saw *Blood Brothers* in London but I found the production a bit moth-eaten. The music was quite iffy, too. I politely told Bill my reservations, but he wasn't discouraged. 'Never mind,' he said. 'Come and see it in New York.'

So, a few weeks later, Bill and I flew to New York and saw the Broadway production at the Music Box Theatre. It had a few British performers – Stephanie Lawrence had just transferred from the London show – but most of the cast were Americans, and I thought they were tremendous. Even so, I still didn't know if I wanted to commit to it.

We had a few days in New York while I went back and forth, agonising over what to do. Bill was gently chipping away at me. Then, one evening, we went for a drink in a bar overlooking Times Square. We were talking about something else entirely when I suddenly looked him in the eye, and said, 'OK. I'll do it.'

What made me do that? A couple of things. Firstly, I had to say *something*: either yes or no. But also, I'd sung in New York so many times and I thought it would be interesting to make my Broadway debut. I'd seen how excellent the American cast were and I knew they'd be great to work with. And I thought that I could do something with the role.

Bill was delighted. *Blood Brothers* had been struggling at the box office but he secured some much-needed publicity when he announced that I was joining the show. On the back of that, he persuaded real-life half-brothers David and Shaun Cassidy to play the twins. Suddenly, it had an all-star cast and the ticket sales picked up dramatically.

We rehearsed for a few weeks and I made my debut as Mrs Johnstone on 16 August 1993. I'd needed a lot of persuasion to take the part but, now that I had, I really enjoyed it. The Cassidy brothers were both great to work with. Even though they were very different.

Shaun was lovely and fairly quiet. David was edgier. He had idolised their father – a very charismatic actor called Jack Cassidy – and been traumatised when he died in a house fire, after falling asleep while drinking and smoking, when David was in his mid-twenties. It took him a long time to get over it, if he ever really did.

Both of the Cassidys had been teen heartthrob singers, but David had never wanted to be a pop star. He longed to be a serious actor, like his dad, and he was very good. I loved working with him, apart from him always trying to change the tempo of the songs. I had to tell him: 'David, you can change *your* parts. Leave mine alone!'

David had a serious monologue at the start of *Blood Brothers*. There'd be excited girl fans in the audience, drawn by his pop-star past, but he'd come on in short trousers, clutching a bicycle pump – not exactly the sexy look that they were hoping for – and speaking in a strong Scouse accent. If he sensed his fans were a bit puzzled, he'd break off and say, 'Sorry, *these* are the jokes, folks!'

I liked being in *Blood Brothers* and I absolutely *loved* being back in New York. I was staying at the Marriott Marquis, virtually on Times Square, and I'd walk to the theatre every day. Those were the days they were really cleaning up the city, but it was as vibrant, exciting and *New York* as ever.

The theatre had a great ex-cop stage-door manager, Steve, who used to take care of us all. He had a real Noo Yawk accent. One day, when I arrived, he said, 'Hey, Petoo-lah. You walk a lot around here! You OK doing that?'

'Yes,' I replied, slightly perplexed. 'Shouldn't I be?'

'Well, some people get scared around here,' he said. 'But they don't need to be. Let me tell you, just about every other person on the street is an undercover cop …'

One afternoon, three French nuns from the Fraternité Notre-Dame turned up at the theatre. They worked in Harlem, running a kitchen for the homeless, people with AIDS, and anybody who needed their help. They were fans of mine and appeared at the stage door asking for me. Steve moseyed up to my dressing room.

'Hey, Petoo-lah, youse got three French nuns downstairs!' he announced, loudly. Heads poked out of the other dressing rooms along the corridor: 'Three French nuns? Huh?'*

I went down to meet the nuns. A few days later, they took me to see their kitchen in Harlem. One of them drove us through the Manhattan traffic like a maniac. This made a huge biker on a Harley-Davidson mad, and he pulled alongside the car to yell at the driver. But when he saw a young nun smiling sweetly at him, he decided not to say anything.

The Fraternité Notre-Dame nuns were terrific. While I was in *Blood Brothers*, Bara and I did quite a lot of work with them to help raise funds for their Haitian and New York missions. I was so glad they had sought me out.

The great thing about Broadway is that you really feel part of a community. The theatres are all very close together. *Les Misérables* was playing right next door. We'd all eat in funky little restaurants together after the shows. At Christmas, the

* Steve was sadly to die too young. After he passed, I played a memorial show for him at Symphony Place on Broadway with Helen Reddy and Carole King, both of whom had followed me into the role of Mrs Johnstone in *Blood Brothers*.

two casts got together and sang carols in the street to raise money for a charity, Broadway Cares.

After a successful eight months in Manhattan, we took *Blood Brothers* on tour around the States. We roamed across the country, visiting cities from Texas to Ohio, and Virginia to California. I loved playing all the different theatres – it keeps you on your toes – and seeing yet more new sides of America.

Somewhere in the Northwest, David Cassidy went off to visit an old friend and invited me to tag along. He was driving, we got hopelessly lost, and we stopped to ask for directions. Ever nervy, always *on*, David marched us into a random road-house and announced our arrival: 'I am David Cassidy, and this is Petula Clark!'

The drinkers enjoying a quiet afternoon beer looked at us as if we were crazy. Which was fair enough, really. We never did find David's friend. But our nine months of playing *Blood Brothers* around the US proved deeply enjoyable.

After the *Blood Brothers* US tour ended in May 1995, Bill Kenwright was aiming to take it back to Liverpool and asked me to go with it. It felt like an honour, to play the role in the city where the play had been born and where it was set: its spiritual home. I was flattered and tempted to do it.

But then something happened.

# CHAPTER 18

# I'M READY FOR MY THOUSAND CLOSE-UPS

I was spending a few days in London after the end of the *Blood Brothers* American tour when I got a phone call from the office of the theatre director Trevor Nunn. For the last year or so, Trevor had directed a West End production of Andrew Lloyd Webber's *Sunset Boulevard* musical at the Adelphi Theatre on The Strand.

And this was what Trevor wanted to talk to me about. He asked if I might be interested in taking on the lead role of fading acting legend Norma Desmond.

*Well!* This was certainly out of the blue … but it was an intriguing offer and my interest was piqued. I agreed to meet Trevor and, because I didn't want to betray Bill or go behind his back, I told him about the approach. It's fair to say that he was not terribly impressed.

'Petula, don't you *dare* do that!' he admonished me. 'You don't want to work for Andrew Lloyd Webber. He won't treat you the way I treat you.' A persuasive man, Bill pulled out all the stops to try to get me to stay with *Blood Brothers*.

In truth, I didn't know what to make of the *Sunset Boulevard* offer. I'd seen the classic 1950 Billy Wilder movie many years before. I'd even once met Gloria Swanson at some Hollywood event or other. She was a tiny woman, not even 5 feet tall, but what a formidable character! I could sense the iconic role had not been a great stretch for her.

I'd also been to Lloyd Webber's *Sunset Boulevard* when it opened in New York the previous November and been rather unmoved by it. It was certainly a spectacular show, with a magnificent set, and the music was wonderful, but the story stirred no emotion in me. I didn't care about Norma, or what happened to her.

Glenn Close was playing Norma in that Broadway production. I went backstage to see her and she was really nice. 'Hi, Petula,' she said. 'I guess they're going to ask you to do this?'

That threw me. It had never occurred to me. 'No. I doubt it,' I replied.

'Ah,' said Glenn. 'Well, if you do it, don't do it for more than eight months. It will drive you mad.' I thanked her kindly for the advice, confident that I would never need it.

After Trevor Nunn phoned me, I went to see the ongoing West End production of *Sunset Boulevard*, with Elaine Paige as Norma. Elaine was wonderful: she even looked like Gloria Swanson. Again, I went to see her backstage when the curtain came down and told her how good she'd been.

'How did you get to this great performance?' I asked her.

'Trevor told me to watch the original movie as often as possible,' Elaine explained.

I was still completely in two minds about what to do when I went to meet Trevor at the Really Useful Company office in Covent Garden. I was there for more than two hours and we went back and forth on whether I should take the part. Trevor was good to talk to and very encouraging.

His opening gambit was to tell me, 'You will be simply marvellous as Norma, darling!'

'What makes you so sure?' I wondered.

'Because you are a fine actress.'

Well, this was all very nice to hear, but I pointed out that I'd never done a role remotely like this one.

'So what? You can certainly do it,' Trevor countered.

'Do you want me to watch the movie a lot?' I asked.

'No, no, not at all!'

'Do you want to hear me sing a song from the show?'

'No. No need!'

Trevor seemed to have made up his mind that I would take the part even before I walked in the door. His confidence in me was heartening if a little baffling. My misgiving was still that I didn't have a feel for what kind of character Norma Desmond was or how I should play her. She was alien to me.

'What do you think I would bring to this?' I asked.

'You will bring humour, and vulnerability,' Trevor said.

Trevor had made a very strong case but I left our meeting still wavering. *What to do?* I hailed a taxi back to my apartment in Chelsea. The driver was a friendly young Cockney skinhead. As I climbed into his cab, he recognised me.

'Hello, Pet, darlin'!' He beamed at me in his mirror. 'How's it going?'

'OK,' I said, and then spilled out my dilemma. I told him that I'd just had a meeting with Trevor Nunn, he'd asked me to star in *Sunset Boulevard* and I didn't have a clue what to do. He nodded along as he drove.

We pulled up outside my building. 'So, what do you think?' I asked, as I paid him (and tipped him royally, for being a good listener).

'Yeah, do it, love!' he said, and drove off.

Free career advice from a taxi driver! Well, it may sound silly but sometimes, if you're agonising over a decision, the smallest thing can tip the scales. And it just had.

I broke the bad news to Bill Kenwright, apologising that I wouldn't be going to Liverpool with *Blood Brothers*. (Bill was upset and wrote me a very angry letter. For some reason, I kept it for quite a while, before deciding I didn't really want it.) And I phoned the Really Useful Company to accept Trevor's offer.

*OK, then.* I was to be Norma Desmond.

* * *

Joining the cast of an established production is different from being in it from the start. Why? Because you're the newbie. The company, and the orchestra, are all in place and know their roles off by heart, and you're the new girl. You have to find your place in the production and work out how to fit in, while bringing your own, new thing to the mix.

My first task after joining *Sunset Boulevard* was to get fitted for my costumes. It was decreed that these clothes had to be made in America, so I was rapidly packed off to New York on Concorde for fittings. In fact, they ended up sending me twice. Showbiz can be very bizarre.

As I got into the rehearsals, my primary problem was still trying to relate to Norma Desmond. As a character, she seemed deluded and bitter – this ridiculous old silent-movie star, side-lined by the talkies, clinging to her golden past and writing a preposterous movie for herself that would never be made. I found her tedious, and rude.

Nevertheless, I made my debut in *Sunset Boulevard* at the Adelphi Theatre on 2 September 1995. I was initially subbing for Elaine Paige for six weeks as she went on holiday. And, on my opening night, I was seriously nervous.

It was the strangest thing. As I've said, I've never greatly suffered from stage fright. I get the odd pre-show nerves, but that's normal. But on my first night in *Sunset Boulevard*, I was truly scared. My mouth was dry and my heart was pounding. *Terror!*

Norma made her big entrance sweeping down the palatial staircase of her Hollywood mansion. I had to climb up a ladder backstage to get to the top. I stood at the top of that ladder, in my costume and beads, listening to the tremolo of the orchestra and the murmurs of the audience awaiting my arrival. *Panic!*

'No, no!' I said to my dresser, Spencer Kitchen. 'I can't do it!'

'Yes, you can,' Spencer whispered. 'Get up there. Now!' And she basically shoved me onstage. And as soon as I was on, of course, I was fine.

Over the ensuing nights, I began to feel my way into the role. If I am honest, for the first six weeks, I was mainly just trying to get through it: to remember my lines and not trip over the furniture. I was groping my way through, getting to know the obnoxious Norma and what she was all about, and it wasn't easy.

And yet then something great happened. After I replaced Elaine full-time, and took on the role in my own right at the start of 1996, I began to understand Norma Desmond. I started to *get* the resentment, and yearning and angst that drove her. The penny dropped.

I realised that Norma, just like Gloria Swanson or Lillian Gish, had been the biggest, brightest, most iridescent silent-movie star of all. Then the talkies had come along, and she'd been forgotten. In denial, she'd stewed in her mansion, hoping the fad would pass, and gone crazy, unable to deal with the reality of her diminished status.

What is it she says? '*I am big. It's the pictures that got small.*'

As I got closer to Norma Desmond, I even, to my surprise, began to *like* her ... and this unexpected, but welcome, development helped me to introduce to her the humour and vulnerability that Trevor Nunn had pinpointed.

Once I had made sense of Norma, I loved playing her. I felt like I was in her corner and rooting for her. Night after night, I looked for ways to make the audience also connect and empathise with this lost, sorry woman and to realise that she wasn't a gargoyle. She was actually very fragile.

Claude flew over to watch me in action a few times. His party piece was coming to my dressing room and crashing out on my chaise longue. His reasoning was the same as when he'd snored his way through the premiere of *Goodbye, Mr. Chips*, right behind the Queen: 'Eet's not my fault! I've seen it before!'

*Sunset Boulevard* came to dominate my life. All through 1996, I was slinking down that palatial staircase, barking caustic one-liners and getting to know poor, doomed Norma better and better. I hardly had time to do anything else ... but I did make one notable exception.

Anthony Newley's manager called me and asked me to record a duet with Tony for his new album. The manager also said that Tony's serious health issues (which he'd told me about on our special night in Miami) had worsened, and hinted that the album might be his last. I was shocked but, obviously, immediately agreed to do it.

Tony and I met in a studio in London and recorded a version of a song called 'The People Tree' from *The Good Old Bad Old Days*, the 1972 stage musical he'd co-written with his creative partner, Leslie Bricusse. Tony was clearly not in the best of health, yet there was nothing sad or sombre about the day. Far from it.

Tony and I found the recording session almost impossible because we were laughing so much. As I've already said, it's very hard to sing if you're laughing or crying. It was to be the last time I ever saw him, but it means that my final memories of Tony are of the two of us singing and laughing together. Which is exactly how I want to remember him.

Anthony Newley was a very important figure in my life. I respected, and loved, him very much. And I suppose, in a way, he will always be the one that got away.*

\* \* \*

Bara had totally turned her life around and now she was starting a family. She was seven months pregnant when she and Roger married in New York in February 1996. On 16 April, she gave birth to a boy, Sébastien. I flew over to see my beautiful first grandchild get christened. He was adorable.

Meanwhile, *Sunset Boulevard* continued to run and run in the West End. It was good that I'd grown fond of Norma Desmond and her idiosyncrasies, because I was getting plenty

---

\* Tony died in Florida, from renal cancer, in 1999. His final album, *The Last Song*, featuring our duet, was not released until 2012.

of chances to portray them. By the time it ended, in April 1997, I'd played Norma at the Adelphi more than 500 times.*

The end of 1997 brought a surprise. I was awarded a CBE for 'services to entertainment' in the Queen's New Year Honours List. It was unexpected and, despite my general ambivalence towards receiving awards, this one felt different. It felt like an honour, and a privilege.

Christmas and New Year were spent in Megève with Claude and the family. Bara, Roger and Sébastien flew in and, on 3 January, Bara and Roger held a beautiful second wedding in the local church. It snowed like crazy. Sébastien, bless him, cried all the way through the service, and somehow it added to the overall joy of the occasion.

After so long on theatre stages, it felt great to begin 1998 on the road with my band. I did six weeks of British dates, finishing in Chichester again. Then it was a tour of Australia which took in not only the major Aussie cities but also more off-the-beaten-track, exotic destinations such as Toowoomba and Coolangatta-Tweed Heads in Queensland, as well as Cairns.

In July, before a second batch of British dates, I went to Buckingham Palace to receive my CBE. I was allowed to take two guests, so Kate and Paddy came with me. In a waiting room, I met people who weren't famous but who had done brilliant, public-spirited things. They made me feel as if I'd achieved nothing by comparison.

Still, it was impossible not to feel proud as the Queen handed me my medal. Until she asked me, 'Are you still active in the entertainment business?' I suppose I could have been

---

* Five hundred and three, to be precise.

offended. However, as I'd previously seen that Her Majesty wasn't even aware that Eric Clapton played guitar, I decided not to take it personally.

And, as it happened, I was about to get extremely active in the entertainment business, yet again. This time back in America.

I'd assumed I was done with Norma Desmond, so I was slightly surprised when Andrew Lloyd Webber got in touch and asked me to reprise the role when *Sunset Boulevard* went on the road in the States that autumn. But this time, I did no agonising over it: I agreed at once. Because, oddly enough, I'd missed the crazy old diva.

These US dates opened at the magnificent theatre at the West Point military academy in upstate New York in November 1998 and were to run for eighteen months. The production had been slightly scaled down because the original set was so lavish that it would cost a fortune to transport. Even selling out every night, the show would have lost money. But it still looked extremely impressive.

Even doing so many shows, for so long, I always enjoyed *Sunset Boulevard*. This was partly because it was such a great touring production. The costumes were brilliant, as were the dressers, the crew … everything. Plus, Lewis Cleale was great as Joe Gillis, the opportunistic young screenwriter with whom Norma ill-advisedly falls in love.

When you're in a long theatrical run, you have to be extra careful. A kind of boredom can set in and it's tempting to alter a scene, even in a small way, just to keep things fresh. But, of course, this is where discipline has to come in. If we made 'improvements' as we went along, the director would come in and take them out again.

The main reason I loved the production so much was that, by now, I was emotionally invested in Norma Desmond. I was playing her in a completely different way than I had in London. I'd finally realised that we never actually saw, in the musical, what a divine, beautiful, bewitching star she'd been in her youth. How brightly she'd shone.

*So, I changed her final big scene.*

At the end of *Sunset Boulevard*, having shot her manipulative young screenwriter lover dead, Norma descends her mansion staircase one last time. Driven utterly mad by now, she mistakes the waiting police and press for her fellow actors and crew, and issues an imperious command: 'Mr DeMille, I'm ready for my close-up!'

In the last few performances of *Sunset Boulevard*, I took her back to those halcyon days of her youth, when she was a glittering Hollywood star on top of the world. I spoke the lines softly, as if she were, again, the fresh, bright ingenue that she once was. Instead of barking them, I breathed them, gently: 'Mr DeMille, I'm ready for my close-up.'

And when I did *that*, I felt that, four years and about one thousand shows after I'd first played Norma Desmond, I'd finally *got* her: captured her essence. Andrew Lloyd Webber never saw me do it that way. He'd probably have told me to change it back, because he liked things to be more camp and over the top. But on this occasion, I didn't agree.

And I think it's what Norma would have wanted.

# CHAPTER 19

# ROCKY, YOU'RE IN MY SEAT!

After I'd spent so long being Norma Desmond, it was probably time to be *me* again. I don't know if that was, subconsciously, why I chose to do it, but my first major project of the twenty-first century was a live tour with a difference: a show that saw me reminisce about, and perform material from, virtually every era of my career.

I suppose the show emphasised that, by now, my life in showbiz stretched to nearly sixty years. And yet, heading into a new millennium, I didn't feel an urge to slow down. I never have. I love performing as much as ever. Nor do I get people's obsession with age. As they say, it's just a number. Doing your job, and doing it well, is all that matters.

I was back in London that autumn, and had a very funny chance encounter at Victoria Station. I was on my way to see my sister, Babs, in Sussex when I suddenly noticed Paul McCartney. He spotted me at the same moment: 'A-ha! Petula!' He didn't have a bodyguard: neither of us had anybody with us. It was just Paul and me.

We stood and chatted for a while. Thousands of people were streaming around the Victoria concourse, as usual. After about five minutes, I said, jokingly, 'Do you realise, not a single person has recognised us?'

Paul pretended to look worried. 'Yes. What shall we do?' he asked. 'Shall I start singing one of your songs?'

'You'd better not.' I laughed. 'I have a train to catch.' It was such a funny little moment.

But there's nothing funny about *this*. On 11 September 2001, I had just done some shopping and returned to my flat when Kate called me from Paris. 'Are you watching TV?' she asked.

'No, why?'

'Put it on!' And we stayed on the phone together as we watched the terrorist attack on New York and the Twin Towers collapsing.

We were both in tears. It was such a terrible thing. Plus, of course, I was worried out of my mind about Bara, Roger and Sébastien. I called and called and called, but all the New York phone lines were down. It was the next day before I was able to make contact and confirm that my eldest daughter and her family were safe.

The 9/11 tragedy had a major effect on me. Like most of the world, I was in shock. I was really in quite a bad way. I went to church, and tried everything I could to get over it, but nothing seemed to help. So, after a couple of weeks, I sat down and I wrote something – I suppose it was a poem – about trying to cope, and to move on.

'Our sorrows will not be in vain / Just as long as the dream stays alive,' I wrote (and hoped). And: 'This could bring out the best in us all.' My Geneva friend and producer, David Hadzis, had just played me a lovely piece of music that he had written, and I thought: *Why not put them together, and make a song?* We called it 'Starting All Over Again' and the next time I toured the States, I played it every night. It was one of the best moments of the shows. I'm really quite proud of it.

New York, and Bara and her family, remained very firmly on my mind at the end of 2001. She was expecting a second child. I'd met Bara's obstetrician on a previous visit to the city, and I began to bombard this poor guy with phone calls as I impatiently waited for any news on the birthdate.

I think he got somewhat annoyed with my constant calls. One time when I rang, he rather crossly told me: 'Look – please stop calling! I am going to get this baby born on 2/2/02.' And that was exactly how it worked out: Bara gave birth to a lovely daughter, Anabelle, on 2 February 2002.

Having two grandchildren was wonderful ... and yet, of course, they were so far away. Despite frequent visits to New York, I never saw as much of Sébastien and Anabelle as babies and toddlers as I would ideally have liked. But they were both gorgeous children and they've grown into beautiful, clever adults.

I flew in for Anabelle's christening and, while I was in New York, I played a role in what was just about the society event of the year, if not the decade. I was a maid of honour at Liza Minnelli's wedding to David Gest.

I'd known David for many years. In the early nineties, he used to host spectacular parties in Los Angeles or, sometimes, Miami. They were quite something: just about any star you could think of would be at those soirees. I never did quite work out exactly how David was so well connected.

David would invite me along and his parties were amazing. We'd all have such a great time. I can't begin to explain how many legendary Hollywood figures I met at those nights. I'd find myself rubbing shoulders with Gregory Peck, or Lauren Bacall, or Elizabeth Taylor.

Sir John Mills used to come to some of them. I'm not at all sure why, because he really was not a fan of LA showbiz schmoozing. At one of these extravagant bashes, at a Beverly Hills hotel, David asked, 'Petula, could you please go and pick up John Mills from his room?'

'Of course!' I said.

I went up and knocked on John's door. He opened it. 'Petula! Oh, thank God it's you.' He sighed, noticeably relieved that it wasn't a gushing Californian showbiz type awaiting him.

John was with his wife, Mary, who I think may already have been fortifying herself in their room for the social ordeal that lay ahead. We all went back down to the party. Mary continued quietly tippling and was just about managing to sit on her chair. She had to go to the toilet and tottered off to the ladies' room.

While she was gone, Sylvester Stallone wandered over and joined our table, sitting on Mary's chair. We were having a nice chat when Mary reappeared. She was most put out that her seat had been taken, and clearly didn't have the first notion who had taken it.

'Young man,' she snapped at Stallone. 'You are sitting in my seat!'

Rocky stood up, bowed to her, said, 'I'm sorry, ma'am,' and made a rapid exit.

David Gest told me that he'd been a fan of mine for years, which was nice, and that he, Michael Jackson and Michael McDonald would hang out and listen to my music (I was flattered by this, as Michael McDonald is my favourite white singer).

David had worked with Michael Jackson a lot and was very close friends with him. At one of his soirees, David asked me if I'd like to speak to Michael. 'Yes, OK,' I said. He got on the phone and then passed me the receiver. I heard a faint, whispery voice coming down the line: 'Hi.'

'Hello,' I said. 'I'm Petula.'

'Oh,' came the gentle reply. 'I love your music.'

I had a feeling that someone might be putting me on. Still, I pressed on. 'Where are you, Michael?' I asked.

'I'm in Neverland,' he breathed.

Well, this confirmed that someone was pulling my leg … until, just in time, I remembered that that was the name of Michael's home. I was later to meet Michael Jackson a few times while in David's company. He was usually surrounded by an entourage of people but he was always very sweet.

It was through Michael that David met Liza Minnelli. Michael had a thing about child stars and was fascinated that not only had Liza been a child star but so had her mother, Judy Garland. However, I had never met Liza before David invited me to their wedding at the Marble Collegiate Church on Fifth Avenue, New York, in March 2022.

I'd never met Liza … but you wouldn't have thought so, to see us together. Which was all down to Liza. She is a force of nature. She will walk into a room and take it over. Every single person in that room becomes her new best friend. And nobody minds because she is so impossibly charismatic.

I really don't know how she does it. It looks exhausting: I wouldn't have the nerve or the energy to attempt it. But Liza grew up in an unimaginably showbiz world and she is showbiz from her head to her toes. She makes everybody she meets feel special and she does it brilliantly.

Despite not really knowing Liza, I was to be one of her maids of honour alongside Janet Leigh, Freda Payne, Jill St. John, Gina Lollobrigida, Mia Farrow and Marisa Berenson. There were thirteen of us in total, and we were all instructed to wear black. Looking back, I guess you could possibly view that as a bad omen.

David's best man was Michael Jackson, and Liza's matron of honour was Elizabeth Taylor. At the rehearsal the day before, Liza was running around arranging everyone – 'OK, stand there!' – as if she was directing a show. Which, I guess, she was. I remember Mia Farrow spent the rehearsal with her nose in Ian McEwan's *Atonement*.

Michael Jackson and Liz Taylor didn't come to the rehearsal and the big question was how to make sure that Liz would be OK. Apparently, she wasn't in the best of health and had a problem with stairs, but the ceremony would require her to walk up a couple of steps. We rehearsed until Liza was happy.

On the day of the wedding, everybody was there except for Elizabeth Taylor. Liz turned up late … in carpet slippers. Somehow, she had managed to forget her shoes. Her poor chauffeur was dispatched back through the Manhattan traffic to her hotel to pick them up and we all had to wait around until he got back.

The wedding was glitzy, choreographed and extravagant. It all went to plan and, when the priest said, 'You may now kiss the bride,' David and Liza chewed each other's faces off. The guest list was ridiculous: Robert Wagner, Kirk Douglas, Anthony Hopkins, Diana Ross, Dionne Warwick, Joan Collins. *Donald Trump* was there, for goodness' sake.

The party afterwards was equally opulent. We all sang and performed: it was a show to die for, yet it wasn't being filmed. I remember talking to Brian May just before he went up to perform with the huge orchestra. 'What are you going to play?' I asked him. 'I have no idea,' he replied, then got up and played like a demon – of course.

It was an unbelievable day. I was to meet up with David and Liza several times over the following few years, most often when they were over in London. Liza was always still so personality-plus, even when it was evident that things were not so good between them. But that, of course, is another story …

* * *

One upside to having a career as long as mine, I suppose, is that there is always plenty of material for compilation albums. In 2002, a record called *The Ultimate Collection* was a top-twenty hit in Britain, and I took it on a lengthy UK tour that included a very enjoyable show at the London Palladium.

I've always chatted to the audience at my shows, and I love to tell the occasional joke, whether they like it or not. 'In *Finian's Rainbow*, I danced with Fred Astaire,' I told the Palladium crowd. 'That's Fred Astaire, not Freddie Starr.' Well, maybe you had to be there.

Of course, one sad consequence of such a long career is that so many artists I have admired, worked with and loved have passed away. And I mean, *so* many. In June 2003, I played New York's magnificent Carnegie Hall for the first time as part of a tribute evening to one of my first musical heroes: Peggy Lee.

The show was called *There'll Be Another Spring* and it was a tremendous evening. It opened with old footage of Peggy singing with Sinatra, Bing Crosby, Judy Garland and Dean Martin. I shared a dressing room with Nancy Sinatra, and a highlight was performing with some of the great musicians who'd worked with Peggy. We repeated the tribute the next year at the Hollywood Bowl.

Three months later, after two shows in magnificent Utah – always one of my favourite US states – I returned to one of the most significant venues in my career: the site of the pivotal concert that ignited my love affair with France, and France's with me, and indirectly led me to quit London and move to Paris. For the first time in nearly forty years, I played the Paris Olympia.

Kate came along and, twenty minutes before my show, she led the band in a meditation session. *That* was a surprise, and a novelty, for them. Then, as I waited in the wings to go on, the crowd suddenly struck up an unexpected, spontaneous chant: 'PET-U-LA! PET-U-LA!' It was extraordinary, and an unforgettable evening.

I believe that, sometimes, you have to remind yourself *why it is that you do what you do*. As I've made music, toured and done theatre shows over the years, I've always had to do promotional interviews. They've never been my favourite activity: you get asked the same boring questions over and over. And, of course, I give the same boring answers. But it has to be done.

Most journalists are OK, but in 2004, I found myself being interviewed by a rather awful woman. She kept chipping away at me, asking, 'What drives you, Petula? Is it fame? Glamour? Money?' I couldn't think of anything to say, and that bothered me for a couple of days: *Why couldn't I answer that question?* And then I wrote a song about it.

The song is called 'Driven by Emotion', and it defines what it is that keeps me going, night after night, year after year. '*I've been getting high on music ever since I was so high,*' it begins. '*And that's the way it's going to stay until the day I die.*' The lyric dismisses that interviewer's concept of what matters: '*Fame and fortune never meant a thing to me, anyway / But when the band starts to play, people, I'm on my way ...*'

And then, the chorus: '*I'm driven by emotion.*' And it's true: I realise I can get *too* involved in a song. I loved writing 'Driven ...' because it explains to people, *and* to me, what I'm about. So, at least *some* good came from that dreadful interview.

Many performers are driven by emotion, of course. Andy Williams was certainly one. Andy was always a brilliantly expressive singer, and in the autumn of 2005 I reunited with him when we played six weeks of shows together at his Moon River Theatre in Branson, Missouri.

Branson is a funny place. It's a kind of Las Vegas without the sin: it's a tiny city but it has about twenty theatres. Andy's was the most beautiful of all of them. He had designed it himself and, because he was a perfectionist and a stickler for detail, it had the very best sound and lighting, not to mention a fantastic band. The female drummer, a Mexican girl called Rosa, played like a demon.

Performing with Andy again was terrific. I'd written a song, 'Together', which I thought might make a nice duet for us. We performed it live and recorded the music there and then. Andy recorded his vocals in Branson, and I added mine once I was back in Geneva. Because you can do that sort of thing nowadays.

Offstage in Branson, I asked Andy if he remembered the two of us getting the giggles when we'd sat in a love seat and attempted to serenade one another on his TV show, nearly forty years earlier. 'Of course!' He smiled. 'That was because we were flirting with each other.' And, you know what? I guess we probably were.

Andy gave me a beautiful house on the golf course for the length of my stay. One day, I was driving home from the theatre when I felt a slight bump. *That's funny*, I thought. *I wonder what that was?* Then, suddenly, the most colossal stench filled the car. It was hard to drive without retching.

When I pulled up at the gates of the golf club, I asked the security guy what the smell could be. He sniffed and grimaced. 'Ah, that is a skunk, ma'am.'

'A *skunk?*'

'Yep. You must have hit one. I'm afraid you'll have to live with the smell for a few days.'

He wasn't joking. The stench had got right into the car's systems and was even coming through the air conditioning. Let me tell you, that is a smell that you *never* forget.

I returned to Branson, and to Andy, the following year, as well as playing other American dates and doing a mini tour of Canada. I was back in the States at the start of 2007 and then played British dates in the springtime, including one particular venue that I fell in love with. It just works that way sometimes.

It was the first and, to date, only time that I performed at Buxton Opera House, but I thought it was wonderful. The backstage area was grotty: falling to bits, really. But the second I walked onstage, I felt as if the place was saying, 'Ah, we've been *waiting* for you!' It had a special vibe. Some old theatres just have that magic.

And then, later that year, I went back to a place that meant a huge amount to me. I returned to the Valleys and the villages of south Wales that I'd loved so much as a child, and which still live so vividly in my memory.

The BBC asked me to film an episode of a series called *Coming Home*, which traced people's family trees and took them back to where they'd grown up. It was an intriguing prospect, so I agreed. And they took me back to Abercanaid and Pontlottyn (although this time, sadly, not by steam train or rickety old bus).

What was it like? It was ... a mixed experience. The Welsh countryside and mountains were – and are – still glorious, of course, and the people as friendly as ever. And yet I also found it quite upsetting how much Abercanaid had changed from how I remembered it. Just about everything that I knew as a child had been pulled down.

The coal tips that Clive and I used to slide down on tin trays have all vanished since the terrible Aberfan tragedy of 1966, when one collapsed and destroyed a village school, killing 116 children and 28 adults. The Colliers Arms, the pub where I'd stand on the table and sing as a girl, was still there, although it seemed so tiny now.

They staged a reunion with a few surviving ex-schoolmates in my old Abercanaid school, where the choir put on a lovely concert for me. But when I made a pilgrimage to visit my grandparents' house, in the *cwm*, it simply wasn't there. Those lovely stone cottages were long gone, replaced by boxy modern houses (which even have inside toilets!).

Well, *what did I expect*? Such is the passage of time ... and, as I said, right at the start of this book, looking back can be painful.

\* \* \*

While this was all going on, Claude and I were still in the same situation as ever. Nothing had changed between us. We were still together but not together. Claude was mainly in Geneva; I was switching between there and London, and travelling all over the world for work, often for weeks at a time. He was going his merry way and I was going mine.

We weren't a husband and wife in the Biblical sense, but when we were in the same place, we did normal things together. We'd go out to dinner, or meet up with friends. In a way, it's very hard to describe the relationship that the two of us had. It was strange, I suppose, but *it was what it was*. And we were both used to it.

I knew Claude had had girlfriends and, given our situation, there was nothing to stop me from entering into a romantic relationship. But I never had. I wasn't remotely looking for anything like that and it didn't appear to be looking for me. But then, suddenly, it happened.

It was someone that I'd known, and worked with, for many years. He was great professionally and we were extremely good friends. One night, we were just about to go onstage for a show when he quietly came up to me, said, 'I love you' … and kissed me.

I could not have expected it less. My head was in a whirl. I don't imagine the audience noticed anything amiss but I was totally distracted that night, knowing that he was onstage just a few feet behind me. And yet this extraordinary beginning led to a full-on romantic relationship. I was in love with him. And it went on for two years.

It was great but also it was difficult, for both of us, because he was already in a long-standing relationship. To his credit, he didn't try to hide this fact: I knew all about it. His partner, his fiancée in fact, found out about us and gave him an ulti-matum: *it's me or her*. After a lot of agonising, and tears, and soul-searching, he stayed with her.

It was tough, of course, as break-ups always are. But I guess, maybe, I'd always known that it had to end. I don't want to name him in this book, or anywhere else, and I won't, because he is a great guy and I still care for him very deeply. He stayed with his lady friend, they patched things up and, eventually, they got married. As they still are.

And I wish them well.

# CHAPTER 20

# *PEACE BE WITH YOU, CHÉRI*

I know I've said this many times in this book, so please forgive me for repeating myself, but I adore playing live. That simple fact has never changed. Appearing in front of an audience, and emotionally connecting with them, is the most exciting thing. For a performer, it's the moment of truth.

I played a lengthy tour of my beloved Australia in 2010. Let's face it, it takes you a long time to get there but when you do, it's worth it. Aussie audiences are invariably warm and generous (plus, it's always a real bonus to escape a freezing British or Swiss winter and enjoy a blast of glorious sunshine).

Ever since 'Downtown', New York City has always been a special place for me to play, and yet, somehow, I hadn't done a show there for many years. I finally put that right at the start of 2012 when I played three weeks at a very upmarket caba-ret venue called Feinstein's in the Loews Regency, a hotel on Park Avenue.

The crowds were as energetic as New York crowds always are, and they particularly relished a new song that I introduced to my repertoire. A New York actor, composer and lyricist named

Barry Kleinbort had written a parody of 'Downtown' and even given New York's anthem a brand-new title: 'Duane Reade'.

Duane Reade is a pharmacy and convenience-store chain that is utterly ubiquitous in New York. You see one on every corner. They always seem to be open and the thing about them is that you can get pretty much anything you want there. You will go in to buy one thing and inevitably come out carrying piles of other stuff.

So, we rewrote one iconic New York institution to celebrate another. 'If on your block, a store has gone out of business, wait a week, there'll be … Duane Reade!' I sang. I then went on to itemise the store's exhaustive inventory: 'The city has a desperate need for condoms and cosmetics / Chocolate chips and paper towels, and Noren diuretics …'

The audience would be falling about as I headed into the song's big chorus: 'So maybe I'll meet you there, you'll find me left of the cookies and men's underwear, at my Duane Reade …' It was very funny and I loved doing it. But you could only get away with it in New York.

I wouldn't call 'Duane Reade' high art, but there are some true artists, and great friends, whose company I've always treasured. One was Charles Aznavour. I'd stayed in touch with Charles, on and off, since first meeting him in France right back in the late fifties. One day in 2012, when I was in Paris, I found myself passing his office and popped in to see him.

Charles had a new *grande passion*. He was very into growing olives and producing olive oil on his estate in Provence. In fact, he was going on and on about it. 'I make the best olive oil in France,' he told me, proudly.

'That's wonderful, Charles,' I said. 'But when are you coming back to perform onstage again?'

'Ah, *non*,' replied Charles. 'That is all finished. I'm not doing *that* again.' (Of course, he didn't keep to that – two years later, he was back at the Albert Hall, pulling the place down.) And he went back to nattering about his olives. But as I was leaving his office, he handed me some lyrics on a piece of paper.

'Write the music for that, Petula,' he said.

'What? For your lyrics?'

'Yes. I love the way you write music. Write some for this.'

*Write music for Charles Aznavour?!* But I took his words away and wrote the music for the song that became '*Pour être aimée de toi*' ('To Be Loved by You'). It's not a jolly little ditty – of course it's not. It's Aznavour! – but it was a privilege to write, and I think it turned out well. I've since released it and performed it live.

Speaking of French culture, at the end of 2012 I was flattered and honoured to be made a commander of the *Ordre des Arts et des Lettres* at a ceremony in Paris. It was lovely, and unexpected, to receive such a prestigious state award. I got it framed and it now has pride of place on the wall of my bathroom in my home in Geneva.

The following year, I released a new album called *Lost in You*. I made it with a very successful and sought-after producer called John Owen Williams (no, not *that* John Williams). At the end of his lovely English garden, at his house in southwest London, John has what looks like a Wendy house. Then you open the door and you are in a state-of-the-art recording studio.

I loved working there. The vocal mic was next to a window. I could watch a cat stroll along a wall as I sang. There were flowers, and birdsong: you could even hear it on some of the tracks. We came up with some interesting material, including a version of Gnarls Barkley's 'Crazy'. I sang it on TV on New Year's Eve on Jools Holland's *Hootenanny*.

My favourite track on the record was the album opener, 'Cut Copy Me', a haunting, ethereal, electronic-music-based track that John had co-written..It is quite unlike the rest of the album. I liked it so much that I released it as a single, and a lot of people described it as 'surprising'. *Good!*

Around this time, I decided that it was time to fall back in love with Switzerland. Because it is true that I used to find living in sedate Geneva, far from the showbiz whirl of New York and Los Angeles, frustrating. But it is still one of the most serenely delightful countries in the world.

I wanted to fully appreciate the country that I live in, and so, with a friend, I jumped on a train from Geneva – which was, of course, spotlessly clean and spot-on time – and went to pictur-esque Interlaken. From there, we journeyed on to Zermatt, the absurdly gorgeous little town nestling in the shadow of the Matterhorn.

What a terrific trip it was. I enjoyed two days of exquisite scenery and great Swiss food, wine and welcome. It gave me a lift, and it reminded me, for all of my previous moans and complaints, how fortunate I am to live in a country as peaceful, hospitable and downright beautiful as Switzerland. It helped me count my blessings.

And another big thing that happened around now was that I met another man. Well, that's rather misleading. I didn't *meet* this man. We had worked together for months and become good friends … until we realised that we were more than just good friends. He is now very much a part of my everyday life, thankfully.

He is a very softly spoken, well-educated man, who loves nature, jazz and classical music. We have so many shared interests that it's no surprise we get on so well. I hope you don't mind, but I don't want to say who this man is in this book. He's not a secret: Claude knew about him. And there is nobody else involved. But he is a person who values his privacy, as do I, and I want to respect that.

I'd been seeing this guy for about two years in 2016 when I went on a British daytime TV programme, *Loose Women*. Presented by four female hosts, it's a very gossipy show and likes to pick through its guests' private lives. 'You've been married for fifty-five years,' one of the women asked me. 'But is that ... no longer?'

I hadn't planned to discuss this issue on national television. But I tackled the question head-on.

'Claude and I are still married,' I said. 'We still live together. But he has his own life and I have mine. And it somehow works. These things are very difficult to talk about in public because it's a very personal thing. But it works.'

Why did I talk so openly, so publicly, about something so intimate? Well, to start with, I didn't have much choice! They put me on the spot. But also, it is not a crime. It's a fact of life ... a fact of *my* life. There comes a point when you just have to tell the truth. To tell it like it is. And, anyway, you realise that the world is not going to stop.

* * *

In 2017, I was back in John Williams's lovely Wendy-house-like garden studio to record a new album called (one of my life's mantras) *Living for Today*. I went on tour in America, then the following year headed back on the road to Canada and did another month-long US jaunt. I was having a whale of a time on the road and everything was going great. And then ... something else happened.

Sir Cameron Mackintosh is one of Britain's greatest theatrical producers. He was about to put on a West End revival of his production of *Mary Poppins*, which he had first staged in 2004. And his office got in touch to ask if I'd play the part of the Bird Woman: the old lady who feeds the birds and, in doing so, teaches children about kindness and love.

*Hmm*. My first thought was that I would, *yet again*, be following in the footsteps of Julie Andrews. But I didn't dwell too much on that this time. Internally, I just shrugged: *ah, well. What can I do about that? Nothing!* I was more concerned, as ever, with what I could do with the role.

Now, the Bird Woman is not the biggest or most exciting part in the world. On the other hand, I trusted Cameron, and the production looked as if it would be fantastic. So, as I always do with these big work decisions, I consulted my family. And Claude and the children all said the same thing.

'Go on, do it!' they told me. 'You'll love it. You know how much you always enjoy being in London. You'll be able to catch up with your friends. You'll have a great time!' And that was a convincing enough argument for me. So, I told Cameron I was in.

*Mary Poppins* opened at the Prince Edward Theatre in the heart of Soho on 23 October 2019. The Prince Edward used to be the Queensberry All-Services Club, where I had appeared at the birthday party for the BBC's Empire Service in 1942:

*seventy-seven years earlier.* As I walked in the door, it was bizarre to think how much time had passed.

The Bird Woman was quite a tricky part to navigate. I had to sing 'Feed the Birds' ('*Feed the birds / tuppence a bag*') but the song was dotted throughout the play: I'd sing a few lines, go off, then come back on later to sing it again. I spent the evenings in my dressing room with my ears cocked so I wouldn't miss my next cue to go on. When I *did* appear, I'm sure a lot of people didn't even recognise me in my weird, frumpy costume and flat hat.

Much as I loved Cameron, and everybody on the show, and the fantastic orchestra, I can't pretend that *Mary Poppins* was a very exciting moment for me. Still, it was a fine production and I was enjoying being in London. As Claude and the kids had said, it gave me an opportunity to get back in touch with that great city.

In fact, my time in London, and in *Mary Poppins*, was bowling along very nicely right up until March 2020. And then the Covid pandemic came along.

I was in my flat in Chelsea when the news broke about the first lockdown: that Britain's theatres, pubs, shops, schools, *everything* would be closed for the foreseeable future. My first thought was that I had to get back to Geneva. I hailed a cab and raced to Heathrow, where one final flight was about to depart.

And British Airways didn't want to let me on the plane. 'You are going to Geneva?' they asked me at check-in.

'Yes. I live there.'

'Do you have any *proof* that you live in Geneva?'

*Disaster!* I didn't. I needed a document called a *permis C,* a Swiss residence permit, and I didn't have it on me. I phoned my personal assistant, friend and producer in Geneva, David

Hadzis.* David rushed to our apartment, found the document and emailed it to Heathrow.

'Ah, this is only a copy,' security tutted. But then, thank goodness, BA relented. They let me on the flight.

\* \* \*

The coronavirus lockdown was such a strange time. Like everyone else's, my life changed overnight. It was like living through a bizarre nightmare. Suddenly, the world was under siege. All you could do was hide at home from the deadly virus, and watch in horror as the news programmes told you each night how many more people had died.

Claude and I were locked down in our apartment in Geneva. We did what everyone else did: wore masks on the rare occasions we had to go out; washed and re-washed our hands with sanitiser; had our jabs. It was the longest we had spent together, just the two of us, for years ... but it was OK.

We were no longer a proper couple, but we were still two people who'd been together for sixty years, knew each other inside out and cared for one another. We may no longer have been in love, but we still loved each other.

Yet Claude was beginning to get ill. He had several different ailments. He had a heart problem, and he'd also had two hip replacements. Then he got lymphoma: a kind of cancer. He was not at all well, and when lockdown finally lifted, he was moved to a clinic just outside Geneva.

---

* David Hadzis has been much more than my trusted assistant for many years. He and his lovely husband, Yves de Matteis, have become a solid source of strength, and I am very grateful to them both. I was their matron of honour when they married in 2016.

Then he was in and out of hospitals and different clinics, one of which was quite beautiful. It had a rose garden and Claude liked it there. I got the bus or an Uber over to see him every single day. Some days, I'd take him smoked salmon, or cook something at home and take it to him. It became our new routine.

He improved a little and came home but it was a desperately difficult time. Once, I sat with Claude in a doctor's office as he had his lymphoma treatment. They gave him a sedative and put him in a room to rest. I sat with him and, when it came time for me to leave, I kissed him goodbye and went to the nurses' office across the corridor to have a word with them.

I didn't know Claude had got up and followed me. He was right behind me, and he passed out and fell on top of me. I was squashed on the floor under him. The nurses heard the commotion, came running out of their room and pulled him up. They were mainly worried about Claude, of course, because he was their patient.

As I gingerly got up, the nurses put Claude into a wheelchair and pushed him off to be examined. A doctor came over to me. 'Are *you* OK?' he asked. 'I don't know,' I answered, truthfully. And, in fact, X-rays showed that the fall had given me a little crack at the bottom of my spine. It can still hurt a bit when I get up from a seat.

In August 2021, I returned to London when *Mary Poppins* reopened. Yet Claude's health travails continued. He continued to be in and out of various hospitals and clinics. Claude also had to deal with Covid, which he'd contracted somewhere along the line. He was very ill but incredibly strong and determined to live through it all. (By some miracle, I never got Covid.)

I was flying back and forth between London and Switzerland to see him. It meant that I had to miss a few shows. I didn't like doing this, as I've always hated letting people down, but Cameron was great. He would just tell me: 'Petula, please don't worry about it. Your husband is ill. You *have* to go.' And off I would go again. I was doing it all the time.

On one occasion, I came offstage and the production manager was waiting for me. 'I'm sorry, Petula,' he said. 'We've had a call from Geneva. Your husband has been rushed into emergency.' Claude had had an accident at home. Luckily, Bara and Roger were with him when it happened, and they stayed with him until I got there.

*Mary Poppins* closed in January 2023 and I returned to Geneva. Claude continued to be in and out of hospitals and clinics: I have no idea how many I went to with him. He was in some of them for a month or more. I would see him every day. And, on 20 March 2024, I was with Claude when he died.

We were sitting in his very nice room in hospital. It was a beautiful afternoon and a light breeze was coming in the open window. We were sitting holding hands, and everything was fine. And then, suddenly, Claude turned his head towards me and it didn't look like him at all.

His face was almost purple. His eyes had turned yellow and he seemed to be foaming at the mouth. He appeared to be having some kind of epileptic fit. It was terrifying. I rushed out to get help.

A doctor and three nurses ran into the room. 'You'd better wait outside,' they told me, and put me in a room next door. I had no idea what was going on. A few minutes later, a doctor came in to see me. 'I'm afraid it is quite possible he will not survive this,' he told me, gently.

The words didn't make sense. 'What do you mean, he won't survive it?' I asked.

'It is quite possible he will die,' he said, then went back to Claude's room. And very shortly afterwards, he reappeared. 'I'm sorry, but he is dead.'

*Dead? It can't be true. He can't be.*

I went back to Claude's room, and … there he was. Except that it wasn't him anymore. It was so strange: *where has he gone?* I sat with Claude for an hour and then … that was it. I think David Hadzis got me home.

I was in shock. I didn't know what to do, or say. I couldn't think straight. I phoned all the children, and then I did what everyone does these days (although it is relatively rare for me). I posted on social media:

> *Our hearts are heavy. This afternoon, Claude, my husband of so many amazing years, passed away, leaving us lost for words to describe this awful emotion – grief.*
>
> *Thank you my lovely children, and friends, for giving me strength to get through this overwhelming sadness.*
>
> *Peace be with you, chéri.* ♥

Claude was cremated in Geneva, and then we held a wonderful reunion of family and friends in his memory. And I set about trying to work out how to make sense of life without him.

* * *

It's been more than a year now since Claude passed and I'm still in mourning for him. I feel his absence so keenly, especially when I'm in our apartment in Geneva, where he lived for so long as I came and went: I still think of it as *Claude's* apartment, really. I cope better with his loss when I'm in London.

Claude wrote his own book a few years ago, called *Il n'y avait pas d'école pour ça! (There Was No School for That!)*. He told his life story – of escaping the Nazis as a boy, of discovering jazz, and Johnny Hallyday, of working in the music industry in Paris … and, of course, of being with me. The story of our life together. Claude wrote this:

> Our life has been punctuated by songs, successes, travel, galas, periods of doubt, lows, rebirths, encounters … I don't think we're meant to spend our entire lives with the same person … [But] we are perfectly aware that there remains a great deal of affection between us, which is probably the definitive form of love. And a deep respect.
>
> And, to this respect, we have always remained faithful.

People reading this book may wonder why I mourn Claude so deeply, when things were not always great between us. They may wonder why I never divorced him when I learned of his infidelities. Even our own children have asked me that. And the answer is simple: *I never really wanted to.*

Claude and I loved each other and we went through so much together. From having no money, we built a life and found success. We saw the world together, and we had extra-ordinary experiences together in France, and across Europe, and in America. And we had three beautiful children. We made a family.

For all his faults (and I had mine, too), Claude was a good man … but were we made to live together forever? Were we made for each other? *Is there even such a thing?* You know, life is complicated. We fumble our way through the days. We try to do our best.

Certainly, I was very much in love with Claude when we met, and I think he was with me. The odd thing is, now he has gone, I feel that I have lost part of my identity. I was Petula Clark, but I was also Madame Wolff. *Always.* Even if things were not good between us, I was still his wife. And, of course, he was the love of my life. I still talk to him every day.

My greatest solace now that Claude has passed is that we made such great children together. I sometimes worry that I was not really a good mother: that I was away with work too much when they were little. Yet I have told them these fears and my kids say they have only happy, exciting memories of their childhoods.

They are all thriving. Bara was born a beauty, and she still is. Her husband, Roger, is a great interior decorator but he is much more than that. He worked with Salvador Dalí and is an expert on all things Napoleonic. Oh, and rock and roll. They are happy in New York and their children, Sébastien and Anabelle, are doing well.

Kate is very different from her sister. She always was. She's what you might call a free spirit. She tried her hand at fashion (for a few seasons) and art. Now, she is a yoga professor and lives between Geneva, Paris and Ibiza, where she has a charming little house (not in the crazy part: it's very tranquil and very zen). She loves her independence.

Paddy has been well into golf since he was a kid. He was part of the Swiss national golf programme and very proud of it. He wanted to be a professional golfer but wasn't quite at that level, but he is extremely happy living in Southern California and working in the golf industry.

Paddy is married to Olivia Burnette, who was a fine movie actress. Olivia now works as a clinical psychologist, but when she was a child star, she played Marti, the daughter that Steve Martin was trying to get home to for Thanksgiving, in *Planes, Trains and Automobiles*. It's still one of the funniest movies I've ever seen.

All three kids have very strong personalities, which can mean things sometimes get lively when we are all together in the same space. I guess that's what families are about.

And, how about me? Well, I'm still here. I would love to be back with you all once more, onstage, singing and connecting with you all again. I hope we can make it happen. If not, know that I love you … and thank you for all our memorable times together.

As I said, right at the beginning of *Is That You, Petula?*, I have never liked looking back. I've always been far keener on living for today. There again, I also said that this was the book that I would never write, yet I appear to have written it. Am I glad that I have?

Can I get back to you on that one?

# ACKNOWLEDGEMENTS

I hope you have enjoyed this. I'm aware that I've left out almost as much as I've put into it: all those 'invisible' people who make it all possible, the thousands of faithful fans, and those random people I've met along the journey who have enriched my life. I once wrote a song called 'Love Is the Only Thing'. Sounds naïve? Maybe. I've been 'in love' a few times but there is the other, immense love that has sustained me even through the hardest times. It has been a blessing, and I wish you all the same.

My thanks to:

Ian Gittins, of course. We have spent long hours together, and on the phone between London and Geneva. He is a lovely man and I think we have become friends!

David Hadzis, a longtime friend and a seemingly bottomless mine of information to boot!

Adrian Sington, who has been so kind and patient with me during this journey.

Grant Sturiale (the maestro!). His love and comradeship have seen us both through the highs and lows (and some tremolos) over many years.

Don Black. Clever, funny and always there for me.

And to so many others who have encouraged me when I needed it the most.

# INDEX

# SONG CREDITS

'(Ah, the Apple Trees) When the World Was Young' – Peggy Lee (Philippe-Gérard/Angèle Vannier/Johnny Mercer)

'April in Paris' – Count Basie Orchestra (Vernon Duke/E. Y. Harburg)

'Downtown' – Petula Clark (Tony Hatch)

'Put a Chrysler Sunbeam in Your Life' and 'Put a Little Sunshine in Your Life' – Petula Clark (Gus Galbraith/Richard Truman/David Climpson/Richard Krupp/Petula Clark)

'Starting All Over Again' – Petula Clark (Petula Clark/David Hadzis)

'Driven by Emotion' – Petula Clark (Petula Clark)

'Duane Reade' – Petula Clark (Tony Hatch/Barry Kleinbort)

'Feed the Birds' – Petula Clark (Richard M. Sherman/Robert B. Sherman)

# IMAGE CREDITS

All from Petula Clark's private collection except for the below.

**Plate Section 1**

P. 1 bottom left © BBC Archive, bottom right © Hulton Deutsch

P. 2 top © BBC Archive, bottom © ITV/Shutterstock

P. 3 top right © Shutterstock, middle left © RGR Collection, middle right © Moviestore Collection Ltd, bottom left © Camera Press

P. 4 top © J.Wilds, middle © Avalon.Red, bottom © Silverside/Daily Mail/Shutterstock

P. 5 top © ZUMA Press, Inc, middle right © Michael Ochs Archive, middle left © Donaldson Collection, bottom right © Harry Benson

P. 6 top left © Mirrorpix, top right © Hermann, Bernard/Fonds France-Soir/BHVP/Roger-Viollet/TopFoto, bottom right © BBC Archive

P. 7 top © Keystone-France, middle © Everett/Shutterstock, bottom © Sergi Griño/Alamy

P. 8 top © ZUMA Press, Inc, middle left © Photo12/Warner Bros/Seven Arts/Alamy, middle right © Ron Galella/Contributor, bottom left © Keystone Press

**Plate Section 2**

P. 1 top left © Everett Collection, top right © Pictorial Press Ltd, middle © Yves LE ROUX, bottom left © Trinity Mirror/Mirrorpix, bottom right © AFP/Gettyimages

P. 2 top left © Swiss National Museum/ASL, LM-149994.7

P. 3 top left © Trinity Mirror/Mirrorpix, bottom left © BBC Archive, bottom right © Mediapunch/Shutterstock

P. 4 top © Michael Ponomarff/Ponopresse/Contributor, middle © Sipa/Shutterstock, bottom left © Peter Brooker/Shutterstock, bottom right © Alan Davidson/Shutterstock

P. 5 top © Nick Skinner/Shutterstock, bottom left © Alison Mcdougall/Shutterstock, bottom right © Karl André

P. 6 top © Photoshot/Topfoto, bottom © Steve Back/Daily Mail/Shutterstock

P. 7 middle left © Joanne Davidson, Camera Press London